BRITAIN IN PICTURES

IMPRESSIONS OF ENGLISH LITERATURE

PRODUCED BY
ADPRINT LIMITED LONDON

✳

*The Editor is most grateful to all those who have so kindly
helped in the selection of illustrations, especially to officials
of the various public Museums, Libraries and Galleries, and
to all others who have generously allowed pictures and MSS.
to be reproduced*

IMPRESSIONS OF
ENGLISH LITERATURE

Introduction by
KATE O'BRIEN

Edited by
W. J. TURNER

With
48 plates in colour
and
125 illustrations in
black and white

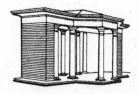

WILLIAM COLLINS OF LONDON
MCMXXXXIV

CONTENTS

DUKE HUMPHREY'S LIBRARY, THE BODLEIAN
Engraving by David Loggan, 1675

LIST OF ILLUSTRATIONS

PLATES IN COLOUR

5

BRITISH HISTORIANS

ENGLISH DIARIES AND JOURNALS

ENGLISH NOVELISTS

BRITISH PHILOSOPHERS

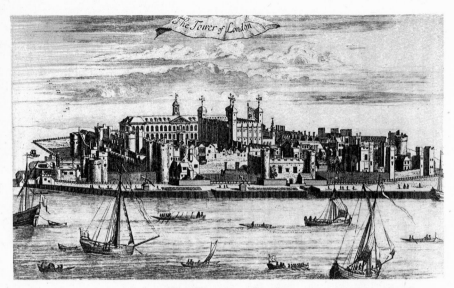

THE TOWER OF LONDON

Engraving from John Stow's *Survey of London and Westminster*. First published 1598

BLACK AND WHITE ILLUSTRATIONS

THE ENGLISH BIBLE

A BRIEF GENEALOGY OF THE ENGLISH BIBLE

1. The *Septuagint :* Greek translation of the Old Testament Scriptures made from the Hebrew and Aramaic for the Jews in dispersion, 3rd century B.C.—c. 2nd. century A.D.

2. The so-called *Vulgate :* a revision by St. Jerome (c. 340-420) of the Old Latin version ; New Testament and Psalter translated from the Greek ; the rest of the O.T. translated from Hebrew (Book of Daniel and Apocrypha) from Aramaic or Chaldee.

3. English Wyclifite or *Lollard* version of the *Vulgate.* 14th century.

4. Hebrew Bible or O.T., which was to displace the Greek and Latin in the 16th century, so-called *Massoretic* text ; complete version printed at Brescia, 1494, and used by Luther whose influence was felt by all English translators.

5. Erasmus's text of the N.T., with Latin translation and copious notes, issued 1516, *et seq.*

6. Luther's German translation : O.T. from Hebrew, N.T. from Erasmus's text, 1522.

7. Tyndale's English N.T., 1528, 1534, 1535, based on Erasmus's texts (2nd and 3rd editions of 1519, 1522) with aid from Luther's version and *Vulgate ;* Pentateuch, 1530 ; Book of Jonah, 1531, from Hebrew.

8. Miles Coverdale's complete translation of the Bible from the *Vulgate* and Luther's version, 1535.

9. Matthew's Bible, "the foundation of all the later English versions," derived mainly from Tyndale and Coverdale, 1537.

10. Cromwell's Bible, April 1539 ; Cranmer's Bible, April 1540, revised November 1540. These constituted the *Great Bible* read in Churches.

11. *Geneva Bible,* "translated according to the Ebrue and Greeke," 1560.

12. *The Bishop's Bible,* 1568, with revision, 1572. Official basis of :

13. *Authorised Version,* 1611.

14. *Revised Version,* "being the version set forth, A.D. 1611, compared with the most ancient authorities and revised." N.T., 1881. O.T. and N.T. together, 1885.

15. More modern versions are : *Twentieth Century New Testament,* based on Westcott and Hort, 1901, revised 1904 ; Weymouth's *New Testament in Modern Speech,* 1902 ; Moulton's *Modern Reader's Bible,* 1907 ; Moffatt's *New Translation,* 1913.

THE ENGLISH POETS

*Illustrations on pp. 69, 79, 83, 87, 91, 93, 95, 98 are reproduced by courtesy of the
National Portrait Gallery; on pp. 71, 82 by courtesy of the Trustees of the British
Museum; on p. 85 by courtesy of the Curators of the Bodleian Library; on p. 97 by
courtesy of Mrs. W. B. Yeats and of Macmillan & Co.*

*Verses from "A Shropshire Lad" from "The Collected Poems of A. E. Housman" by
permission of Jonathan Cape, Ltd.; "The End of the Episode" from "The Collected
Poems of Thomas Hardy" by permission of the Trustees of the Hardy Estate and of
Messrs. Macmillan & Co.; "I love all beauteous things" from "The Shorter Poems
of Robert Bridges", by permission of The Clarendon Press, Oxford; "A Dream of
Death" from "The Collected Poems of W. B. Yeats" by permission of Mrs. W. B. Yeats
and of Messrs. Macmillan & Co.; "The Scribe" by Walter de la Mare by permission
of the Author and of Constable & Co.; Verses from "Murder in the Cathedral" by
T. S. Eliot by permission of the Author and of Faber & Faber, Ltd.*

DESIGN FOR *THE WINTER'S TALE*
Drawing by Albert Rutherston, 1928

BRITISH DRAMATISTS

Illustration on p. 103 reproduced by courtesy of Trinity College, Cambridge and the Roxburghe Club ; on pp. 125, 139, by courtesy of the National Portrait Gallery ; on p. 117 by courtesy of the Trustees of the British Museum ; on p. 115 by courtesy of the Garrick Club, London ; on pp. 127, 131 by courtesy of the Victoria & Albert Museum ; on p. 132 by courtesy of the Trustees of the Lady Lever Collection ; on p. 135 by courtesy of Graham Robertson Esq., and the Garrick Club, London ; on p. 141 by gracious permission of H.M. The King and on p. 10 by courtesy of Albert Rutherston, Esq. and the Hon. Charles Tennyson.

BRITISH HISTORIANS

Illustration on p. 145 by courtesy of the Walpole Society ; on p. 151 by courtesy of the Master and Fellows of Clare College, Cambridge ; on p. 152 reproduced by courtesy of Corpus Christi College, Cambridge ; on p. 161 by courtesy of the Curators of the Bodleian Library, Oxford ; on p. 181 by courtesy of Oriel College, Oxford.

SEVENTEENTH CENTURY FRIENDS MEETING HOUSE
In the Time of George Fox

ENGLISH DIARIES AND JOURNALS

*Illustrations on pp. 191, 211 are reproduced by gracious permission of H.M. The King ;
on pp. 195, 201, 205, 209 by courtesy of the National Portrait Gallery ; on pp. 12,
197, by courtesy of the Society of Friends ; on p. 198 by courtesy of Dr. R. E. H.
Woodforde; on p. 203 by courtesy of Sir Robert Witt ; on p. 207 by courtesy of the
Earl of Durham ; on p. 214 by courtesy of the Trustees of Dr. Williams's Library ;
on p. 221 by courtesy of Miss Sybil Awdry.*

ENGLISH NOVELISTS

*Illustrations on p. 253 reproduced by courtesy of the Victoria & Albert Museum ;
on pp. 235, 239, 254, 255, 259, 267, by courtesy of the National Portrait Gallery ;
on p. 257 by courtesy of Messrs. Macmillan & Co. Ltd. ; on p. 261 by gracious
permission of H.M. The King ; on p. 269 by special permission of David Low Esq.*

BRITISH PHILOSOPHERS

INTRODUCTION

THE seven pieces of writing collected in this volume embrace between them—broadly indeed and with an elasticity imposed by their form, the whole field of English achievement in literature. And as literature has undoubtedly been England's paramount gift to human life, it follows that this book, seeking—in less than one hundred thousand words to re-introduce the whole tale, from the English Bible backwards and forwards through philosophy, history, verse and imaginative prose, may seem to take *two* risks : on the one hand, it may appear to the learned an absurdity ; on the other, the uninformed and eager may think that it will necessarily assume too much knowledge in its readers, and so only confuse and depress them.

In fact, neither of these dangers has overtaken this collection. As that one of the seven writers represented here who has made incomparably the *least* important contribution to the book—and that, as I shall later make clear, is *not* a perfunctory flourish of false modesty—I feel free to introduce this book with enthusiasm. The first general impression which arises in me from reading it as a whole is of a harmony of feeling and conclusion which can only be accidental, but is all the more persuasive for that, all the more likely to reflect truth and to win the assent of the cautious. This harmony is salutarily interrupted and enlivened, again and again, by flashes of eccentricity or captiousness which Mr. Kenneth Matthews, Lord David Cecil or Mr. E. L. Woodward would readily accept as part of the English genius. But harmony, agreement as to the English essence, rings reassuringly across the pages, from author to author. Says Mr. Kenneth Matthews : "The native characteristics of British philosophy are these : common sense, dislike of complication, a strong preference for the concrete over the abstract and a certain awkward honesty of method in which an occasional pearl of poetry is embedded." Says Mr. Woodward, of British historians : "A certain quietness of mind ; a strong visual imagination ; a clear style, not without poetic quality ; a shrewd, tolerant judgment ; a greater interest in character and action than in ideas." And Miss Elizabeth Bowen says : "Looking back, we may say that the English novelists have, from the eighteenth century up to some years ago, excelled in the creation of character, and secondarily, in the drawing of scenes, rather than in the analysis of ideas and passions."

These statements are sometimes qualified by their authors, in some brilliant portraits of non-conforming genius which they give us ; and they may seem indeed to be swept away in Lord David Cecil's shining procession of English Poetry, of which he rightly says that "no generalisation is uniformly true." Sir Herbert Grierson tells us that a major influence of the Bible on English literature is "the great background of story, characters, teachings, proverbs, parables, poetry made familiar as their daily bread to the mass of the people." Daily bread. Lord David Cecil seems, among the poets, to find the relationship of high inspiration to the plain here and now clearly defined only—in one sense—in Chaucer, and in another in Cowper. But Mr. Graham Greene, speaking for the dramatists, points to this very link as one of the stupendous certainties of Shakespeare, ". . . these lines of Shakespeare's are *realistic ;* they refer to the common, known life, they have the uneven rhythm of speech and grammatically they are simple." So I think that what Sir Herbert Grierson embraces in his phrase, "daily bread"—realism, reaction to the five senses, and awareness of routine and the common day—is, as these writers mainly find it, the anchor holding English letters to its proper place. Genius has tugged eternally against it, and sometimes broken loose—but in the main, even in escape, even in revulsion, it derives what it is from that ancient hold and stay, from that vast harbourage.

Space denies me the pleasure of examining other parallels of idea between these collected papers. All I may do is present them with brief suggestions as to what may be found most characteristic in each one. The English Bible is something about which I suspect—arguing guiltily from myself—we are all disposed to think we know very much more than we do. And if I am right, no pleasanter or clearer way of breaking that illusion can be found than by a reading of Sir Herbert Grierson's essay, which opens this volume. It is a model of compressed learning, presented with a mingling of justice and warmth which at once establishes confidence in the writer's scholarship and attracts us to his personal surmises. He sketches the great history of the Bible in English, from Caedmon and Bede to *The New Testament in Basic English ;* briefly, somewhat too briefly, he discusses it as literature ; and, very stimulatingly, in conclusion, he traces its influence as the Word of God, *i.e.* in its moral and social application, in Milton, Bunyan, the hymn-writers, Methodists and Evangelists, through Lord Byron, surprisingly and persuasively, in the Romantic period, to the social conscience and preachings of Ruskin.

Mr. Kenneth Matthews carries his learning wittily and, I suspect a fellow philosopher might say, with a touch of arbitrariness. But certainly he has here condensed the history of British philosophy in a manner to delight and attract all who come innocent and untrained to that vast field —and I imagine that much of his matter should stimulate the learned to argument, and to new lines of reflection. He claims Francis Bacon as the founder, rather than Descartes, of modern European philosophy; he stresses the realistic and practical character of the English philosopher; but he reveals too, a little, even to those who will never skirt its lowest foothills, of the high, abstract passion of pure thought. "No modern thinker touches like Hume that nerve of the spirit which caused Alcibiades to say of philosophy that it stings like a viper when it gets hold of a young and not insensitive mind."

To write of the whole of English poetry in fourteen thousand words is a staggering task, and only a scholar blessed with real lucidity of style as well as with exceptional power to select and eliminate could attempt it. Lord David Cecil is such a scholar, and one reads him with the odd pleasure of almost complete agreement, and with no sense at all of the labour and thought required to reduce so much richness and such life-long, sympathetic familiarity with it to this shining, limpid quintessence.

Differently, Miss Elizabeth Bowen confronts a similar problem. For though the English novel proper has only about one-third the history of English verse, it is the most widely known, among the averagely literate, of all English writing forms—a condition which sets particular problems of selection and comment. Yet he will be captious or stupid indeed, I think, who reads this brilliant estimate of English novelists without great pleasure, and the refreshment to be taken from individual and witty judgment. One might ask, perhaps, for more about Dickens and less about Trollope; one may question the setting of *Jane Eyre* above *Villette*, and wonder why in an essay that rightly embraces Henry James and Virginia Woolf no space has been found for James Joyce. But these are mere breaths of opinion, and the text as a whole delights by reason of its qualities of justice, delicacy and grace.

Mr. Graham Greene brings an alertly critical mind to the subject of British Dramatists—and also a large share of that captiousness which satisfactorily leavens this book. In order to praise Shakespeare he deems it necessary to be unjust to Marlowe; and by what rule does he decide that *Twelfth Night* is the most perfect of the former's plays? (No matter how you define "perfect," the decision still seems arbitrary.) One must quarrel too with this—that "Sheridan's style has the smooth unoriginal proficiency of a Parliamentary orator"; and with the—shall I call it cynicism—which, dismissing Shaw in a few hinted insults, describes the farces of Vernon Sylvaine as "serious in the aesthetic sense." A new way this to *épater le bourgeois*. But *British Dramatists* is brilliantly and vividly written to a somewhat forced thesis.

English Diaries find their place here only as a mild footnote to English letters. They have a varied charm, and for students of social history they are very valuable. But as literature they must be questioned. It has been pointed out, with some justice, that a writer unable to love Pepys is not the right person to discourse on English Diaries—yet I hope

17

that my pages may be found in some sense contributory and entertaining —though inessential perhaps to the main stream of this book.

In *British Historians* Mr. Woodward gives us a clear and satisfactory summing-up. From Bede, Matthew Paris, Holinshed right through to Trevelyan and Powicke, he packs together in the little space a very great deal of information and illuminative comment, and all he tells us supports the suggestion which dominates this book, that English genius is rooted in realism and derives from the least common multiple of every day, and of things understandable by the least of us. He offers no easy answer to the long labours of historians, ". . . a satisfactory clue has yet to be found to the meaning of the strange acts of the strangest of living creatures." He reminds us at the end of his book of Bede's image for man, of the bird that flies into a warm room in winter and then flies out again into the storm—"*de hieme in hiemem regrediens.*"

KATE O'BRIEN

THE ENGLISH BIBLE

SIR HERBERT GRIERSON

THE TRANSLATORS: WYCLIF TO MOFFATT

"VERY sort of doctrine which is to be delivered to the faithful," says the Catechism of the Council of Trent, "is contained in the Word of God, which is divided into Scripture and Tradition." And the Scripture had always, at least in theory, held the first place. In his exposition and defence of Christian doctrine Thomas Aquinas has two courts of appeal,—firstly Scripture, and secondly "the Philosopher," that is Aristotle, in matters scientific, but the latter is subject to correction by the former. The Scriptures were represented, for those who could read, by the Vulgate, St. Jerome's Latin translation of the Old and New Testament. The rhythm of the English Bible, as that finally emerged, owes not a little to the Latin of St. Jerome, though Tyndale will assert that both Hebrew and Greek are more easily rendered into English than into Latin.

The influence of the Scriptures, Old and New Testament, on English literature goes back to the earliest extant records of that literature—the Caedmonian poetic version of the books of *Genesis* and *Exodus* and of the apocryphal *Judith* (which in the Vulgate is included among the historical books) followed later by the *Crist* of Cynewulf, a noble poem. Just before his death the Venerable Bede was engaged on a translation of the Gospel of St. John, and the last work of King Alfred was a translation of the Psalter. If from the date of the Norman Conquest to the fourteenth century there were fewer English versions of Biblical literature that was because English was the language of a conquered people. Those who could read at all could also read Latin and French. Yet in many ways the main story of the Old and New Testament was made familiar to the people. The *Ormulum*, our oldest poem in a regular syllabic metre, is an exposition of the Gospels for each day. There were poetical paraphrases of *Genesis* and *Exodus*, and the *Cursor Mundi* told in rude accentual verse a history of the world, including the main episodes which were made familiar to the people in the popular Miracle Plays. The great English mystic of the fourteenth century, Richard Rolle of Hampole, made two prose versions of the Psalms with commentaries, as well as extracts from the Books of Job and Jeremiah. The didactic alliterative poem *Piers Plowman* is pervaded with the Spirit of the Bible and enforces its teaching with excerpts from the Vulgate. Caxton in his translation of the *Golden Legend* included stories from the Old Testament. The general story of the Bible was fairly well known in the fourteenth century; but "save for the Psalms, of all that is not story, notably the Prophets in the Old Testament and the Epistles in the New, there was small opportunity for any one ignorant of Latin to gain knowledge, and this was the case also with the whole Bible in respect of its text as distinct from its general purport." (Pollard.)

It was with the first stirrings of reform, the revolt against the corruptions of the Mediaeval Church (and one may confine the word to corruptions which the Roman Church admitted and in great part set itself to correct later) that a new importance began to be attached to the Bible, a movement which might, without irreverence, be described as Swift does in the *Tale of a Tub*, as a determination to see if the Will was being faithfully observed. We sometimes hear it suggested that it was the translation of the Scriptures that led to the Reformation. It might be more justly said that the Reformation led to a renewed and closer study of the Scriptures. The Church, at least in its higher orders, but in all to some extent, had like Jeshurun waxed fat and kicked, with results that were felt in all ranks of society from the king upon his throne to the peasant preyed upon by friars and summoners and pardoners. "Everything," as a Commission of 1537 reported to the Pope, "could be obtained for money, however hurtful it might be to the general welfare of the Church." Moreover, what has been said above, that those who could read could also read Latin and French, must be qualified by the fact that not many, even of the clergy, could understand Latin, even the Latin of the services which they read.

The translation of the Bible into English was thus coincident with, and a consequence of, a revolt against the practices, and in the wake of that against the dogmas, of the Catholic Church, an attitude which was, as we shall see, often emphasised by the glosses which accompanied the translation. In estimating, therefore, the influence of the Bible on our people and literature there are two things to be kept in mind : firstly, the purely literary effect of possessing in the vernacular such a magnificent body of literature, narrative and poetic—for the prophetic is also the poetic

'THE MARTYRDOME OF MASTER WILLIAM TINDALL IN FLANDERS BY VILVORD CASTLE'
Engraving from Foxe's *Acts and Monuments of Martyrs*, 1684

whether one thinks of Isaiah or St. Paul: secondly, the effect on the mind of the English people, represented by some prominent figures in our literature, of the acceptance of this literature, rich in narrative and poetry but entirely devoid of science, as the inspired Word of God, all in that respect on the same, or practically the same, level.

The new approach to the Bible began with the first complete translation, the Wyclifite or Lollard Bible of the fourteenth century, for to Wyclif the Bible was not only the ultimate but the only authority on matters of religious belief and practice : and to this he added the other doctrine fundamental to Protestantism, the right of every man, learned or ignorant, to examine the Bible for himself.

The Lollard Bible is not now thought to be the work of Wyclif himself. Wyclif's own versions are rather to be found in his homilies, where, if the homily were removed, we should have a valuable and fairly continuous translation of the New Testament. "In one set of *Epistolae Dominicales* Wyclif expressly states that his motive was to tell in English Paul's

Epistles." (Workman : *Life of Wyclif*.) The Bible has come down to us in, for the greater part of it, two versions, both of course from the Vulgate; the time for Greek and Hebrew was not yet come. The first of these is attributed to a Nicholas Hereford, one of Wyclif's supporters at Oxford; the other, on less probable grounds, to a John Purvey, another friend of the reformer. The interest of this second version is that the translator, whom we may call Purvey, breaks away from the too literal rendering of Latin idiom in the direction which Tyndale was to follow, the acceptance of the native English idiom and order of words, the use even of colloquial expressions. Purvey, who describes himself as "on symple creature of God," explains among many other things, in a long, interesting, and very Wyclifite, prologue, in what various ways a translator may deal with different Latin idioms, such as *e.g.* the ablative absolute.

The Lollard Heresy was suppressed on the accession to the throne of Henry IV, the son of that John of Gaunt who, for political purposes, had been a supporter of Wyclif against the prelates. It was suppressed, but not annihilated, by the passing of the act *De Heretico Comburendo* and the persecution which ensued. The Lollard Bible circulated continuously, as is proved by the survival of some hundred and eighty manuscripts ; and it kept alive the temper which accepted the Bible as the sole and supreme authority in religion, a spirit which reasserted itself so soon as the influence of the new heresy of Luther began to flow in from the Continent. It was in this spirit that the work of translation was resumed in the sixteenth century. Meantime the Renaissance had come. Hebrew and Greek had to be reckoned with. The Vulgate was being subjected to criticism. Erasmus published a Greek text of the New Testament in 1516, and a Latin translation in 1519 ; and it was from Erasmus's text that Luther made his German translation which was published in September 1522.

The hero and martyr of the English Bible as we have it is William Tyndale (or Hutchins), born about 1494 and educated at Oxford and Cambridge, where, especially at the latter, he came in contact with the new learning and acquired an impatience with the old, and with the restrictions attached to a knowledge of the genuine Scriptures. As a tutor in a family in the Cotswolds he continued his studies and translated both the *Enchiridion Militis Christiani* of Erasmus and, from the Greek, a speech of Isocrates. When finally, provoked by the ignorance of the clergy whom he met at his master's table, and by accusations of heresy, he resolved to "cause a boy that driveth the plough" to know more of the scripture than they, and went to London to seek the patronage of the Bishop of London, Cuthbert Tunstall, he took the latter translation with him as a proof of his competence. But he found that neither London nor England was a safe place for such a task, and he went to Germany. Settling at Cologne, with a rather talkative and troublesome colleague, William Roye, he began to prepare a quarto edition of the New Testament

'THE MIRACULOUS DRAUGHT OF FISHES'
Woodcut from Tyndale's Bible. St. Luke, chapter 5.

with a prologue and very Lutheran glosses. What was being prepared was discovered by an English spy, and Tyndale fled to Worms, where he issued a complete translation, but without prologue or glosses, in octavo form, about February 1526. Of this early edition three copies survive. A carefully revised edition was issued by Tyndale in 1534 with prefaces general and special, references, glosses, and including the epistles taken from the Old Testament and the Apocrypha as used in the service-book of Salisbury. A further edition, slightly revised, was published in 1535, Tyndale's final text. But in the interval between the completion of the first New Testament and this latter year he had been busy with the Old Testament, and in 1530 printed his version of the *Pentateuch* in 1530 and of *Jonah* in 1531. In 1535 he was seized by treachery, imprisoned in the castle of Vilvorde and a year later "he was brought forth to the place of execution, was there tied to the stake, and then strangled first by the hangman, and afterwards with fire consumed . . . crying thus at the stake with a fervent zeal and a loud voice : Lord, open the King of England's eyes." (Foxe.) His chief opponent in controversy, Sir Thomas More, had suffered a similar fate a year earlier.

Of Tyndale's version I shall shortly print an extract or two beside those of later ones with a view to show how the one led on to the others, and what a composite piece of work the Authorised version of 1611 is. But there are some features of Tyndale's work which it is only fair to indicate at once, for his sake and for that of his opponents, such as Sir Thomas More ; for Tyndale's sake, because the later changes were not all for the better. His is the racier style if it includes some questionable devices, as varying the word by which one word in the original is rendered, and using contemporary words not always applicable : "We sailed away from Philippos after the ester holydays" (Acts xx. 6.); "on a Sondaye" (Rev. i. 10.). But how racy and colloquial are such phrases as : "Then said the serpent unto the woman: 'Tush ye shall not die,'" "And the Lord was with Joseph and he was a lucky fellow," "When ye pray bable not much," "a void ground and a roaring wilderness," (The "howling wilderness" of the Authorised has become common usage.) and many others. To Tyndale we owe the word "Jehovah" to which we are now taught to prefer the barbaric "Javeh." To him also we owe some fine Hebraisms : "To die the death," "in the sweat of thy face," "the living God," "sick unto death," "uncircumcised lips."

Against all this and more must be set, from a Catholic point of view, his use of tendencious forms as "congregation" for "Church," "senior" and later "elder" to translate "presbuteros" rather than "priest" which was kept for "hiereus," "repentance" for "penance," etc. More justifiable was the complaint of Tyndale's tendencious notes. Some are simply doctrinal, Calvinistic, as the note at the beginning of the benedictions (Matth. v.) intended to correct any thought of human merit : "All these deeds here rehearsed, as to nourish peace, to shew mercy, to suffer persecution and so forth, make not a man happy and blessed, neither deserve reward of heaven: but declare and testify that we are happy and blessed, and that we shall have great promotion in heaven, and certify us in our hearts that we are God's sons, that the Holy Ghost is in us, for all good things are given to us freely of God for Christ's blood's sake and his merits." Others, which a modern critic describes as "amusing," were to a Catholic very offensive : "How shall I curse whom God curseth not" ("The pope can tell how"). "Neither bring the hire of a whore nor the price of a dog in to the house of the Lord thy God" ("The pope will take tribute of them yet, and bishops, and abbots desire no better tenants"). "And they blessed Rebecca" ("to bless a man's neighbour is to pray for him, and to wish him good : not to wag two fingers over him"). "They shall make them no baldness upon their heads" ("Of the heathen priests therefore took our prelates the ensample of their bald pates"). "And these words which I command thee this day shall be in thine heart, and thou shalt whet them on thy children, and shalt talk of them at home in thine house &c." ("It is heresy with us for a lay man to look of God's Word or to read it"). "And he [Joseph] appointed the people, unto the cities, from one side of Egypt unto the other, only the land of priests bought he not. For there

24

FIRST PAGE OF ST. MATTHEW'S GOSPEL

Fifteenth century illuminated MS. of the Wyclifite Bible

By courtesy of the University Library, Cambridge

WILLIAM TYNDALE 1492 - 1536
Oil painting by an unknown artist
By courtesy of the Principal and Fellows of Hertford College, Oxford

was an ordinance made by Pharaoh for the priests, etc." ("The blind guides get privileges from bearing with their brethren, contrary to Christ's law of love. And of these priests of idols did our compassing ivytrees learn to creep up little by little and to compass the great trees of the world with hypocrisy, and to thrust the roots of idolatrous superstition in to them and to suck out the juice of them with their poetry, till all be seer boughs and no thing green save their own commonwealth"). "Ye shall put nothing unto the word which I command you neither do aught there from etc." ("No ; nor yet corrupt it with false glosses to confirm Aristotle's false lerning therwith"). The last note shows Tyndale's sympathy with the new learning which was in revolt against Aristotle. But it is little wonder that Sir Thomas More distrusted a translation animated by such a spirit. On the other hand it must be remembered that behind Tyndale's passionate notes lay a century of persecution and burnings.

Meantime another pioneer of translation, Miles Coverdale, no scholar such as Tyndale, nor with the same racy and vigorous style, but master of a pleasing and readable English, had made a complete translation which he described as "faithfully and truly translated out of Douche and Latin," that is from the Vulgate and Luther. The reference to Luther was soon dropped. This was published in 1535 with an unauthorised dedication to the King : "Josias commanded straitly (as your grace doth) that the law of God should be read and taught unto all the people." It was probably printed at Zurich, and is the first complete Bible in English and the first entirely by one man. Coverdale has some interesting renderings of his own. I quote from Mr. Isaac's chapter in *Ancient English Versions of the Bible* (1940) not having Coverdale's at hand. In the sections of which his is the first modern translation: Jer. viii. 22, "There is no more triacle at Galaad" ; Ps. xc. 5, "Thou shalt not need to be afraid for eny bugges by night" ; Isa. xxiv. 9, "the beer shal be byter to them that drinke it" etc. Coverdale's version was followed in 1537 by what is known as Matthew's Bible. This was (for Henry had now broken definitely with the Pope and declared himself Supreme Head of the Church) issued "with the Kinge's most gracyous lycence" and is therefore our first Authorised version. It is a composite Bible,—Tyndale's Pentateuch and New Testament, Coverdale's Apocrypha and version of Ezra to Malachi, and a new version of Joshua to Chronicles now believed to be that left by Tyndale in manuscript. It is from the Hebrew and has all his peculiarities, as the varying of the word to render the same word in the original. But the whole book has been edited by one John Rogers or so it is generally accepted, a competent editor whoever he was. On these were based the so called Great Bibles including Cromwell's 1539, Cranmer's (he having contributed a prologue) 1540, and the King's. This was the Bible appointed to be used in Churches. It was revised with each issue ; but more popular and more important for later versions was the Geneva Bible, the New Testament issued in 1557, the Psalms in 1559, and the Bible in 1560 with a dedication to the Queen, Elizabeth. This is known sometimes as the Breeches Bible because of the verse in Genesis : "and they sowed figge leaves together and made themselves breeches." Tyndale's word had been "apurns" to which the Authorised reverted as "aprons." Tyndale's spelling is interesting for the pronunciation of the time. He always spells "childeren" and "bretheren" ; and "childern" was Milton's spelling in the first edition of *Paradise Lost*.

The Geneva Bible was the work of Protestant refugees from the Marian persecution, especially William Whittington, a fellow of All Souls College, Oxford. The New Testament is based on Tyndale, the Old on the Great Bible ; but the work was done with a scholarly regard to the Hebrew and Greek and there are divergencies from the Tyndale-Coverdale tradition, some of which have found their way into the Authorized text. All these later versions, from Matthew's onwards, owe a good deal to the French translations of Lefevre (1534) and Olivetan (1535). To the Geneva Bible in its first edition was prefixed a prologue by Calvin ; and the translation is accompanied from the first verse to the last with a running commentary in marginal glosses. So far as the present writer can judge from some study of them in very small print in a copy of 1610, these are not so pointedly savage as those of Tyndale. The worst of the fight was over. But all the contents of the Apocalypse are interpreted as applying to the Church of Rome. Some of the glosses seem sensible and humane : "And they called Rebecca and said unto her, Wilt thou go with this man ? " ("This showeth that parents have not authoritie to marry their children without consent of the parties.") "I demand then, hath God cast away his people ? God forbid, etc." ("Now the Apostle sheweth how this doctrine is to be applied to others abiding still in his propounded case. Therefore he teacheth us that all the Jews are not cast away, and therefore we ought not to pronounce rashly of private persons whether they be of the number of the elect or not, etc.")

This was the popular Bible, that read by Shakespeare for example, though the Great Bible was that read in Church. Between the Geneva and the Authorised of 1611 there came one more revision of the Great Bible, the so-called Bishop's Bible issued in 1568, and with some revision in 1572. It has been described as "a backward looking Bible usually ignoring the improvements in music and accuracy of the Geneva version in favour of the traditional readings of the Great Bible." (*The Bible in its Ancient and English Versions*. Edited by H. Wheeler Robinson, 1940.) But it does not always follow either. In the Psalms especially, so far as the present writer has examined them, it has often a text of its own of a not very attractive character musically. Nevertheless it is the source, the issue of 1572, of several phrases familiar to us from the Authorised : "the voice of one crying in the wilderness," "less than the least of all

TITLE PAGE OF THE GENEVA BIBLE
English reprint of 1614

saints" (for ἐμοὶ τῷ ἐλαχιστοτέρῳ παντων ἁγίων), "Rend your hearts and not your garments" and some others.

It was on the one hand the feeling that the Geneva Bible was a better translation than any of the Great Bibles, and on the other the dislike of many, including King James, for the tendencious glosses, that led to the resolve, at the Hampton Court Conference, to prepare yet another version. Three committees were appointed, for Oxford, Cambridge and Westminster, and the work divided among them. Instructions were issued of which only one or two need be cited : the Bishop's Bible (1572) was to be followed as closely as possible. The older ecclesiastical words were to be kept instead of Tyndale's innovations ; there were to be no marginal glosses except to explain some Hebrew or Greek word. Tyndale remains the hero of the English Bible. His rendering was the raciest. All that is best in the final version of the New Testament derives from Tyndale. It is regrettable that his text of 1535 is accessible only in the rather heavy Hexapla of Bagster.

The Roman Catholic version known as the Douay Bible, of which the New Testament appeared at Rheims in 1582, the Old Testament at Douai in 1609-10, lies a little out of the main current but was consulted by the revisers. It is from the Vulgate, and the translators retained the technical terms in their original form ; "Pasch" (passover), but also "make the phase" (keep the passover) ; "loaves of proposition" (shew bread) ; "scenopegia" (feast of tabernacles) etc. A number of Latin words are also retained from the Vulgate as "inquination," "potestates," "longanimity" (which may explain its frequent use by Donne). But none of these peculiarities has found its way into the language. It is more interesting to note the claim in the introduction that the Latin of the Vulgate is based on older Hebrew texts than those available in the sixteenth century. This is quite true. All the extant Hebrew texts of the Old Testament derive from one and the same source. But St. Jerome may have known older manuscripts or Jewish traditional readings, and the Greek Bible known as the Septuagint "was made from the Hebrew text over a thousand years before the date of the earliest existing copy of the Hebrew text." (David Daiches : *The King James Version of the Bible*, 1941.) These are important facts for revision, at any time, of the text ; not for the history of the English Bible and its influence.

The revision of the Authorised Version of 1611 in the nineteenth century was the outcome of a growing body of criticism which is summarised by Professor Cadoux : "Not only had successive printers introduced into it [the Authorised] numerous small alterations, so that there was no fixed standard for its wording, but it was replete with increasingly obscure archaisms and—what was worse—inconsistencies and errors innumerable, which the progress of scholarship was rendering more and more intolerable. Nor indeed was it free from the dogmatic bias to which

JAMES I
The King responsible for the Authorised Version of 1611
Oil painting by Paul van Somer, 1576-1621

different groups of its translators had been (perhaps in part unconsciously) subject." (Robinson, *op. cit.*) The work began in 1870, separate committees being appointed for the Old and the New Testament. The New Testament was issued in 1881, the Old and New together in May 1885. The translation was rather savagely attacked by Dr. Burgon, Dean of Chichester, and others including the late Professor Saintsbury in his *History of English Prose Rhythm*, his fine ear jarred by the changes in old and familiar cadences. It is not for the present writer to enter into a now old controversy. There can be no doubt that for certain of the books of the Old Testament, as the *Book of Job* and the Prophets generally, a study of the Revised version is indispensable by anyone interested in the meaning as well as the rhythm. Nor should the marginal readings be overlooked. But the main theme of the present volume is the Bible in England in the hey-day of its acceptance as the entire and unchallenged Word of God.

But the Revised version was an experiment, or more truly a double experiment, firstly to alter the Elizabethan English just sufficiently to secure accuracy and clearness; and secondly to correct the Authorised so far as seemed essential in the light of advanced Hebrew and Greek scholarship. In both respects the result was a compromise, especially as regards the latter aim. The Masoretic text of the Hebrew Scriptures is in places, Dr. Moffatt declares, very corrupt. The text of the New Testament adopted by the translators is not thought to be so trustworthy as that which was being worked out by Westcott and Hort. The present writer is not qualified to discuss these questions, nor is this the place to attempt any such estimate. He records the opinion of scholars to explain why the work of the revisers was soon followed by various attempts to go further in both directions, a closer approximation to modern English, a bolder treatment of the original source, Hebrew and Greek. The best known and most revolutionary is that of Dr. James Moffatt, late of the Theological Seminary, New York. The New Testament appeared in 1913, the Old Testament in 1924, the complete Bible in 1926, and revised in 1935.

Moffatt's English is colloquial and familiar with frequent clichés. Admitting his scholarship to be sound, one gets often the sense of passages formerly found obscure, and for certain books, as the Epistles of St. Paul, he does provide a more intelligible text. This is probably also true of the difficult prophetic books, which, too, he boldly breaks up in accordance with the dating and dividing of scholars, which must be conjectural in character. Poetically to one familiar with the older versions there is undoubtedly loss or apparent loss. It is just a question how far such an experiment as Moffatt's here or Lawrence's in the *Odyssey* can be successful. At times, too, some overfamiliarity or unhappy association produces a reading which jars badly, *e.g.* Matthew xxvi. 34.

The New Testament in Basic English, 1941, is an experiment in using a limited range of language, avoiding synonyms at all costs. For this particular work one thousand words was allowed in place of the usual eight hundred and fifty of the official Basic English vocabulary. The rendering is not wanting in dignity. There are fewer clichés than in Moffatt's. But the disadvantage is that, when there are apparently several synonyms, there are generally different shades of meaning and one may lose by adhering to the same word or phrase throughout. "One of you will be false to me," "Judas who was false to him." There are more ways of being false to a friend than actually betraying him to his mortal foes. Similarly there are more ways of being "untrue in married life" than actually committing adultery.

It is strange at first sight that Scotland, which accepted so completely the Reformation as that came to it from Geneva, failed to secure a version of the Scriptures in the vernacular. Under Knox, Scotland accepted the Genevan version; and later the authorised Jacobean Bible. The use of an English version of the Scriptures and the currency of Knox's controversial pamphlets "were the most effective agents . . . in undermining the position of the Scots tongue as a literary dialect." (J. H. Millar: *A Literary History of Scotland*).

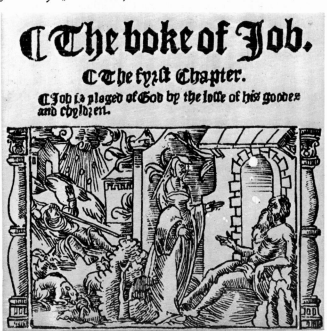

WOODCUT FROM THE GREAT BIBLE, 1539

EFORE going into any detail as to the influence of the English Bible as literature I propose to give in consecutive order short extracts from the various versions, the same passage or passages in the Lollard, in Tyndale, in the Geneva version and in the Authorised : but it might be well to begin with the Vulgate :

"Si linguis hominum loquar et angelorum, critatem autem non habeam, factus sum velut aes sonans, aut cymbalum tinniens. Et si habuero prophetiam, et noverim mysteria omnia, et omnem scientiam ; et si habuero omnem fidem ita ut montes transferam, caritatem autem non habuero, nihil sum. Et si distribuero in cibos pauperum omnes facultates meas, et si tradiderim corpus meum ita ut ardeam, caritatem autem non habuero, nihil mihi prodest . . . Nunc autem manent, fides, spes, caritas, tria haec ; major autem horum est caritas."

This is the immediate source of the Lollard rendering :

"If I speke with tonges of men and angels, and I have not charite, I am made as bras sowninge or a cymbal tinklynge, and if I have profecie, and know alle mysteries, and al kynninge, and if I have al feith so that I meve hills fro her place, and I have not charite I am nought, and if I departe alle my godis into metis of pore men, and if I bitake my bodi so that I brenne, and I have not charite it profiteth me no thing . . . and now dwellen feith hope and charite ; but the most of these is charite."

Tyndale's version follows in which it will be noticed he uses the past subjunctive for the present in both Greek and Latin, probably to heighten the hypothetical cast of the statement :

"Though I spake with the tonges of men and angels and yet had not love I were even as sounding brass or as a tynklynge Cymball. And though I coude prophesy and understode all secretes and all knowledge : yea if I hade all fayth so that I coude move mountaynes oute of ther places and yet had no love I were nothynge. And though I bestowed al my goodes to fede the poore ; and though I gave my body even that I burned and yet had no love, it profiteth me nothing . . . Now abydeth fayth hope love even these three but the chief of these is love."

Tyndale changes "charity" to "love" for the Greek "agape." There are two Greek words, *agape* and *eros*, the latter the love of passion. But the English "charity" has also acquired misleading implications. The Geneva version runs :

"Though I speake with the tongues of men and Angels, and have not love, I am as sounding brasse or a tinkling cymball. And though I had the *gift* of prophesie, and knew all secrets and all knowledge, yea, if I had al faith, so that I could remove mountains, and had not love, I were nothing. And though

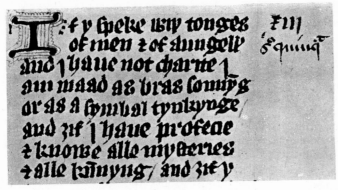

A 15TH CENTURY ILLUMINATED Ms.
OF THE WYCLIFITE BIBLE
I Corinthians, chapter 13, 1-2

I feede the poore with all my goodes, and though I give my body, that I bee burned, and have not love, it profiteth mee nothing . . . And now abideth faith, hope, and love, *even* these three ; but the chiefest of these is love."

Here the present and past interchange. Here too begins the custom of printing in italics any words added for the sense. Finally here are the Authorised and Revised versions :

"Though I speak with the tongues of men and of angels and have not charity, I am become *as* sounding brass or a tinkling cymbal. And though I have *the gift of* prophesy, and understand all mysteries, and all knowledge ; and though I have all faith, so that I could remove mountains, and have not charity, I am nothing. And though I bestow all my goods to feed *the poor*, and though I give my body to be burned, and have not charity, it profiteth me nothing . . And now abideth faith, hope, and charity, these three ; but the greatest of these is charity."

Notice "the most," "the chief," "the chiefest," "the gretest." The principal changes made in the Revised version, which I need not print at length, were "love" for "charity," a reversion to Tyndale, and "clanging" for "tinkling." The former provoked much protest.

Of the Prophets the version till the Authorised of 1611 had been in the main Coverdale's, and it may be well to take a short extract from the Lollard version and Coverdale's, giving the Vulgate version first for comparison again with that of the later text—the beautiful verses which close the fortieth chapter of Isaiah :

"Numquid nescis, aut non audisti : Deus sempiternus Dominus, qui creavit terminos terrae, non deficiet, neque laborabit, nec est investigatio sapientiae ejus ? Qui dat lasso virtutem, et his qui non sunt fortitudinem et robur multiplicat. Deficient pueri, et laborabunt, et juvenes in infirmatate cadent. Qui autem sperant in Domino mutabunt fortitudinem, assument pennas sicut aquilae, current et non laborabunt, ambulabunt et non deficient."

Purvey's version of this runs:

"Whether thou knowest not, ether herdest thou not? God everlasting Lord, that made of nouht the endis of erthe, schal not faile, nether schal travele, nether enserching of his wisdom is: That gyreth vertu to the weeri, and strength to hem that ben not, and multiplieth stalworthnesse. Children schulen faile, and schulen travele, and yonge men schullen falle doun in her sicknesse. But thei that hopen in the Lord schulen chaunge strengthe, thei schulen take fetheris as eglis: thei schulen renne and schulen not travele, thei schulen go, and schulen not faile."

Coverdale's, as it stands in Matthew's Bible and again in the Great Bible of 1539, runs:

"Knowest thou not, or hast thou not hearde, that the everlasting God, the Lorde which made all the corners of the earth, is nether weery nor faynt? and that his wysdom cannot be comprehended: but that he geveth strength unto the weery and power unto the faynte? Children are weery and faynt, and the strongest men fall: But unto them that have the Lord before theyr eyes shal strength be encreased. Aegles winges shal grow upon them: when they runne, they shall not fall; and when they go they shall not be weery."

It is with some help from the Genevan that the Authorised achieves its magnificent rendering:

"Hast thou not known? Hast thou not heard, *that* the everlasting God, the Lord, the Creator of the ends of the earth, fainteth not, neither is weary? There is no searching of his understanding. He giveth power to the faint; and to *them that have* no might he increaseth strength. Even the youths shall faint and be weary, and the young men shall utterly fall. But they that wait upon the Lord shall renew *their* strength; they shall mount up with wings as eagles; they shall run and not be weary; *and* they shall walk, and not faint."

The Revised version of 1884 reads for "them that have" "him that hath." But Coverdale's great achievement was his version of the Psalter which is still used in the Anglican Prayer Book. That final version was the result of a good deal of revision. The text of Coverdale's own Bible and of Matthew's Bible is not quite that of 1539 which is the Prayer Book's text. The changes are often small but occasionally considerable, *e.g.* in the well known twenty-third: "The Lord is my shepherd."

What then is to be said of the influence of the English Bible on our own prose and verse? Some things must be set aside as erroneous. It is, I think, Mr. Somerset Maugham who in a recent volume lays it to the charge of our reading the Bible so much that we acquired the ideal of prose represented by Dr. Johnson and Gibbon, which is absurd. The prose of the Bible, it has often been pointed out, is not the prose of the century in which the final version was made, the period of Hooker and Bacon and Milton and Browne. That ideal had another source, in Latin

Though I spake with the tonges of men and aungels, and haue no loue, I am euen as soundyng brasse: or as a tynklynge cymball. And though I coulde prophesy, and vnderstande al secretes, and all knowledge : yea, yf I had a*all fayth, so that I could moue moūtayns out of their places, and yet had no loue, I were nothynge. And though I bestowe all my goodes (to fede the poore) and though I gyue my body euen that I burned, and yet haue no loue, it profeteth me nothynge.

Though I speake with the tongues of men ⁊ of Angels, and haue not charity I am become as sounding brasse or a tinkling cymbal.

2 And though I haue the gift of prophesie, and vnderstand all mysteries and all knowledge : and though I haue all faith, so that I could remooue mountaines, and haue no charitie, I am nothing.

3 And though I bestowe all my goods to feede the poore, and though I giue my body to bee burned, and haue not charitie, it profiteth me nothing.

TYNDALE'S BIBLE, 1528 : I Corinthians, chapter 13, 1-3
AUTHORISED VERSION, 1611 : I Corinthians, chapter 13, 1-3

prose and ultimately in the Greek orators and Plato. The narrative prose of the Bible is at the delightful early stage represented also by Sir Thomas Malory or Berners' *Froissart*. Nothing could be more delightful in its own way than the manner of telling the stories in Genesis and the historical books generally, *e.g.* the story of the finding of Rebecca as a wife for Isaac : "And the servant took ten camels of the camels of his master and departed ; for all the goods of his master were in his hand : and he arose and went to Mesopotamia unto the city of Nahor. And he made his camels to kneel down without the city by a well of water at the time of the evening, even the time that women go out to draw water. And he said, O Lord God of my master Abraham, I pray thee, send me good speed this day, and shew kindness to my master Abraham. Behold I stand here by the well of water ; and the daughters of the men of the city come out to draw water : and let it come to pass, that the damsel to whom I shall say, Let down thy pitcher, I pray thee, that I may drink ; and she shall say, Drink, and I will give thy camels drink also ; let the same be she that thou hast appointed for thy servant Isaac ; and thereby shall I know that thou hast shewed kindness to my master. And it came to pass" etc.—and so it flows on with the successive "and," "and," "and." There is much worse narrative prose, but to write just so would be affectation though it has been used for translation of Homer. But the kind of prose which the English were learning in the sixteenth century had another origin. It was with their practice of dialectic that the Greeks learned and taught others the prose of exposition and demonstration. That is not the way of the East. The Oriental teacher imparts his intuitions to his pupils in brief sentences as in the *Book of Proverbs, Ecclesiastes* and even the Sermon on the Mount. St. Paul was learning a new dialectic, yet it is not difficult to note how he struggles to give the form of dialectic, demonstration, to his intuitions. No ; it is elsewhere than in the *form* of prose or verse that one must look for the influence of the Bible on our literature.

There is firstly the great background of story, characters, teachings, proverbs, parables, poetry, made familiar as their daily bread to the mass of the people. Of course all this does not come direct from the text of the Bible. Much of the Bible story had been made, as has been said above, familiar from the Miracle plays and other sources. But this was a strange medley of what was Biblical and what the fancy of the dramatiser had added to enliven the play. The mediaeval peasant had heard of Noah and his wife :

> Hastow not herd, quod Nicolas also,
> The sorwe of Noah with his felawshipe,
> Ere that he mighte gete his wife to ship ?
> Him had be lever, I dar wel undertake,

At thilke tyme, than alle his wethers blake,
That she had had a ship herself allone.

He knew of Herod and Pilate as notorious braggarts, and had pictured
to himself the shepherds of the Nativity as English peasants blowing
their nails on a cold night and complaining of landlords and tax-collectors.
With Shakespeare that is all changed. He is not a religious poet like
Milton, shaping to himself the story of man's fall as he accepts it from
the Scriptures, though Bishop Wordsworth has no difficulty, in his
interesting volume *Shakespeare and the Bible* (1880), in showing how
essentially Christian and Biblical are the sentiments his characters
give expression to throughout. In another chapter he shows that Shakespeare's use of Biblical stories, of Adam and Eve, Cain and Abel, Noah,
Jacob, Joseph, Jeptha, David and Goliath and so on are obviously known
to him from the Bible, so that he as often as not uses the very language
of the Scriptures. Occasionally Wordsworth falls into the not uncommon
error of attributing to Shakespeare's memory of the original what he has
got more shortly from Holinshed or other source. He also failed to notice
that the text with which Shakespeare was familiar is that of the Geneva
version. This has been much laboured of late, but one example is
conclusive proof. Discussing the speech of Shylock : "Yes to smell
pork ; to eat the habitation which your prophet the Nazarite conjured
the devil into," the Bishop asks : "Had our poet any reason for making
use of the name Nazarite rather than Nazarene . . . or was it a mistake ?"
If he had looked at the Genevan version of Matthew ii. 23, he would
have found that where the Authorised reads: "He shall be called a Nazarene," the Genevan Bible reads : "That hee should be called a Nazarite."

Of Shakespeare's effective use of Bible incidents it may suffice to cite
two instances : the application of the story of Jacob and the "eanlings
streak'd and pied" to the subject of interest on money in a spirit both
Biblical and Aristotelian, and the comment of Antonio, reminiscent of
the story of the Temptation :

> The devil can cite Scripture for his purpose.
>
> (*Merchant of Venice*)

Perhaps the most moving is the passionate speech of the forsaken Richard :

> Give sorrow leave awhile to tutor me
> To this submission. Yet I well remember
> The favours of these men. Were they not mine ?
> Did they not sometime cry "All hail" to me ?
> As Judas did to Christ : but he in twelve
> Found truth in all but one ; I in twelve thousand none.
>
> .   .   .   .
>
> Nay all of you that stand and look upon,
> Whilst that my wretchedness doth bait myself,

37

> Though some of you with Pilate wash your hands,
> Showing an outward pity ; yet you Pilates
> Have here delivered me to my sour cross,
> And water cannot wash away your sin.
>
> *(Richard II)*

Shakespeare may be taken for many others who in the course of our literature, not writing on devout themes, have found in Scriptural allusion and phrasing some of the most moving of their effects. For with the stories and wisdom and poetry came new words and effective phrases applicable to many circumstances. To Tyndale we owe, as has been said, the form Jehovah which we are now asked to abandon for the more barbaric-sounding Javeh. The late Henry Bradley, in that delightful book, *The Making of English*, attributes to him "long-suffering" and "peacemakers" (for "eirenopoioi"), and points out that the word "beautiful" has not been found used by any writer before Tyndale : "He certainly did not invent it, but there is no doubt that by introducing it into the People's Book he helped to bring it into general use." To Coverdale he attributes "lovingkindness" and "tender mercy." But besides words there are innumerable phrases which have become applicable beyond their first use : "A perfect Babel," "the Prophet's chamber," "the wise and foolish virgins," "to cast pearls before swine," "Gallio-like behaviour," "the eleventh hour" and many others. The whole tone of the Old and the New Testament is one of elevated and passionate sentiment that could not but quicken the imagination of a poet. There is not a great deal of purely picturesque and sensuous poetry, if there are some lovely passages. The "luscious" imagery of which Mr. Somerset Maugham complains is to be found in the *Song of Solomon*, both luscious and quaintly oriental: "Thy neck is as a tower of ivory; thine eyes like the fishpools in Heshbon by the gate of Bath-rabbim ; thy nose is as the tower of Lebanon which looketh toward Damascus." In the Apocalypse precious stones abound. Yet sensuousness is not the note of Biblical imagery. Even in the *Song* we get a more passionate strain : "Love is strong as death ; jealousy is cruel as the grave . . . Many waters cannot quench love." "Thou art beautiful, O my love, as Tirzah, comely as Jerusalem, terrible as an army with banners." "Until the day break, and the shadows flee away." Realism and passion are the note of Biblical imagery. It was to the Greek and Latin classics, especially Ovid, Virgil and Homer, that our poets went for sources of picturesque description such as one gets in the *Merchant of Venice* :

> The moon shines bright, in such a night as this
> When the sweet wind did gently kiss the trees,
> And they did make no noise, in such a night
> Troilus methinks mounted the Troyan walls
> And sigh'd his soul toward the Grecian tents

NOAH'S ARK
Woodcut from Caxton's *Golden Legend*, 1483

Where Cressid lay that night.   In such a night
Did Thisbe fearfully o'ertrip the dew . . .
                              In such a night
Stood Dido with a willow in her hand,

and so on in story after story from Ovid ; and Milton can write in the
same vein :

This saying, from her husband's hand her hand
Soft she withdrew, and like a Woodnymph light
Oread or Dryad, or of Delia's train,
Betook her to the groves, but Delia's self
In gait surpass'd and Goddesslike deport.

There is little of that kind of painting in the Scriptures.   The metaphors and hyperboles and personifications of Hebrew poetry breathe
something of what Grote calls the terrible intensity of the Semitic mind,
(the "ferocious strength of will") : "the mountains melted from before
the Lord," "the stars in their courses fought against Sisera," "the beauty

of Israel is slain upon thy high places : how are the mighty fallen,"
"Saul and Jonathan were lovely and pleasant in their lives, and in their
death they were not divided : they were swifter than eagles, they were
stronger than lions," "woe unto them that draw iniquity with cords of
vanity, and sin as a cart-rope," "But the wicked are like a troubled sea,
for it cannot rest, and its waters cast up mire and dirt," "for he that
wavereth is like a wave of the sea driven with the wind and tossed,"
"they sow the wind and they shall reap the whirlwind," "As the shepherd
rescueth out of the mouth of the lion two legs or a piece of an ear so shall
they be rescued that sit in Samaria in the corner of a couch and on the
silken cushions of a bed" ; but there is no end to these sublime and
passionate figures. They are of the kind to which Shakespeare approxi-
mated in the great tragedies, *Hamlet, Macbeth, Othello, Lear*, and in some
of those gathered in Wolfgang Clemens' interesting study of Shakespeare's
imagery it seems to me that, consciously or half-consciously, the nucleus
of the figure has come to the dramatist from his memory of a Biblical
image : "The sun of Rome is set" (J.C. V. 3. 61) recalls "her sun
is gone down while yet day" (Jer. xv. 9); "conjures the wandering stars
and makes them stand" (Ham. V. i. 278), "Sun stand thou still upon
Gibeon, and thou Moon in the valley of Ajalon." (Josh. x. 12) ; "Life's
but a walking shadow" (Macb. V. v. 20), "Man that is born of woman
is of few days and full of trouble. He cometh forth like a flower and is
cut down ; he fleeth also as a shadow and continueth not." (Job. xiv. 1-2) ;
"His virtues will plead like angels trumpet-tongued against The deep
damnation of his taking off" (Macb. I. vii. 19), "And he shall send his
angels with a great sound of a trumpet, etc." (Matth. xxiv. 31) ; "for fear
the very stones prate of my whereabout" (Macb. II. i. 58), "The stones
shall cry out of the wall" (Hab. ii. 11). "A man . . . That thunders,
lightens, opens graves and roars" (J.C. I. iii. 72) is an obvious reference
to "and the earth did quake and the rocks rent, and the graves were opened"
(Matth. xxvii. 51-2). The long speech in Hamlet about "some vicious
mole," "some habit that too much o'er-leavens The form of plausive
manners, etc." is an elaboration of the text "A little leaven leaveneth the whole
lump," the thought of leaven as corrupting coming from the belief, expressed by Plutarch, concerning leaven, "itself the offspring of corruption
and corrupting the mass of dough."

If Shakespeare's metaphors seem at times to derive from the Bible,
and are of the same realistic, passionate kind, Milton in his last poems
more deliberately cultivated a style Biblical in its eschewing of decorative
writing. In *Paradise Lost* he had allowed himself a free use of the epic,
elaborate simile drawn in about equal measure from Nature, the Classics
and the Bible. In *Paradise Regained* there is not a single figure of this
kind in the first three books. In *Samson Agonistes* there is only one of a
decorative kind, and that in the ironical description of his wife :

'THE JUST UPRIGHT MAN IS LAUGHED TO SCORN'

Illustration to the *Book of Job*

Water colour by William Blake, 1757 - 1827

By courtesy of the Pierpont Morgan Library

JOHN RUSKIN 1819 - 1900

Water colour by Sir Hubert von Herkomer, 1881

By courtesy of the National Portrait Gallery

That so bedeckt ornate and gay,
Comes this way sailing
Like a stately ship
Of Tarsus, bound for the Isles
Of Javan or Gadire
With all her bravery on, and tackle trim,
Sails fill'd, and streamers waving,
Courted by all the winds that hold them play,
An amber scent of odorous perfume
Her harbinger.

The few others are realistic and charged with feeling: "grow up and perish as the summer fly," "so much of adder's wisdom I have learned,"

Why are his gifts desirable: to tempt
Our earnest prayers, then given with solemn hand
As graces, draw a scorpion's tail behind?

But Milton's deliberate use of the very words of Scripture requires and repays careful study. Underneath the classical cast of his sentence and verse lurks, or is obvious, a so exact use of the actual words that he is able to leave ambiguous the sense in which he himself understood them, which, as the *De Doctrina* shows, was not always the orthodox interpretation.

THE WORD OF GOD: MILTON TO RUSKIN

S has been said above, there are two things to be studied in estimating the effect of the Bible on English thought and literature—the translation regarded as a piece of literature, its influence on the diction and rhythm of our verse and prose, secondly, the Bible itself, accepted as the Word of God, superseding any claim of the Church as interpreter or as a vehicle of authoritative tradition. In the seventeenth century a great part of the English people, were, it has been said, "intoxicated with the poetry of the Bible and with the hope for a heaven on earth." In the great revival of the eighteenth century, Wesleyan and Evangelical, the influence of the Bible was still supreme, but its effect was softened and sentimentalized by what the earlier century had regarded with great suspicion, the appeal of hymns which were "merely human compositions." In the nineteenth century, cross-currents begin to flow.

To Milton the meeting of the Long Parliament, and opening of the Presbyterian attack upon the Prelates, was no merely political or even ecclesiastical event, it contained the hope of a Second Coming: "Come forth out of thy royal chambers, O Prince of all the Kings of the earth, put on the visible robes of thy imperial majesty, take up that unlimited sceptre which thy Almighty Father hath bequeathed thee; for now the voice of thy Bride calls thee, and all creatures sigh to be renewed." In his controversy on the side of the Presbyterians Milton early became aware that the appeal to Antiquity, to history, was dangerous: "we both forsake our own grounds and reasons which led us at first to part from Rome, that is to hold the Scriptures against all antiquity; we remove our cause into our adversaries' own court." The safest line for the Protestant is to allow no appeal from the Scripture: "Let them chant while they will of prerogatives, we shall tell them of Scripture; of custom, we of Scripture; of Acts and Statutes, still of Scripture, till the quick and piercing word enter to the dividing of their souls, and the mighty weakness of the Gospel throw down the weak mightiness of man's reasoning." "Wherefore should we not urge only the Gospel, and hold it ever in their faces like a mirror of diamond till it dazzle and pierce their misty eyeballs? Maintaining it the honour of its absolute sufficiency and supremacy inviolable." Accordingly Milton set himself in the *De Doctrina Christiana* to work out for himself and "all Christians" a creed based on the Scriptures alone: "since I enroll myself among the number of those who acknowledge the Word of God alone as the rule of faith." "Let us then discard reason in sacred matters, and follow the doctrine of Holy Scripture exclusively." For the form of the great poem he was to make his life-work Milton chose as his models the classical poems of Greece and Rome; for his critical guide "that sublime art which in Aristotle's Poetics, in Horace, and the Italian commentaries of Castelvetro, Tasso, Mazzini and others teaches what are the laws of a true epic poem, what of a dramatic, what of a lyric, what decorum is which is the grand masterpiece to observe." Yet even as early as this (1642) he finds in the Scriptures counterparts to each of these forms, and in lyrical poetry, "those frequent songs throughout the law and prophets . . . not in their divine argument alone, but in the very critical art of composition, may be easily made appear over all the kinds of lyrical poesy to be incomparable." Accordingly if *Paradise Lost* is a Virgilian epic, and *Samson Agonistes* a Sophoclean tragedy, *Paradise Regained* is modelled on the *Book of Job;* and, in the final reply of the Saviour to Satan's eulogy of Athens, Milton finds in the Scriptures not only the fountainhead of truths unknown to the Greek Philosophers:

Ignorant of themselves, of God much more,
And how the world began, and how man fell
Degraded by himself, on grace depending;

JOHN MILTON, 1608-1674
Engraving by George Vertue

but he finds also poetic beauty and originality :

> Or if I would delight my private hours
> With music or with poem, where so soon
> As in our native language can I find
> That solace ? All our law and story strew'd
> With hymns, our psalms with artful terms inscrib'd,

Our Hebrew songs and harps in Babylon,
That pleas'd so well our victors' ear declare
That rather Greece from us these arts deriv'd.

In the *De Doctrina* Milton developed some heresies of his own. It cannot be said that even his Arianism intrudes itself obviously into the three poems in which he set forth the Christian doctrine of the Fall of Man, forfeiting or corrupting the divine gift of reason; the Atonement by the perfect obedience and the death of the Son of God; or thinking, if of himself also of the English people, the way of recovery ever open through repentance, "a broken and a contrite heart." But Milton's reading of Christian doctrine and experience was a stern one, emphasises the pessimistic strain which is not wanting in the Scriptures: "the regenerate are few," "Strait is the gate and narrow is the way, and few there be that find it," an aspect of Christian teaching which to the emotional convert, whose approach is more of the heart than of the intellect, is lost to sight in the entirety of his love and trust.

Such a more emotional approach was that of John Bunyan, for whom also the Bible was the sole and entire source of truth. His regard for the Bible made him as suspicious of the Quakers' "inner light" as of prelatical authority. In learning Bunyan was at the opposite pole from Milton, who read his Scriptures in the original Hebrew and Greek. The Latin translations in the *De Doctrina* are his own, certainly not those of the Vulgate; Bunyan's quotations are from the Authorised version. In his *Grace Abounding to the Chief of Sinners*, where he describes the storms through which he passed between his first conviction of sin and the assurance of salvation, texts hum round his head like flies on a summer day, or like mosquitos on a damp evening, for they are as often alarming as consoling. They dart in through an open window, or sound in his ear like the voice that cried to Macbeth, "Sleep no more"—"now about a week or fortnight after this I was much followed by this Scripture, *Simon, Simon, behold Satan hath desired to have you*, Luke xxii. 31, and sometimes it would sound so loud within me, yea, as it were, call so strongly after me that once, above all, I turned my head over my shoulder thinking verily that some man had, behind me, called me being at a great distance methought he called so loud." And when, at length, assurance came to his tormented soul it was borne on the wings of a text: "Suddenly this sentence fell upon my soul, *Thy Righteousness is in Heaven*; and methought withal, I saw with the eyes of my soul Jesus Christ at God's right hand, there, I saw, was my righteousness so that where ever I was, or whatever I was doing, God could not say of me *He wants my Righteousness*, for that was just before him." And so later Bunyan translated his experience, and the Scripture as he read it, into the well known allegory, *The Pilgrim's Progress*, in two parts, of Christian and of his wife Christiana, the marginal notes to which keep the reader in constant touch with the

44

JOHN BUNYAN, 1628-1688
Drawing by Robert White

Scriptural authority. Thus four great imaginative works of the century, *Paradise Lost, Paradise Regained, Samson Agonistes* and *The Pilgrim's Progress* are the expression of a reaction intellectual and spiritual to the text of the Bible, read as the sole and complete word of God to men.

In the second great religious and puritan movement, of the following century, which is connected with the names of Watts, Whitefield, the Wesleys, Newton and Cowper, to say nothing of others, the Bible is once more the supreme revelation. The movement began, indeed, within the Church of England, at least as regards the Wesleys. In fact it was their regular, weekly attendance at the Eucharist which won for Charles and his small group of friends the title of "Methodists," before John had joined him at Oxford. It was this which evoked the scorn of their fellow-students, and the disapproval of the authorities. John Wesley had no desire to leave the Church, and had a regard for the history and authority of the Church. But this is not the place to sketch even in outline the history of Methodism. Wesley passed through a less agitated, but almost as painful, an experience as Bunyan before he found assurance of salvation, through the influence of the Moravians, in the doctrine of the conviction of sin and acceptance of salvation through the merits and death of Christ, an experience which could be, and more often than not was, instantaneous, and was followed at once by the duty of preaching to others. His final conviction, and escape from the fear of death, which he had expressed to himself shortly before in the words of Donne :

> I have a sin of fear that when I have spun
> My last thread I shall perish on the shore,

was followed at once by the out-of-door preaching which, with the attendant phenomena of instantaneous conversion, was the great feature of Methodism. But if like Bunyan in this experience, he resembled Milton in another. He became gradually convinced that he had attached too much authority to Antiquity and Councils. In September 1713 he began reading over Bishop Beveridge's *Pandectae Canonum Conciliorum* (1672) and came to the conclusion that "Nothing could so effectually have convinced me that both particular and general councils may err, and have erred ; and of the infinite difference between the decisions of the wisest men and those of the Holy Ghost recorded in his word."

But the eighteenth was a less heroic, a more humanitarian, century than the seventeenth, and the most characteristic product of the Evangelical movement, whether without or later within the Church of England, was no Scriptural epic or allegory but a flood, one might almost say, of hymns. There had been much religious poetry in the former century, witness not Milton only but Donne, Herbert, Vaughan, Traherne and others ; but even the lyrical poems of such ardent souls were not hymns, not the expression of the Church, the Congregation, as such but of the individual mind and experience of the particular poet. The reason was, of course, the conviction of the Puritan, whether within or without the Church, that there must be no introduction into the service of the Church of merely human compositions, "adeoque nefas esse Christianorum aliquem ad ullum religionis cultusve actum cogi cuius ratio ex Scripturis reddi nequit aperta" (Ames : *Puritanismus Anglicanus*, 1658.) Our earliest post-Reformation hymns are the morning, evening and midnight hymns of Bishop Ken included in his *Manual of Prayers for Winchester Scholars* (1695). But our first great hymn-writer was Isaac Watts (1674-1748), whose earliest hymn was composed in the same year, 1695, "Behold the glories of the Lamb." He was not a Wesleyan but a Nonconformist minister in London. That he was aware of the innovation implied in the suggestion that hymns of "meer human composure" might be introduced into the worship of the Church is shown by the Preface to the *Hymns and Spiritual Songs* (1707) and by the title which he gave to his second volume, *The Psalms of David Imitated in the Language of the New Testament, and Apply'd to the Christian State and Worship* (1719). To

'CHRISTIAN MEETING EVANGELIST'
Illustration from Bunyan's *Pilgrim's Progress*, 1767 edition

this also is prefixed an *apologia* for his boldness, in which he claims that the Psalms of "the Royal Author" are not the fittest expression of the feelings of a Christian : "Moses, Deborah and the Princes of Israel and all the Saints under the Jewish State, sung their own Joys, and Victories, their own Hopes and Fears and Deliverances . . . and why must we, under the Gospel, sing nothing else but the Joys, Hopes and Fears of Asaph and David ? Why must Christians be forbidden all other Melody but what arises from the Victories and Deliverances of the Jews." "Some of them [the Psalms] are almost opposite to the spirit of the Gospel : Many of them foreign to the State of the New Testament, and widely different from the present circumstances of Christians . . . Thus by keeping too close to David in the House of God the Veil of Moses is thrown over our hearts." It is thus as a paraphrase of the first five verses of the ninetieth psalm that the best of his hymns, which might well replace any national anthem : "Our God, our help in ages past," appears in the 1719 volume. The other well-known hymn "When I survey the wondrous cross" belongs to the collection intended for use at the Communion service. The *Divine Songs Attempted in easy Language for the Use of Children* (1715) include some of a terrifying character :

> There is a dreadful Hell
> And everlasting pains
> Where sinners must with Devils dwell
> In darkness, fire and chains ;

but also the charming "Hush my Dear, lie still and slumber" and the once well-known " 'Tis the voice of the sluggard," "How doth the little busy bee," and "Let dogs delight to bark and bite." There was no thought in Watts's mind of disparaging the Scriptures : "I grant 'tis necessary and proper that in translating every Part of Scripture for our Reading or Hearing the Sense of the Original should be exactly and faithfully represented for there we hear what God says to us in his Word." But in singing it is *our* feelings that we are expressing, just as Asaph and "the Royal Author" had done.

Among the Wesleyans the best hymn-writer was Charles Wesley, though John made his contributions. To Charles we owe "Hark the Herald Angels sing," which in his own version ran "Hark through all the welkin rings," "Love divine all love excelling," "Lo he comes with clouds descending," "Christ the Lord is risen to-day," and others. The Wesleyans were in time divided into the Wesleyan Methodists and the Calvinist Methodists or Countess of Huntingdon's Connection. The leader of the Calvinists was the very emotional preacher Whitefield, John Wesley of the other division. But the most impassioned champion of Calvinism, Predestination, was not a Wesleyan but an evangelical minister in the Church of England, Augustus Toplady, a bitter opponent of John Wesley.

JOHN WESLEY PREACHING
Oil painting by P. J. de Loutherbourg, 1740-1812

It is in one of his impassioned defences of his doctrine that he bursts into his own great hymn, two verses of which express the quintessence of the Calvinist refusal of all merit except the imputed merits of Christ :

> Nothing in my hand I bring,
> Simply to thy cross I cling.

John and Charles Wesley, like Milton and Foxe earlier, rejected the doctrine but it was the faith of the two chief hymn writers of the Evangelical wing of the Church of England, Newton and Cowper. The *Olney Hymns* not infrequently, like those of Watts, refer to the text on which the hymn is based, *e.g.* "There is a fountain filled with blood" (Zech. xiii. 1.), "Hark my soul it is the Lord" (John xxi. 16.) But William Cowper has a larger interest than merely as the author of the above hymns as well as of "God moves in a mysterious way." He, in a way, linked Evangelical religion with the Nature poetry of the century which, influenced by Newton's discoveries, tended in Thomson's *Seasons*, towards a rhetorical Deism. In Cowper's poems the Methodist rejection of the world and its enticements and "laying up treasures on earth" readily blended with the invalid's love of retirement and of the country :

49

God made the country and man made the town.

None of the landscape poets of the century came so near to the mood of Wordsworth as Cowper :

> Oh nature ! whose Elysian scenes disclose
> His bright perfections at whose word they rose,
> Next to that Power who form'd thee and sustains,
> Be thou the great inspirer of my strains.

In *A Winter Walk at Noon* in the *Task* Cowper anticipates a mood of Wordsworth :

> No noise is here, or none that hinders thought.
> The redbreast warbles still, but is content
> With slender notes, and more than half suppress'd :
> Pleas'd with his solitude, and flitting light
> From spray to spray, where'er he rests he shakes
> From many a twig the pendent drops of ice,
> That tinkle in the wither'd leaves below.
> Stillness accompanied with sounds so soft
> Charms more than silence. Meditation here
> May think down hours to moments. Here the heart
> May give an useful lesson to the head,
> And learning wiser grow without his books.

That is Wordworth's :

> Books ! 'tis a dull and endless strife :
> Come hear the woodland linnet !
> How sweet his music ! On my life,
> There's more of wisdom in it !

But Cowper will not go the whole way with Wordsworth. A retired life in contact with the beauties of Nature may produce a mood conducive to meditation and acceptance of the Truth. But to find that Truth, and a saving knowledge of God, one must go to a Book. The cottage wife may be wiser than Voltaire, for she :

> Just knows, and knows no more, her Bible true—
> A truth the brilliant Frenchman never knew,
> And in that charter reads with sparkling eyes
> Her title to a treasure in the skies.

Knowing his Bible Cowper knows that the geologists, who were later to trouble Tennyson, are just wrong :

> some drill and bore
> The solid earth, and from the strata there
> Extract a register, by which we learn

WILLIAM COWPER, 1731-1800
Pastel by George Romney, 1792

That He who made it and reveal'd its date
To Moses was mistaken in its age.

It was, a French historian tells us, the Evangelical influence which
more than anything else saved us from the horrors of the French Revolution.
Nor did the influence quickly pass away in the century which followed.
The definite teaching about Sin and Guilt, Heaven and Hell (not least the
latter), Conversion and Sanctification remained a power which, accepted

or rebelled against, formed a great part of the background of English feeling and habits. The Bible and Watts's hymns, including the *Divine Songs for Children*, were what, a recent writer says, "all right-minded parents" brought up their children on. So dominant was Evangelical Christianity that any definite attack, whether by a Paine or a Shelley, practically outlawed the writer here and, as Paine found, in America. To Lamb even, it seemed that Shelley's theories were "miching malice and mischief." To Charles Kingsley, Byron's poetry seemed less dangerous to a Christian than Shelley's. To an Evangelical like Richard Cargill, if we may trust Crabb Robinson, Wordsworth in the *Excursion* was anti-Christian: "It is only faith in the Redeemer that constitutes Christian feeling. Everything else is opposed to that." To another, Byron is much closer to the Christian truth: "He saw in his works the profoundest views of the depravity of human nature—not indeed spiritual views, but though not spiritually minded Lord Byron has described the human heart, and the intense truth of all his poetry is its great excellence." Byron, in fact, had been educated on the Bible in Calvinist Scotland and Methodist England, and he never outgrew the effect: "Send," he writes to Murray in 1821, "a common Bible, of a good legible print (bound in Russia). I *have* one; but as it was the last gift of my Sister (whom I shall probably never see again) I can only use it carefully, and less frequently, because I like to keep it in good order. Don't forget this, for I am a great reader and admirer of those books, and had read them through before I was eight years old—that is to say, the *Old* Testament, for the New struck me as a task, but the other as a pleasure. I speak as a *boy*, from the recollected impression of that period at Aberdeen in 1796." Poor Fletcher's illiterate letter to Augusta tells how the convulsive attacks which led up to the final illness "Made my Lord Doubley attentive Both to the Maxim of Low Living and the More Greater Duty of a good Christian which I am verry Happy to say My Lord Studyed most Ferventley for the Bible was Placed on his Lordship's Breakfast table has reagularly has his Simple Cup of tea which his Lordship always Drank with out either Cream or Suger." Augusta's gift and Fletcher's record are more characteristic of the period than significant as to Byron's mind. But indeed it needs no psychologist to discover what is written so clearly over all he composed. It is the Orthodox Evangelical doctrine of sin and guilt and retribution with which Byron is always inwardly at war:

> Our life is a false nature—'tis not in
> The harmony of things,—this hard decree,
> This ineradicable taint of sin,
> This boundless Upas,—this all-blasting tree,
> Whose root is earth—whose leaves and branches be
> The skies which rain their plagues on men like dew—

Disease, death, bondage—all the woes we see,
And worse, the woes we see not—which throb through
The immedicable soul, with heart-aches ever new.

"Of the Immortality of the Soul it appears to me that there can be little doubt. . . A material resurrection seems strange, and even absurd, except for purposes of punishment ; and all punishment which is to revenge rather than to correct must be morally wrong. . . Human passions have probably disfigured the divine doctrines here, but the whole thing is inscrutable. It is useless to tell me *not* to *reason* but to *believe*. You might as well tell a man not to wake but *sleep*. And then to *bully* with torments, and all that. I cannot help thinking that the *menace* of Hell makes as many devils as the severe penal codes of inhuman humanity make villains." "Man is born *passionate* of body, but with an innate though secret tendency to the love of Good in his Mainspring of Mind. But God help us all ! It is at present a sad jar of atoms." (*Detached Thoughts*). The motive running through Byron's tales and tragedies is clear. Good and evil in human nature are too strangely blended for pious judgements. All the heroes of his early melodramatic tales in verse are, or are meant to be, "great, bad men." It is the same with the more readable of the dramas. Sardanapalus is a voluptuary but courageous and humane. Cain is a noble if passionate creature. Cain's descendants, in *Heaven and Earth*, are superior to those who are content to live on when all their fellows are to perish, to live on to repeat the same sins and endure the same woes. "If the whole world were going to Hell," he told Kennedy, "he would prefer going with them." Southey's ridiculous poem provoked a rather scurrilous opening to the *Vision of Judgement*, but neither in that brilliant poem nor the greater *Don Juan* is Christianity treated with Voltairean levity. His last journey to Greece may, if one wishes, be regarded as a fresh bid for popularity; his motives were always mixed. A charitable mind would see in it, at least *also*, a desire to do something worthy before his death, even a note of penitence : "Poverty is wretchedness ; but it is perhaps to be preferred to the heartless, unmeaning dissipation of the higher orders. I am thankful I am now clear of that, and my resolution to remain clear of it for the rest of my life is immovable."

If Byron was the only one of the greater romantics whom Biblical, Evangelical Christianity had got *inside*, so that he might rebel but could never ignore or entirely reject, the Victorian whose work was shaped and coloured by the same influence, whether he wrote on painting and architecture or on economic and social problems, was John Ruskin. "Walter Scott and Pope's *Homer* were reading of my own election, but my mother forced me, by steady daily toil, to learn long chapters of the Bible by heart, as well as to read it every syllable through, aloud, hard names and all, from Genesis to the Apocalypse, about once a year : and to that discipline

53

—patient, accurate, and resolute—I owe, not only a knowledge of the Book, which I find occasionally serviceable, but much of my general power of taking pains, and the best part of my taste in literature. From Sir Walter Scott's novels I might easily, as I grew older, have fallen to other people's novels ; and Pope might, perhaps, have led me to take Johnson's English, or Gibbon's, as types of language ; but once knowing the 32nd of Deuteronomy, the 119th Psalm, the 15th of 1st Corinthians, the Sermon on the Mount, and most of the Apocalypse, every syllable by heart, and having always a way of thinking with myself what words meant, it was not possible for me, even in the foolishest times of youth, to write entirely superficial or formal English ; and the affectation of trying to write like Hooker and George Herbert was the most innocent I could have fallen into." (*Praeterita*). But it was not only to know good English prose from less good that Ruskin learned from this extraordinary (surely even in those days) idolatry of the Bible. It was much more. His mother had " 'devoted me to God' before I was born ; in imitation of Hannah . . . Devoting me to God meant, as far as my mother knew herself what she meant, that she would try to send me to college and make a clergyman of me ; and I was accordingly bred for the Church." While a small child he preaches to his mother and her friends, "the sermon some eleven words long . . . and I still think must have been the purest gospel, for I know it began 'People, be good.' " Once begun Ruskin was never. to cease preaching, and on the theme that people must be good if they are to do any good work, that all good art and architecture must have been the work of good men, of good social conditions. And "good" Ruskin understood in the narrow Evangelical sense of the word : "All my first books, to the end of the *Stones of Venice*, were written in the simple belief I had been taught as a child." In *Modern Painters* his praise of Turner for the truth of his representation of nature, and his own minute studies of different aspects of trees, rocks and mountains, are in the spirit of Cowper, and the objective style of Scott, rather than in the pantheistic mood of Wordsworth. And texts come almost as readily to his mind as to Bunyan's. The General Index to that work alone shows some two hundred and fifty references, and those from Genesis to Micah in the Old Testament and from Matthew to the Apocalypse in the New. His works on architecture were inspired by the same religious spirit : "In all my past work, my endeavour has been to show that good architecture is essentially religious—the production of a faithful and virtuous not an infidel and corrupted people. But I have had also to show that good architecture is not ecclesiastical . . . Good architecture has always been the work of the commonality, not the clergy . . It is the manly language of a people inspired by resolute and common purpose, and rendering resolute and common fidelity to the legible laws of an undoubted God." (*Crown of Wild Olives*.) If Ruskin gradually fell away from his Evangelical

'THE SLUGGARD'
Engraving by H. Fitzcook
Illustration to Watts's *Divine and Moral Songs for Children*

religion, the religion of conversion and salvation by faith, it was in the main because he felt so acutely the interval between Christian teaching, the Sermon on the Mount, and Christian Capitalist society. But that did not alter the Christian spirit of his work nor his use of the Bible: *Unto This Last* (1860), his first "heretical" work, owes its title and tenor to the Gospels. If his interest in the Bible altered it was, as with many others, that it shifts from the Law to the Prophets in the Old Testament, from the Epistles of St. Paul, who to Bunyan was "one of a thousand; he can beget Children, travel in Birth with Children, and nurse them himself when they are born" (*Pilgrim's Progress*), to the more practical Catholic Epistles, which Luther despised but which, Ruskin tells the workmen of Sheffield "are written to you . . as much as anyone else— the Pauline epistles being only to special persons. . . . But the Catholic epistles are directly addressed to you—every word vital for you; and the most vital of these is the one that is given in nearly the same words by two of the Apostles, Peter and Judas (not Iscariot) namely 2 Peter i. 19, to end of epistle and the epistle of Jude entire . . . For if you understand those two epistles . . . you will also understand the definition of true religious service by St. James the Bishop . . . to wit 'Pure service and undefiled . . . before God and the Father is this, to visit the fatherless and widows in their affliction, and to keep himself unspotted from the world.'"

The falling away of Ruskin from the Evangelical, Biblical religion in which he had been educated, and in which he had set out to preach and to open the eyes of readers to the moral and spiritual significance of art, is symptomatic of what I have called the cross-currents which in the century began to flow. On the one hand was the reversion to the authority of the Church in Christian teaching and order, represented among other symptoms by the Oxford Movement of the middle of the century, a movement, which, like the Methodist revival a century before, was the effect of a reaction against the increasing secularity of political and social life, but also of a growing suspicion, quickened by the reports blowing in from the country of Luther, that the Bible itself was not to remain exempt from criticism. The second current was just this of criticism, the application to the Scriptures of the same critical spirit as had been applied to the poems of Homer and other writings come down from antiquity. It is not my intention to enter at length on either of these. For thousands of people, here and in America and the Dominions, the Bible remained and remains the Word of God much as it was to Milton and Bunyan. What the Bible, read as the Word of God, in the last three centuries has been to the British people has been well stated by a Catholic: "Who will not say that the uncommon beauty and marvellous English of the Protestant Bible is not one of the great strongholds of heresy in this country? It lives on the ear like music that can never be forgotten—like the sound of a church-bell which a convert hardly knows he can forgo. . . It is part

MOUNTAINS ABOVE LAKE ANNECY
Drawing by John Ruskin from his *Studies in both Arts*, 1895

of the national mind and the anchor of national seriousness. The memory of the dead passes into it. The potent traditions of childhood are stereotyped in its verses. The dower of all the gifts and trials of a man's life is hidden beneath its words. It is the representative of the best moments ; and all that there has been about him of soft and gentle, and pure and penitent and good, speaks to him for ever out of the English Bible. It is his sacred thing which doubt has never dimmed and controversy never soiled. [Here, in quoting, Ruskin interjects "Doctor ! " for certainly there has been much controversy, and Christians have spoken of Christians in language which is a disgrace to humanity.] In the length and breadth of the land there is not a Protestant with a spark of righteousness about him whose spiritual biography is not his English Bible." (Faber, quoted in Ruskin's *Fors Clavigera*. Letter LXXVI. Notes.)

Moreover, if criticism has for some, perhaps many, people robbed the Bible of some of what might be called the magical character it had for those whom we have had in view, the feeling that could make even a man like John Wesley seek guidance from a casual opening of the book, it has for many others by no means weakened its religious value and appeal. It has rather, by showing the various constituents of the Book in better perspective, made it easier, in the words of a great critic: "to separate dead tradition from living truth and to feel a Spirit not their own working through and upon the ancestral institutions and practices of Israel, upon tribal and local ideas of God . . . lifting up and transforming these to a degree which justifies the divine claim, *Behold I make all things new.*" (George Adam Smith : *Teaching of the Old Testament in Schools.*) Of one aspect of the new perspective the interest and importance for to-day may excuse a few words. I have already come near to it in speaking of the swing over of Ruskin from the Evangelical concentration on the individual's conversion and salvation by faith to the demand for a Christian economic and social reform. As a consequence of the new criticism, says the writer quoted above, "in particular the prophets came to their own with us." The swing over has been stated more strongly by the late C. J. Montefiore: "To our forefathers, Amos, Hosea and Isaiah were all later than the Law in time and inferior in greatness and authority ... to us they are earlier in time and superior in greatness and authority." The prophets had been studied in the centuries on which I have touched (I speak subject to some correction, there were doubtless exceptions) mainly to trace the predictions of the Messiah, and of the future, as far as might be, of the Church and the World. What had been in great measure overlooked was their social implications, the significance of the cry of Amos and Micah and Isaiah: "I hate, I despise your feastdays, and I will not smell in your solemn assemblies. Though ye offer me burnt offerings and your meat offerings, I will not accept them.... Take thou away from me the noise of thy songs; for I will not hear the Melody of thy viols. But let judgement run down as waters, and righteousness as a mighty stream." (Amos v. 21-4.) "Will the Lord be pleased with thousands of rams or with ten thousands of rivers of oil? Shall I give my firstborn for my transgression, the fruit of my body for the sin of my soul? He hath showed thee, O man, what is good; and what doth the Lord require of thee, but to do justly and to love mercy, and to walk humbly with thy God." (Micah vi. 7, 8.) It was in just such a spirit that Ruskin made up his mind that it was not for him enough to be pious and to subscribe largely to charities at home or abroad, but that the first duty of a Christian was to work for the reconstruction of society on a basis of justice and mercy: "For my own part I will put up with this state of things passively not an hour longer. I am not an unselfish person, nor an Evangelical one; I have no particular pleasure in doing good; neither do I dislike doing it so much as to expect to be rewarded for it in another world. But I simply cannot paint, nor read, nor look at minerals, nor do anything else that I like, and the very light of the morning sky, when there is any—which is seldom now-a-days near London—has become hateful to me, because of the misery that I know of, and see signs of, where I know it not, which no imagination can interpret too bitterly." (*Fors Clavigera*, Letter I.) That the same revolutionary spirit lurked in the Prophets was so little suspected that poor Tom Paine could abuse the prophets in *The Age of Reason* without a suspicion that they had been fighting in their day the same battle as himself, against the exploitation of the poor by the rich: "Woe unto them that join house to house, that lay field to field, till there be no room, and ye be made to dwell alone in the midst of the land." "Woe unto them that decree unrighteous decrees, and to the writers that write perverseness: to turn aside the needy from judgement, and to take away the right of the poor of my

"`. . . . To whom thus Adam called`
`'Haste hither, Eve, and worth thy sight behold`
`Eastward among those trees, what glorious shape`
`Comes this way moving . . . .'`"

ILLUSTRATION TO MILTON'S *PARADISE LOST* BY JOHN MARTIN, 1827

people, that widows may be their spoil, and that they may make the father-less their prey!" But I need not accumulate instances. The protest of Ruskin against the doctrine of *laisser faire*, that doctrine of "liberty in the interests of the employing and commercial classes" (Nietsche), aroused so much outcry that the editor of the *Cornhill Magazine* had to discontinue the publication of his *Unto This Last*, and the publishers of *Fraser's Magazine* had to compel the editor to do likewise with the essays which became *Munera Pulveris*. "Only a genius like Mr. Ruskin could have produced such hopeless rubbish" was one line of criticism, but the rubbish was also alarming. If to-day we hear Ruskin's condemnation of a purely profiteering industry echoed from every side, from Archbishops to the humbler clergy, it is a compliment to Ruskin. But it is more. It is a proof that, if in different senses to different people and times, the Bible has proved itself the word of God in its unfailing witness to the demands of justice and mercy. "I am thankful," wrote a Scottish divine to Carlyle, apropos of Ruskin's articles, "for any unveiling of the so-called science of political economy, according to which avowed selfishness is the rule of the world. It is indeed most important preaching—to preach that there is not one God for religion and another God for human fellowship—and another God for buying and selling—that pestilent polytheism has been largely and confidently preached in our time, and blessed are those who can detect its mendacities, and help to disenchant the brethren of their power." "Let not the wise man glory in his wisdom, neither let the mighty man glory in his might, let not the rich man glory in his riches : but let him that glorieth glory in this, that he understandeth that I am the Lord which exercise lovingkindness, judgement, and righteousness in the earth: for in these things I delight, saith the Lord." (Jeremiah ix. 23-5.)

"In assuming that the English Bible may yet be made the rule of faith and conduct," wrote Ruskin, long after he had abandoned the faith of his early training, "much more is of course accepted as the basis of our future education than the reader will find taken for granted in any of my writings on political economy previous to the year 1875. It may partly account for the want of success of those writings that they pleaded for honesty without praise, and for charity without reward ;—that they entirely rejected, as any motive of moral action, the fear of future judgement ; and—taking St. Paul in his irony at his bitterest word,—*Let us eat and drink, for to-morrow we die*, they merely expanded that worldly resolution into its just terms : Yes, let us eat and drink—what else ? but let us *all* eat and drink, and not a few only, enjoining fast to the rest." (*Fors Clavigera*, Letter LXXXVI).

THE ENGLISH POETS

LORD DAVID CECIL

I

EVERY great nation has expressed its spirit in art: generally in some particular form of art. The Italians are famous for their painting, the Germans for their music, the Russians for their novels. England is distinguished for her poets. A few of these, Shakespeare, Milton, Byron, are acknowledged to be among the supreme poets of the world. But there are many others besides these. Shakespeare is only the greatest among an array of names. Seven or eight other English poets deserve world-wide fame : in addition to them, many others in every age have written at least one poem that has made them immortal. The greatness of English poetry has been astonishingly continuous. German music and Italian painting flourished, at most, for two hundred years. England has gone on producing great poets from the fourteenth century to to-day : there is nothing like it in the history of the arts.

That the English should have chosen poetry as the chief channel for their artistic talent is the result partly of their circumstances, partly of their temperament.

English is a poet's language. It is ideally suited for description or for the expression of emotion. It is flexible, it is varied, it has an enormous vocabulary ; able to convey every subtle diverse shade, to make vivid before the mental eye any picture it wishes to conjure up. Moreover its very richness helps it to evoke those indefinite moods, those visionary flights of fancy of which so much of the material of poetry is composed. There is no better language in the world for touching the heart and setting the imagination aflame.

English poetry has taken full advantage of its possibilities. Circumstances have helped it. Nature placed England in the Gothic North, the region of magic and shadows, of elves and ghosts, and romantic legend. But from an early period she has been in touch with classic civilisation, with its culture, its sense of reality, its command of form. In consequence her poetry has got the best of two traditions. On the whole Nature has been a stronger influence than history. Most good English poets have been more Gothic than classical ; inspired but unequal, memorable for their power to suggest atmosphere and their flashes of original beauty, rather than for their clear design, or their steady level of good writing. For the most part too, they write spontaneously, without reference to established rules of art. But they have often obeyed these rules, even when they were not conscious of them : and some, Milton and Chaucer for instance, are as exact in form and taste as any Frenchman. No generalisation is uniformly true about English poetry. It spreads before us like a wild forest, a tangle of massive trees and luxuriantly-flowering branches, clamorous with bird song : but here and there art has cut a clearing in it and planted a delicate formal garden.

II

ROUGHLY speaking English poetry divides itself into four phases. The first, the medieval period, is a short one. During most of the Middle Ages neither language nor the laws of versification were sufficiently developed to be a vehicle for the best poetry. Only towards the middle of the fourteenth century were they ready. Even then, it is to be doubted if they would have revealed their possibilities without the genius of one man. Geoffrey Chaucer (1340-1400), the friend of Petrarch, is the first great English poet ; and he has remained one of the greatest. He was a story-teller. Of the two works for which he is remembered, the first, *Troilus and Criseyde*, re-tells a love romance about the siege of Troy ; the second, the *Canterbury Tales*, is a collection of stories, serious and comic, supposed to be told by a troop of Pilgrims on their way to the Shrine of St. Thomas of Canterbury. Chaucer is a curious mixture of the old and the new. In his subject matter he looks back to that world of medieval Christendom which was approaching its end. His stories were old stories ; legendary romances and popular anecdotes. And he tells them in the straightforward spirit in which they were created. On the other hand his smooth easy style is something quite new ; in his work we find the English language used for the first time to produce effects as delicate, artful and economical as those of the great writers of Greece and Rome. What is the life of man, he laments,

> Now with his love, now in the colde grave,
> Alone, withouten any company.

The sad fleetingness of mortal life, the solitude of death, is conveyed in thirteen words.

But Chaucer's mastery of style is only one of his gifts. He makes his stories enthralling, and his characters alive. The Canterbury Pilgrims, the fat, genial, gap-toothed wife of Bath, the gay young Squire, "as fresh as is the month of May," the brutal miller with his red scaly neck, are as vivid as people we have met. And he can trace with the subtle sympathy of a psychological novelist the guilty waverings of poor frail Criseyde. Indeed, of all his talents, it is his sympathetic spirit that most compels our admiration. Here again his spirit shows a curious mixture of old and new. Chaucer approaches life with the innocent zest of an earlier civilisation. He delights in spring flowers, in youthful beauty, in the animal humours of the body ; a fresh gale, racy with the smell of earth, blows through his pages. But his attitude to life is not unsophisticated. He is a man of the world. He knows human nature well and has no illusions about it. Acuteness and charity combine in an ironical wisdom which sparkles over his pages in a silvery sunlight.

Chaucer left no followers to compare with himself. During the fifteenth century, medieval civilisation collapsed in a series of civil wars, and wars, as we know too well to-day, do not provide a favourable climate for poets. The only voices that made themselves heard above the storm were those of the anonymous, humble composers of popular ballads and carols. These, however were enough to make the period memorable. The childlike sweetness of the carols, the wild lilt of the ballads, with their stark, tragic stories shrouded in an atmosphere of Gothic enchantment, disturbed the imagination and thrilled the heart with a direct sharpness, denied to most sophisticated poetry :

THE UNQUIET GRAVE

The wind doth blow to-day, my love,
And a few small drops of rain ;
I never had but one true-love,
In cold grave she was lain.

I'll do as much for my true-love
As any young man may ;
I'll sit and mourn all at her grave
For a twelvemonth and a day.

The twelvemonth and a day being up,
The dead began to speak ;
"Oh who sits weeping on my grave
And will not let me sleep ?"

" 'Tis I, my love, sits on your grave,
And will not let you sleep ;
For I crave one kiss of your clay-cold lips,
And that is all I seek."

"You crave one kiss of my clay-cold lips ;
But my breath smells earthy strong ;
If you have one kiss of my clay-cold lips,
Your time will not be long.

" 'Tis down in yonder garden green,
Love, where we used to walk,
The finest flower that ere was seen
Is withered to a stalk.

"The stalk is wither'd dry, my love,
So will our hearts decay ;
So make yourself content, my love,
Till God calls you away."

With the beginning of the sixteenth century, professional poetry began to raise its head again, led by the fantastic, playful Skelton and the graceful amorous verses, modelled on classic and Italian poetry, of Wyatt and Surrey. But it was not till the reign of Elizabeth, that it emerged into full sunlight. The world that met its eyes was a changed world. England had broken with the Catholic Church, had established a new triumphant monarchy, and was on the way to lay the foundation of an Empire. Her new-born vitality and self-confidence expressed itself in a tremendous outburst of poetic talent. For a hundred years England was alive with poets, lyric poets, dramatic poets, narrative poets, philosophic poets ; and among them the greatest she ever produced. Their work reflects the age they lived in, the Renaissance ; a multi-coloured age, cruel, fantastic and glorious, mingling in a bewildering complexity, horror and beauty, barbarism and subtlety.

It passed through two phases. The first, the early Renaissance, was hopeful and joyous. After the darkness of the preceding age, man rioted in his newly discovered sense of life's splendour. This poetry is sumptuous and musical in form, in mood it is ideal and magnificent. The chief figure among non-dramatic poets is Edmund Spenser (1552-1599). His great work, *The Faerie Queene*, is a long symphonic poem, in the form of a fairy-tale romance about knights and ladies, composed in celebration of Queen Elizabeth, and in praise of those noble qualities to which it should be the aim of her subjects to aspire. Still medieval in its feeling for the magical and the marvellous, it blends the idealism of chivalry, its belief in piety and heroism and poetic love, with a pagan delight in sensuous beauty. It is a strange mixture. Venus and King Arthur, the arch-angel Gabriel

GEOFFREY CHAUCER 1340–1400
Oil painting by an unknown artist

JOHN DONNE 1573–1631
Miniature by Isaac Oliver
By gracious permission of H.M. The King

and Queen Elizabeth, jostle one another in an endless confusion of fabulous adventure. But this confusion is more than made up for by Spenser's poetic intensity. An iridescent glow of beauty suffuses his whole canvas, harmonising its most incongruous elements, and breathing forth its spirit in a stream of melody, honeyed, dreamy, and intricate ; which lulls the critical mind to sleep, like a spell woven by one of the poem's own sorcerers.

SPENSER'S MARRIAGE

Open the temple gates unto my love,
Open them wide that she may enter in,
And all the posts adorn as doth behove,
And all the pillars deck with garlands trim,
For to receive this Saint with honour due,
That cometh in to you.
With trembling steps and humble reverence,
She cometh in, before th'Almighty's view ;
Of her ye virgins learn obedience,
When so ye come into those holy places,
To humble your proud faces :
Bring her up to th'high altar, that she may
The sacred ceremonies there partake,
The which do endless matrimony make ;
And let the roaring organs loudly play
The praises of the Lord in lively notes ;
The whiles, with hollow throats,
The choristers the joyous anthem sing,
That all the woods may answer, and their echo ring.

From EPITHALAMION

At the same time a school of courtly poets arose—Sir Walter Raleigh and Sir Philip Sidney are the most famous of them—who expressed a similar spirit on a smaller scale. In mellifluous and flowered phrase, they carol of silken dalliance and Arcadian shepherds, of winged Cupid and the rose of pleasure that must be plucked ere it withers. In a sense, these poems are artificial productions ; sentiment and imagery alike are conventional ; in another sense they are as natural as the song of birds ; spontaneous outpourings of youthful fancy, intoxicated by the loveliness of the world.

The fields breathe sweet, the daisies kiss our feet,
Young lovers meet, old wives a-sunning sit,
In every street these tunes our ears do greet—
Cuckoo, jug-jug, pu-we, to-witta-woo !
Spring, the sweet Spring !

From SPRING by Thomas Nashe

A similar intoxication permeates the other great literary form of the period, the drama. Otherwise it was very different, not courtly and formal, but haphazard, racy and popular. The Elizabethan theatre was, at its inception, a very humble affair, controlled by troops of vagabond mummers, who roamed about from inn to great house providing entertainment for any one they could attract to their performances. It was a crude sort of entertainment too; its lighter pieces were a mixture of coarse farce and naïve, fairy-tale plot, relieved by singing and dancing; while its more serious efforts were incoherent melodramas made lively by as many ghosts and massacres and maniacs as could be packed into them. Such a drama did not rise to the level of literature at all. Indeed it might never have done so, had it not been that a poor bohemian scholar, Marlowe (1564-1593), turned to the theatre as a means of making a living. Considered purely as a playwright, Marlowe was not much improvement on his predecessors. He had no sense of character and no gift of construction. But he was a dramatic poet of genius: and, in his hands, these rough melodramas were transfigured into a vehicle for the soul-stirring expression of human passion.

> Ah Faustus,
> Now hast thou but one bare hower to liue,
> And then thou must be damnd perpetually:
> Stand stil you euer moouing spheres of heauen,
> That time may cease, and midnight neuer come:
> Faire Natures eie, rise, rise againe, and make
> Perpetuall day, or let this houre be but
> A yeere, a moneth, a weeke, a naturall day,
> That Faustus may repent, and saue his soule,
> *O lente, lente currite noctis equi :*
> The starres mooue stil, time runs, the clocke wil strike,
> The diuel wil come, and Faustus must be damnd.
>
> *From the last soliloquy of DOCTOR FAUSTUS*

In line after line of triumphant eloquence, Marlowe trumpets forth Elizabethan pride in man's strength and beauty, his insatiable thirst for every joy, sensual and intellectual, that life could offer.

He was followed by a writer who, to a poetic genius even richer than his own, added that talent for design and character drawing that he lacked. The peculiar significance of Shakespeare (1564-1616) in the history of English literature arises from the fact that it was he alone who had the capacity to impose order on the brilliant chaos of Elizabethan drama. He was not a revolutionary. His comedies and tragedies are compounded of the same elements as those of his contemporaries. They are the same extraordinary mixture of beauty and farce and improbable horrors. But the apparent defects of the form become in his hands virtues. The breadth

and flexibility of his imagination enabled him to unite these elements
into a whole, and to make use of their diversity to present a wider range
of experience than could have been included in any stricter form.

> To die, to sleep ;
> To sleep : perchance to dream : ay, there's the rub ;
> For in that sleep of death what dreams may come
> When we have shuffled off this mortal coil,
> Must give us pause : there's the respect
> That makes calamity of so long life ;
> For who would bear the whips and scorns of time,
> The oppressor's wrong, the proud man's contumely,
> The pangs of despised love, the law's delay,
> The insolence of office and the spurns
> That patient merit of the unworthy takes,
> When he himself might his quietus make,
> With a bare bodkin ? who would fardels bear,
> To grunt and sweat under a weary life,
> But that the dread of something after death,
> The undiscover'd country from whose bourn
> No traveller returns, puzzles the will
> And makes us rather bear those ills we have
> Than fly to others that we know not of ?

From HAMLET

In his most characteristic plays, *Hamlet* and *Antony and Cleopatra*,
he shows us life in its variety ; he ranges from tragic passion to ironical
comedy, from solid realistic portraiture to ethereal lyric beauty. Yet all
is fused into a whole, by the life-giving form of his imagination. It does
not matter if his stories are improbable : the people in them are so living
that we believe anything that we are told of them. It does not matter
that his plays are such a mixture : we only feel them truer to the hetero-
geneous nature of life. He has his limitations. Absorbed as he was in
the huge spectacle of human existence moving before his gaze, his eye
never wanders to explore the realms of spiritual light and darkness extending beyond the brief span of mortal experience.

> We are such stuff
> As dreams are made of. And our little life
> Is rounded with a sleep.

So runs the brief, baffled comment in which, in his last play, he seems to
sum up his final conclusions on the riddle of human destiny. He is the
supreme spectator ; content to report what he sees, and to let us draw
a lesson from it, if we can.

His specifically poetic quality is of a piece with the rest of his work.
Shakespeare's is a dramatic style, designed to convey as realistically as

possible, the flux of thought and feeling passing through the minds of his characters. To achieve this object he uses every means ; breaks the ordinary rules of grammar and syntax, coins words of his own and employs any sort of language, from slang to the most ornate poetic diction, without regard to conventional canons of style. He can write with classic restraint ; but his genius is of the English and Gothic type, bold and fantastic, its simplest statement thickly embroidered with the images of his exuberant fancy. On occasion, his invention over-reaches itself. In his efforts to extend the frontiers of expression, he becomes obscure or bombastic ; sometimes, too, his delight in his command over words leads him into playing tricks with them, inexcusable by any standard of good taste. But when all is said he has the most wonderful style in the world, able to convey at once a subtler and wider range of feeling than any other and in which word and thought are so closely identified that it is impossible to paraphrase his lines without losing their essential significance ; while to crown all, he writes with a natural imperial magic that makes the work of other writers seem pale or laboured by comparison.

SONNET

When, in disgrace with Fortune and men's eyes,
I all alone beweep my outcast state,
And trouble deaf heaven with my bootless cries,
And look upon myself, and curse my fate,
Wishing me like to one more rich in hope,
Featured like him, like him with friends possest,
Desiring this man's art and that man's scope,
With that I most enjoy contented least ;
Yet in these thoughts myself almost despising—
Haply I think on thee : and then my state,
Like to the Lark at break of day arising,
From sullen earth, sings hymns at Heaven's gate ;
For thy sweet love rememb'red such wealth brings
That then I scorn to change my state with kings.

Shakespeare's early work is gorgeous and sunshiny ; in maturity it is complex, sombre, weighed down with the burden of thought. Here his work is a bridge between the first Renaissance period and the second. For the golden confidence of Spenser and Marlowe did not last long. How should it ? "The glories of our blood and state, are shadows, not substantial things." And those who pursue them most recklessly, are the soonest to discover their vanity. The poets of the later Renaissance retained the vitality of the earlier : life to them remained equally fascinating. But they did not trust it in the same way. With anguish they recognised that its pleasures and achievements are transitory ; they are

SIR WALTER RALEIGH 1552 ?-1618
Oil painting by an unknown artist

incessantly aware of the inevitability of death, the mysterious uncertainty
of fate, the appalling possibilities of sin and suffering inherent in the very
nature of human existence. The dramas of the great playwrights who
followed Shakespeare : Webster, Tourneur, Ford, are glittering night-
mares in which figures of baleful splendour, burn their lives out against
a lurid background of blood and mania and supernatural darkness. Even
the one great comedian of the period, Ben Jonson (1573-1637), is touched
with the same spirit. With fierce laughter, he ruthlessly exposes the
monstrous pageant of human vice and folly.

Non-dramatic poetry shows the same change of heart. It is dominated
by one man, John Donne (1573-1631). Donne is the epitome of the new
age. In youth a passionate amorist, in age a passionate mystic, he thirsted
as unappeasably as Marlowe himself for the absolute and the perfect. But
a darker temperament, reinforced by the questionings of a restless powerful
intelligence taught him that such perfection is never achieved in this
world. Now and again he reaches his ideal ; passion and intellect fuse
together to attain a white heat of sensual or spiritual ecstasy unique in

69

English poetry. More often, however, they struggle with one another in labyrinths of baffled thought. His mode of expression faithfully mirrors his divided spirit. Gone is the smooth sweetness of Spenser and his friends.

Donne's language is colloquial, his rhythms complex, his imagery audacious and grotesque. For pages together he speaks in harsh and puzzling riddles; then suddenly comes a passage whose every word quivers, shining and transparent as a living flame.

> Dear Love, for nothing less than thee
> Would I have broke this happy dream,
>   It was a theme
> For reason, much too strong for fantasy.
> Therefore thou waked'st me wisely; yet
> My dream thou brok'st not, but continued'st it.
> Thou art so true that thoughts of thee suffice
> To make dreams truths and fables histories;
> Enter these arms, for since thou thought'st it best
> Not to dream all my dream, let's act the rest.
>
> As lightning, or a taper's light,
> Thine eyes, and not thy noise, waked me;
>   Yet I thought thee—
> For thou lov'st truth—an angel, at first sight;
> But when I saw thou saw'st my heart,
> And knew'st my thoughts beyond an angel's art
> When thou knew'st what I dreamt, when thou knew'st when
> Excess of joy would wake me, and cam'st then,
> I must confess it could not choose but be
> Profane to think thee anything but thee.
>
> *From THE DREAM*

"Donne," said Ben Jonson, "was the first poet in the world in some things." Certainly his contemporaries thought so. His influence was overwhelming. He had made lyrical poetry modern, individual and intellectual: after him it was almost impossible to go on writing in the conventional mode of the previous age. A host of writers appeared, ranging from pious clergymen to flaunting cavaliers, who sought to emulate Donne's boldness of style and fantastic ingenuities of thought. None of them was of his calibre of genius. But he had managed to communicate to them something of his intensity. So that they all have occasional flashes equal to the work of the greatest poets. Among the religious poets is the tender Herbert, the mystical Vaughan, the fiery Crashaw. The most famous of the secular are King, Carew, Suckling and the gallant Lovelace. Andrew Marvell (1621-1678) is the least unequal of Donne's followers.

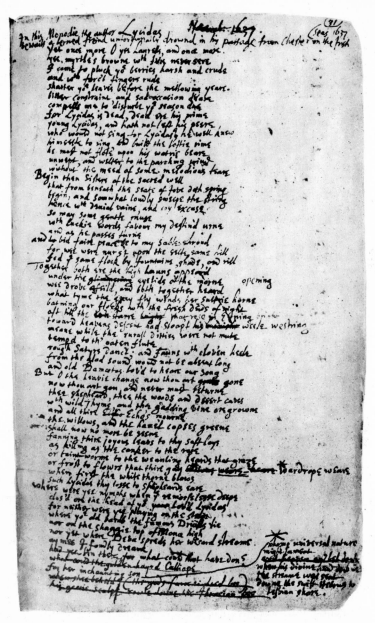

FACSIMILE EXTRACT FROM *LYCIDAS*
An elegy on the death of his friend Edward King, by John Milton

Had we but World enough, and Time,
This coyness Lady were no crime.
We would sit down, and think which way
To walk, and pass our long Loves Day. . .

But at my back I alwaies hear
Times winged Chariot hurrying near :
And yonder all before us lye
Deserts of vast eternity.
Thy Beauty shall no more be found ;
Nor, in they marble Vault, shall sound
My echoing Song : then Worms shall try
That long preserv'd Virginity :
And your quaint Honour turn to dust ;
And into ashes all my Lust.

From TO HIS COY MISTRESS

Only two important writers withstood Donne's spell, Herrick and Milton. Herrick (1591-1674) is the least solemn of English poets. His pagan spirit was cheerfully impervious to melancholy thought. Gaily he continued to sing of springtime revels and light love, of curds and cream and nosegays. But he enjoyed them so freshly, he wrote with such a fanciful felicity that, touched by his hand, these withered flowers of poetry bloom anew, with a dewy and immortal sweetness.

UPON JULIA'S CLOTHES

Whenas in silks my Julia goes,
Then, then (me thinks) how sweetly flowes
That liquefaction of her clothes.

Next, when I cast mine eyes and see
That brave Vibration each way free ;
Oh how that glittering taketh me !

There is nothing trifling about Milton (1608-1674). A scholar, a philosopher and a puritan, he thought all except the most elevated type of poetry, not worth the writing, and from an early age he made it his object to be the great English master of such poetry, to enshrine in imperishable words the highest truths known to man. Such an ambition revealed an awe-inspiring confidence in his own powers. But it was justified. Milton's genius united, in a unique way, heroic loftiness of spirit with the most delicate sensibility to every kind of sensuous beauty. He was also, alike in design and detail a master of his craft. His early work is jewelled and fanciful ; the great religious poems of his later years are sublime and austere. But each is equally remarkable for the grandeur with which it is conceived and the lucid perfection with which it is executed.

PRODESSE NON PRÆESSE

RICHARD LOVELACE 1618–1658
Oil painting attributed to John de Critz

ANDREW MARVELL 1621–1678
Oil painting by Hanneman

DESCRIPTION OF SATAN AND THE FALLEN ANGELS

                          He above the rest
In shape and gesture proudly eminent
Stood like a Towr; his form had yet not lost
All her Original brightness, nor appear'd
Less than Arch Angel ruind, and th' excess
Of Glory obscur'd : As when the Sun new ris'n
Looks through the Horizontal misty Air
Shorn of his Beams, or from behind the Moon
In dim Eclipse disastrous twilight sheds
On half the Nations, and with fear of change
Perplexes Monarchs. Dark'n'd so, yet shon
Above them all th' Arch Angel : but his face
Deep scars of Thunder had intrencht, and care
Sat on his faded cheek, but under Browes
Of dauntless courage, and considerate Pride
Waiting revenge.

From PARADISE LOST

Milton is the great example in English literature of that un-English type, the conscious artist ; whose every effect is carried out in accordance with the rules of a refined and disciplined taste. His style is all marble and precious stones ; it lacks Shakespeare's flexibility and still more his natural magic ; but it is incapable of Shakespeare's lapses.

AT A SOLEMN MUSICK

Blest pair of Sirens, pledges of Heav'ns joy,
Sphear-born harmonious Sisters, Voice, and Vers,
Wed your divine sounds, and mixt power employ
Dead things with inbreath'd sense able to pierce,
And to our high-rais'd phantasie present,
That undisturbed Song of pure content,
Ay sung before the saphire-coloured throne
To him that sits thereon
With saintly shout, and solemn Jubily,
Where the bright Seraphim in burning row
Their loud up-lifted Angel trumpets blow,
And the Cherubick host in thousand quires,
Touch their immortal Harps of golden wires,
With those just Spirits that wear victorious Palms,
Hymns devout and holy Psalms
Singing everlastingly ;
That we on Earth with undiscording voice
May rightly answer that melodious noise ;

As once we did, till disproportion'd sin
Jarr'd against natures chime, and with harsh din
Broke the fair musick that all creatures made
To their great Lord, whose love their motion sway'd
In perfect Diapason, whilst they stood
In first obedience, and their state of good.
O may we soon again renew that Song,
And keep in tune with Heav'n till God ere long
To his celestial consort us unite,
To live with him, and sing in endless morn of light.

III

MILTON marks the end of the great age. His life coincided with those civil and religious wars, in which the English Renaissance sank to extinction. The period which succeeded it was without the sensual and spiritual splendour of its predecessor ; it lacked, also, its confusion and its extravagance. England in the late seventeenth and eighteenth centuries was a society settled in civilised equilibrium, untroubled by fundamental issues, and in which questions of conduct and manners were discussed by the standards of good sense and good taste. Such a society expressed itself in a very different sort of poetry from what had gone before ; so different that subsequent generations, dazzled by the glories of the age of Shakespeare, have often denied that it was poetry at all.

This shows, however, a foolishly narrow conception of poetry. The poets of this third phase may not be of the highest kind ; but they have expressed perfectly certain aspects of human experience, not treated by other English poets. Theirs is predominantly social poetry. It deals not with the elemental passions of man, nor with his solitary dreams and visions, but with those subjects that interest him as a member of an organised society with established standards and conventions. It is the poetry of home and town and fashionable life, of friendship, flirtation and worldly wisdom : it voices the normal person's affections and his reflections on the way of the world. Its most characteristic forms are satire, didactic verse and poems of graceful compliment. When it fails it is commonplace and conventional ; it is successful by reason of its wit, elegance and rhetorical force.

Dryden (1631-1700), who introduced the new style of poetry, is the least personal of English poets. He was a great critic ; and even in his creative work he seems stimulated to write less by desire to communicate an individual vision, than by his pleasure in practising the craft of letters.

In consequence he is at his best in satire, where his wit and vigour of mind compensates for any lack of more imaginative qualities. But he tried his hand at many other forms, songs, plays, stories ; and always with a fair degree of success. His most commonplace thoughts are warmed into poetry by the sheer virile accomplishment of his writing, the swing and snap of his superb versification.

ZIMRI

Some of their chiefs were princes of the land ;
In the first rank of these did Zimri stand,
A man so various that he seemed to be
Not one, but all mankind's epitome ;
Stiff in opinions, always in the wrong,
Was everything by starts and nothing long ;
But in the course of one revolving moon
Was chymist, fiddler, statesman, and buffoon ;
Then all for women, painting, rhyming, drinking,
Besides ten thousand freaks that died in thinking.
Blest madman, who could every hour employ,
With something new to wish or to enjoy !
Railing and praising were his usual themes,
And both, to show his judgment, in extremes :
So over violent or over civil
That every man with him was God or Devil.
In squandering wealth was his peculiar art ;
Nothing went unrewarded but desert.
Beggared by fools whom still he found too late,
He had his jest, and they had his estate.

His most famous successor, Pope (1688-1744), is also a master of his craft ; not so varied but with an extremely delicate sense of style which he polished to the last degree of gleaming finish. Like that of the spider in one of his own poems, Pope's touch : "So exquisitely fine, feels in each thread and lives along the line." As Dryden represents the strength of the new school, so Pope represents its elegance, its acute perception of detail in character and custom, and all intensified by the fire of his peculiar and waspish temperament. In his satires hate becomes positively beautiful, a glittering rapier piercing the heart of its victim with one graceful deadly thrust ; his lighter poems, notably the *Rape of the Lock*, a fantasy about fashionable life, are the very triumph of artifice. The frills and airy frivolity of the beau monde are crystallised into sparkling immortality by the brilliance of his art.

75

THE LADY'S DRESSING TABLE

And now, unveil'd, the Toilet stands display'd,
Each silver Vase in mystic order laid.
This casket India's glowing gems unlocks,
And all Arabia breathes from yonder box.
The Tortoise here and Elephant unite,
Transform'd to combs, the speckled, and the white.
Here files of pins extend their shining rows,
Puffs, Powders, Patches, Bibles, Billet-doux.
Now awful Beauty puts on all its arms ;
The fair each moment rises in her charms,
Repairs her smiles, awakens every grace,
And calls forth all the wonders of her face.

From THE RAPE OF THE LOCK

Pope set the standard of taste for his age. Indeed for sixty years after his death, writers, some of them very gifted, like Goldsmith and Doctor Johnson, took him as their model. He had, however, reached perfection in his kind ; and none of his followers equalled him. Fortunately, some poets did not try. The eighteenth century saw the rise of a number of authors—Thomson and Gray, Collins and Cowper, are the most famous of them—who turned from the urban and social subjects which had engaged the pens of Pope and Dryden, to sing in quieter strains of the pleasures of retirement. They represent no violent break with the prevailing tradition. As much as Dryden and Pope, they were rational and civilised persons, accepting the standards of society in which they lived : as much as Dryden and Pope they spoke for the average intelligent man of their day. Only they spoke for him in his more contemplative and sentimental moods. They express his love for friends and home, his sober piety, his pleasure in the peaceful beauty of the countryside. As life becomes more urban, people grow more consciously appreciative of nature as such. Spenser and Milton do not draw any careful distinction between natural beauty and other beauty ; they enjoy both because they are beautiful. To Thomson (1700-1748) and Cowper (1731-1800), the untutored charm of the rural and the rustic makes a peculiar appeal ; living in a sophisticated world, the unsophisticated has for them the attraction of contrast, and their eighteenth-century eye for reality makes them describe it with delightful accuracy. The English landscape appears in their pages just as it is, undisguised by the extravagance of poetic fancy. Thomson, with his grassy distances stretching beneath sun-lit or cloudy skies, paints the broader view of it : Cowper's is more delicately exact in detail. He is memorable too as the only distinguished poet who has found his chief inspiration in domesticity, in the Englishman's characteristic tenderness for the simple pleasures and steadfast affections of home life, his sentiment for his own house, his own garden, his own pet animals.

EPITAPH ON A TAME HARE

Here lies, whom hound did ne'er pursue,
    Nor swifter greyhound follow,
Whose foot ne'er tainted morning dew,
    Nor ear heard huntsman's halloo ; . .

Old Tiney, surliest of his kind,
    Who, nursed with tender care,
And to domestic hounds confined,
    Was still a wild Jack hare. . .

His diet was of wheaten bread,
    And milk, and oats, and straw ;
Thistles, or lettuces instead,
    With sand to scour his maw. . .

But now beneath this walnut shade
    He finds his long last home,
And waits, in snug concealment laid,
    Till gentler Puss shall come.

Gray (1716-1771) and Collins (1721-1759) are less fertile writers. Their combined works only make up a slender volume of elegiac verses, in most of which pensive reflection is diversified by occasional vignettes of landscape. In Collins' poems these vignettes play the largest part ; he was the more imaginative of the two. Gray had a greater mastery of design, strengthened by a deeper note of sentiment.

In neither do we find the warmth of temperament necessary to raise them to the highest levels of poetry. But both have achieved a permanent place in English letters, by the purity of their inspiration, and the scholarly grace with which they have clothed it.

Some village-Hampden, that with dauntless breast
    The little Tyrant of his fields withstood,
Some mute inglorious Milton here may rest,
    Some Cromwell guiltless of his country's blood.

Th' applause of list'ning senates to command,
    The threats of pain and ruin to despise,
To scatter plenty o'er a smiling land,
    And read their hist'ry in a nation's eyes,

Their lot forbad : nor circumscrib'd alone
  Their growing virtues, but their crimes confin'd ;
Forbad to wade through slaughter to a throne,
  And shut the gates of mercy on mankind,

       *   *   *

Far from the madding crowd's ignoble strife,
  Their sober wishes never learn'd to stray ;
Along the cool sequester'd vale of life
  They kept the noiseless tenor of their way.

From Gray's ELEGY IN A COUNTRY CHURCHYARD

How sleep the brave, who sink to rest,
By all their countries wishes blest !
When Spring, with dewy fingers cold,
Returns to deck their hallow'd mould,
She there shall dress a sweeter sod,
Than Fancy's feet have ever trod.
By fairy hands their knell is rung,
By forms unseen their dirge is sung ;
Their Honour comes, a pilgrim gray,
To bless the turf that wraps their clay,
And Freedom shall awhile repair,
To dwell a weeping hermit there !

William Collins

Both the urban and the country schools have left their mark on the work of the last important writer in the eighteenth-century tradition. George Crabbe (1754-1832) was not a polished artist. The long bleak narratives of rural life, which make up the greater part of his work are often written in a style as bare as a guide-book ; but there is something compelling about them. The patient accuracy with which he observes the world, the unillusioned wisdom with which he judges it, make one listen to his words and forbid one to forget them.

From the general tradition of this period of English verse, two names stand apart. Robert Burns (1759-1796), a Scottish peasant, founded his work on the popular songs of his own Lowland countryside, and it has the direct infectious zest and songfulness of a ballad. But heaven had made him a great artist; he added to the natural qualities of folk-poetry, a grace, a finish and a humour of his own. The elemental feelings of humanity, the massive fun and pathos and passion of the natural man become, in his hands, the stuff of immortal poetry :

Ye flowery banks o' bonnie Doon,
  How can ye blume sae fair !
How can ye chant ye little birds,
  And I sae fu' o' care.

WILLIAM BLAKE 1757-1827
Oil painting by Phillips, 1807

Thou'll break my heart, thou bonnie bird,
   That sings upon the bough :
Thou minds me of the happy days,
   When my fause luve was true.

William Blake (1757-1827) is a more unusual type. He is in every respect a sensational contrast to his contemporaries. Possibly insane, and certainly inspired, he passed most of his time in a realm of mystical visions from which the material world was hardly visible, but which was astir with mysterious figures of demon and angel. An experience so remote from that of ordinary people makes much of Blake's work strange, and even unintelligible. But he had a lyrical gift of such unearthly power as to render this of almost no consequence. His fleeting fragments of song, his wild prophetic rhapsodies contain the distilled essence of poetry. They set the readers nerves athrill with the inexplicable force of some natural manifestation, the cry of the birds, or the rush of the wind in the tree-tops.

JERUSALEM

And did those feet in ancient time
　Walk upon England's mountains green ?
And was the holy Lamb of God
　On England's pleasant pastures seen ?

And did the Countenance Divine
　Shine forth upon our clouded hills ?
And was Jerusalem builded here
　Among these dark Satanic Mills ?

Bring me my bow of burning gold !
　Bring me my arrows of desire !
Bring me my spear ! O clouds, unfold !
　Bring me my chariot of fire !

I will not cease from mental fight,
　Nor shall my sword sleep in my hand,
Till we have built Jerusalem
　In England's green and pleasant land.

IV

BLAKE lived before his time.　His own age could not be expected to appreciate him ; but in the forty years that followed his death, once more a revolution took place in English letters.　Under the double shock of the Industrial and French Revolutions, the fabric of eighteenth-century civilisation crumbled ; its standard of taste and conduct lost their hold, and people turned for guidance to the instinctive movements of the heart and imagination.　In politics and practical life this led to a good deal of confusion.　Poetry however profited by the change. For passion and imagination are essential ingredients of the best poetry. Now, after a hundred years repression, they flared up in the brightest blaze of poetic splendour since the Renaissance.　It was marked by many of the same qualities.　Glamour and mystery, extravagance and irregularity, fantasy and naïvety came thronging back into literature.　But the poets of this new Romantic school, as it was called, were more consciously individualistic than the Elizabethans ; reacting violently against the conventions that had governed their fathers, they deliberately followed the light of their vision wherever it might lead them.　And they concentrated more on the inner life.　They turned from the humdrum world to seek inspiration in the secret dreams of the fancy and the adventures of the solitary soul.

JOHN MILTON 1608–1674
Oil painting by Van der Gucht
By courtesy of the Viscount Harcourt

JOHN DRYDEN 1631–1700
Oil painting by an unknown artist
By courtesy of the Curators of the Bodleian Library

Wordsworth (1770-1850), the first great poet of the period, was a mystic of nature. The mountains of that Lake country of north-west England which was his home, its still waters and wooded silences communicated to him the sense of an indwelling spirit of the Universe, divine and beneficent, who would, if man listened to its voice, illuminate him with its own ineffable wisdom. To interpret this voice to mankind was the aim of all Wordsworth's poetry; and he thought this was best done by expressing himself in the plainest language, undisguised by the artificial ornaments of conscious art. Only a writer with the most impeccable natural taste could follow this principle without danger. Wordsworth was far from being such an author. The result is that his work is ludicrously unequal. Often it is as flat as the flattest prose. But now and then inspiration seizes him: and he rises to a height of serene, spiritual sublimity unparalleled in English poetry. Moreover, unlike Blake, he is never so wrapt into the world of his vision as to lose sight of the common earth. He is the supreme poet of spiritual experience, who can both convey those moments of celestial glory, in which man penetrates beyond the veil of the flesh, and also show them in their true relation to the confined prosaic round of every day existence.

> But now, like one who rows,
> Proud of his skill, to reach a chosen point
> With an unswerving line, I fixed my view
> Upon the summit of a craggy ridge,
> The horizon's utmost boundary ; far above
> Was nothing but the stars and the grey sky.
> She was an elfin pinnace ; lustily
> I dipped my oars into the silent lake,
> And, as I rose upon the stroke, my boat
> Went heaving through the water like a swan ;
> When, from behind that craggy steep till then
> The horizon's bound, a huge peak, black and huge,
> As if with voluntary power instinct
> Upreared its head. I struck and struck again,
> And growing still in stature the grim shape
> Towered up between me and the stars, and still,
> For so it seemed, with purpose of its own
> And measured motion like a living thing,
> Strode after me. With trembling oars I turned,
> And through the silent water stole my way
> Back to the covert of the willow tree ;
> There in her mooring-place I left my bark,—
> And through the meadows homeward went, in grave
> And serious mood ; but after I had seen
> That spectacle, for many days, my brain
> Worked with a dim and undetermined sense
> Of unknown modes of being ; o'er my thoughts

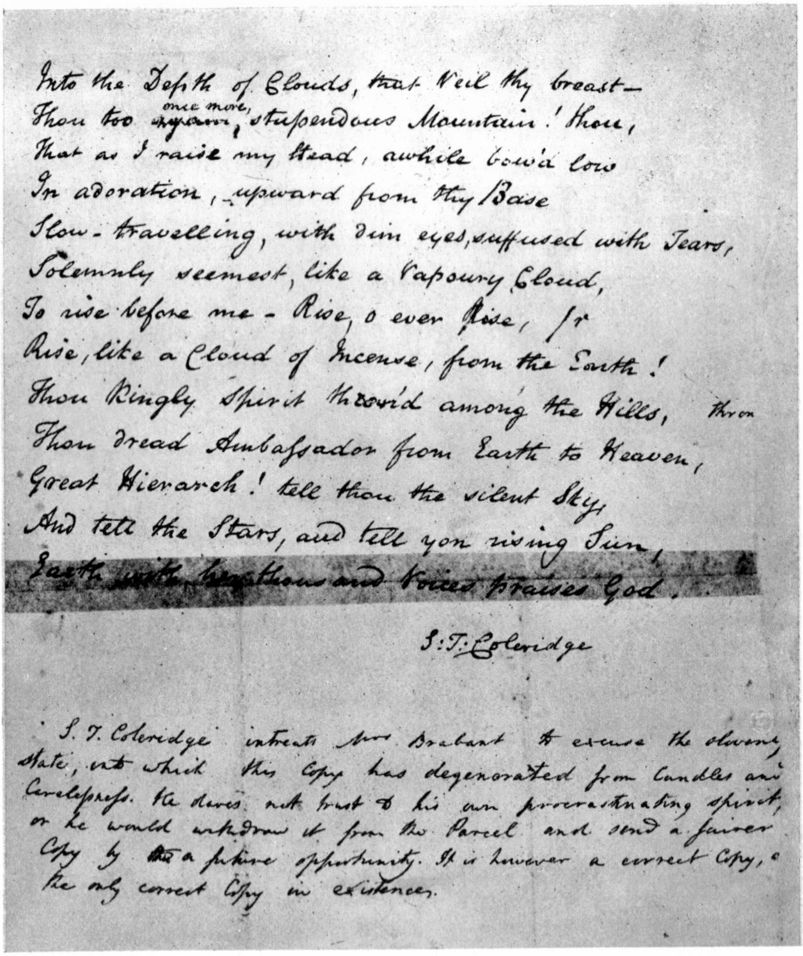

Into the Depth of Clouds, that Veil thy breast—
Thou too once more, again, stupendous Mountain! thou,
That as I raise my Head, awhile bow'd low
In adoration, upward from thy Base
Slow-travelling, with dim eyes, suffused with Tears,
Solemnly seemest, like a vapoury Cloud,
To rise before me - Rise, o ever Rise,
Rise, like a Cloud of Incense, from the Earth!
Thou Kingly Spirit thron'd among the Hills,
Thou dread Ambassador from Earth to Heaven,
Great Hierarch! tell thou the silent Sky,
And tell the Stars, and tell yon rising Sun,
Earth with her thousand voices praises God.

S. T. Coleridge

'S. T. Coleridge' intreats Mrs Brabant to excuse the slovenly State, into which this Copy has degenerated from Candles and Carelessness. He dares not trust to his own procrastinating spirit, or he would withdraw it from the Parcel and send a fairer Copy by a future opportunity. It is however a correct Copy, & the only correct Copy in existence.

HYMN BEFORE SUNRISE
Coleridge's original MS

There hung a darkness, call it solitude
Or blank desertion. No familiar shapes
Remained, no pleasant images of trees,
Of sea or sky, no colours of green fields ;
But huge and mighty forms, that do not live
Like living men, moved slowly through the mind
By day, and were a trouble to my dreams.

From THE PRELUDE

WILLIAM WORDSWORTH 1770-1850
Drawing by Robert Hancock, 1798

Wordsworth's friend, Coleridge (1772-1834), had no such definite gospel to expound. He was a man of the most varied gifts, critic and philosopher as well as poet. And in each capacity, he exhibited gleams of extraordinary genius. But, owing to some inexplicable inability to concentrate his powers, they only found complete fulfilment in a handful of poems. The most famous of these, *The Ancient Mariner*, and *Christabel*, reveal another aspect of the romantic impulse, its sensibility to the imaginative appeal of the remote and the marvellous. In a succession of pictures, preternaturally vivid as those of a dream, and set to a haunting word music, they evoke the eerie enchantment of medieval legend.

> The moving Moon went up the sky,
> And nowhere did abide ;
> Softly she was going up,
> And a star or two beside—
> Her beams bemock'd the sultry main,
> Like April hoar-frost spread ;
> But where the ship's huge shadow lay,
> The charmed water burnt alway
> A still and awful red.

Beyond the shadow of the ship,
I watched the water-snakes :
They moved in tracks of shining white,
And when they rear'd, the elfish light
Fell off in hoary flakes.

Within the shadow of the ship,
I watch'd their rich attire :
Blue, glossy green, and velvet black,
They coil'd and swam, and every track
Was a flash of golden fire.

From THE ANCIENT MARINER

A similar sensibility, but this time to the picturesque appeal of true history, is the outstanding characteristic of Sir Walter Scott's poems. Scott (1771-1832) was primarily a novelist ; his rousing ballad tales in verse are poetry for boys rather than men. As such, however, they are as good as possible, stirring and gallant as the sight of a regiment stepping out to the sound of drum and bugle. The other romantic poets, Keats, Shelley, Byron, rise higher. Keats (1795-1821) like Coleridge responded to the attraction of medieval literature. But in him this was only one expression of a feeling for beauty of every kind. "I have loved the principal of beauty in all things," he said, and the object of his poetry was to express this love. He was equipped to do it. Not only could he appreciate beauty in its most varied manifestations, but he had an extraordinary faculty for detecting precisely the qualities, in which each specific manifestation consisted. Keats died very young, at the age of twenty-five, before he had learnt to discipline his exuberant talent ; and some of his work is marred by a youthful floridity. But he had a gift for the right word, for the exact visualising phrase that can only be compared to Shakespeare's.

ON FIRST LOOKING INTO CHAPMAN'S HOMER

Much have I travell'd in the realms of gold,
   And many goodly states and kingdoms seen ;
   Round many western islands have I been
Which bards in fealty to Apollo hold.
Oft of one wide expanse had I been told
   That deep-brow'd Homer ruled as his demesne ;
   Yet did I never breathe its pure serene
Till I heard Chapman speak out loud and bold :
Then felt I like some watcher of the skies
   When a new planet swims into his ken ;
Or like stout Cortez when with eagle eyes
   He stared at the Pacific—and all his men
Look'd at each other with a wild surmise—
   Silent, upon a peak in Darien.

PERCY BYSSHE SHELLEY 1792-1822
Crayon portrait attributed to Beyerhaus after Clint

In his pages, spring and autumn, the sensuous grace of classic myth, the moon-lit forests of fairy-tale, rise before the mental eye in all the detailed, breathing loveliness of reality.

Shelley (1792-1822) is the lyrical poet of the movement. Take it all in all, he is the most wonderful lyrical poet England has ever produced. In flight after flight of soaring, full-throated song he gives voice to those aspirations after an ideal freedom alike in love and politics, which surged in the breasts of the youth of his time. Youthfulness is one of Shelley's outstanding qualities. He has all youth's enthusiasm, its dreamy exaltation, its refusal to compromise with evil. Indeed, his idealism often made him very unhappy. His mood hovered between rapture at life as he wished it to be and despair at life as he found it. This division of spirit was, however, to the advantage of his poetry. For it kept it from becoming inhuman. His songs glow with an ethereal radiance, but they also throb with the poignancy of a soul who has known what it is to suffer.

85

Asia. The rocks are cloven, and through the purple night
 I see cars drawn by rainbow-winged steeds
 Which trample the dim winds : in each there stands
 A wild-eyed charioteer urging their flight.
 Some look behind, as fiends pursued them there,
 And yet I see no shapes but the keen stars :
 Others, with burning eyes, lean forth, and drink
 With eager lips the wind of their own speed,
 As if the thing they loved fled on before,
 And now, even now, they clasped it.
 Their bright locks
 Stream like a comet's flashing hair : they all
 Sweep onward.
Demogorgon. These are the immortal Hours,
 Of whom thou didst demand. One waits for thee.

From PROMETHEUS UNBOUND

  There is nothing of Shelley's innocence about Byron (1788-1824).
A dynamic, theatrical personality, ruthlessly observant of other people
and morbidly sensitive to their opinion of himself he both lived and wrote
with one eye fixed upon his audience. They returned his gaze. The
figure of the beautiful Lord Byron with his reckless brilliance, and his
shocking thrilling career of love and lawlessness, caught the imagination
of the public as no poet ever has before or since. Since then a reaction
has set in. Byron, in his own day far more admired than Keats or Shelley,
is now rated below them. This is partly just ; there is something coarse
and stagey about his talent. But the decline of his reputation is also
due to a passing fashion in taste. During the nineteenth century the
standard of poetry was set by the other romantics ; writers were admired
in so far as they exhibited their sort of merit. Although Byron's life was
romantic, his literary gifts were nearer those of Dryden and Pope. Like
them he was a brilliant and eloquent commentator on the active life of
man. And he was their equal. His best works, *Don Juan* and *The Vision
of Judgment*, are written with a careless scintillating mastery that keep
them as vital now, as the day they were written.

ON HIMSELF

My days of love are over ; me no more
 The charms of maid, wife, and still less of widow,
Can make the fool of which they made before,—
 In short, I must not lead the life I did do ;
The credulous hope of mutual minds is o'er,
 The copious use of claret is forbid too,
So for a good old-gentlemanly vice,
I think I must take up with avarice.

ALFRED LORD TENNYSON 1809-1892
Oil painting by S. Laurence

Ambition was my idol, which was broken
    Before the shrines of Sorrow, and of Pleasure ;
And the two last have left me many a token,
    O'er which reflection may be made at leisure :
Now, like Friar Bacon's brazen head, I've spoken,
    "Time is, Time was, Time's past ;"—a chymic treasure
Is glittering youth, which I have spent betimes—
My heart in passion, and my head on rhymes.

From DON JUAN

One other poet of this period must not be forgotten. Walter Savage
Landor (1775-1864) is one of those authors who seem to have been created
by Providence to show that there is an exception to every rule. He is
equally far from the school of Pope and the school of the Romantics.
The chief influence we can trace in his work is that of the ancient Latin
writers. The epigrams which are his chief claim to fame, so grand in
conception and so tersely expressed, are like antique inscriptions carved
in marble to last for ever.

SEPARATION

There is a mountain and a wood between us,
  Where the lone shepherd and late bird have seen us
Morning and noon and eventide repass.
Between us now the mountain and the wood
Seem standing darker than last year they stood,
  And say we must not cross—alas ! alas !

Meanwhile the tide of romanticism swept irresistibly on. Its first dazzling outburst came to an end with Byron. But the movement did not spend itself for a century and more ; and produced a succession of poets who, if they never rose as high as their masters, maintained nevertheless a very high level. The first phase was distinguished by three figures, Tennyson, Browning and Matthew Arnold. Tennyson (1809-1892) was, poetically speaking, the child of Keats; stimulated to write by a similar sensibility to beauty and with a natural gift for the lovely evocative phrase. He was a more accomplished craftsman, and his best work is a miracle of finished art. Only—he lacked Keats' divine fire. Perfectly though he expresses it, his vision of beauty has not the same inspired intensity ; after Keats the best of Tennyson seems a little undistinguished. This lack of distinction was increased by the fact that he seldom allowed himself to concentrate exclusively on his vision. By the time he reached his maturity the Victorian age had begun to dawn over England. The Victorian age, strenuous and puritanical, took the view that poetry should teach a moral lesson. Tennyson yielded to the pressure of his age : he set up to be preacher as well as poet. And since his preaching did not spring from his native creative impulse, it was uninspired ; a mere polished repetition of opinions held by serious persons of his day. All the same Tennyson is a great poet. No one since has left a volume of verse covering so wide a range of subject, with such consistent mastery of the art of writing. Moreover he has a special interest as one of the best painters of the English scene. Eastern and southern England are portrayed in his verses with the detailed accuracy of Cowper and a silvery exquisiteness of phrase, all his own.

Now fades the last long streak of snow,
  Now burgeons every maze of quick
  About the flowering square, and thick
By ashen roots the violets blow.

Now rings the woodland loud and long,
  The distance takes a lovelier hue,
  And drown'd in yonder living blue
The lark becomes a sightless song.

ROBERT BROWNING 1812-1889
Oil painting by G. F. Watts

Now dance the lights on lawn and lea,
  The flocks are whiter down the vale,
  And milkier every milky sail
On winding stream or distant sea.

From IN MEMORIAM

No one ever accused Browning (1812-1889) of yielding to convention. In him, we find the wilful determination of the romantic to be himself at all costs, carried to its limit. The sort of poem he wrote—it was usually some spasmodic lyric or a dramatic monologue, put into the mouth of some curious imaginary character—is his own invention ; so is his philosophy, a defiant optimism, boisterously welcoming disaster as a test of its strength. Most individual of all is his actual style ; conversational, slap-dash, and freaked all over with the grotesque quips of Browning's fancy. So aggressively eccentric an author will never please every one. And it must be admitted Browning is often obscure and ugly. But he is most exciting reading : bursting with life and passion and possessed of a subtle insight into the processes of men's minds. He is also a most important influence, for what is looked on as the very "modern" type of poetry, the complex, realistic, intellectual poetry of Mr. T. S. Eliot and his followers, derives directly from Browning.

Room after room,
I hunt the house through
We inhabit together.
Heart, fear nothing, for, heart, thou shalt find her,
Next time, herself !—not the trouble behind her

Left in the curtain, the couch's perfume !
As she brush'd it, the cornice-wreath blossom'd anew :
Yon looking-glass gleam'd at the wave of her feather.

Yet the day wears,
And door succeeds door ;
I try the fresh fortune—
Range the wide house from the wing to the centre.
Still the same chance ! she goes out as I enter.
Spend my whole day in the quest,—who cares ?
But 'tis twilight you see,—with such suites to explore,
Such closets to search, such alcoves to importune !

Matthew Arnold (1822-1888) was a less original writer. He was a serious-minded academic person, learned in the literature of the past ; his style is a careful blending of Wordsworth and the classics. In consequence it never stirs us with the first-hand creative freshness of Browning or Tennyson. But this deficiency is partly counterbalanced by a greater depth of sentiment. In words of restrained and poignant eloquence, Arnold voices the profound melancholy which was beginning to permeate the more thoughtful minds of his time. For, in spite of its outward prosperity, and the extraordinary advance of material improvement which it witnessed, the Victorian age was not serene. Intellectually it was disordered ; the revolutionary movement, which preceded it, had failed to establish any foundation of commonly accepted ideals, on which confidence in life might securely rest itself ; religious faith was shaken by the discoveries of science. Darkly, the huge energy of material progress swept onwards to no certain end. This uncertainty affected the writers of the age and it was rendered still more painful for them by the fact that the new industrial civilisation, which was bit by bit superseding the old England, tended to look on literature as a frivolous luxury, unrelated to the serious business of life. In consequence, the poets themselves grew more and more to feel at odds with the world in which they lived. Some turned their backs on it to take shelter in some secluded monastery of the imagination, constructed by themselves : others, embracing the philosophy of pessimism, openly repudiated life as a cheat. They can hardly be blamed. But it was a pity. It is not healthy for the artist to feel himself out of tune with the people round him. He becomes cranky or narrow or both. Whether for this cause or not, the poets of the later nineteenth century seem built on a smaller scale than their predecessors.

DANTE GABRIEL ROSSETTI 1828-1882
Self portrait, drawn 1846

However they remained very good in quality. And there were a great many of them. The Pre-Raphaelite group, led by Rossetti (1828-1882) and William Morris (1834-1896) in his earliest most fruitful phase, found refuge in an artistic dreamland founded on the art and literature of the Middle Ages and early Renaissance. It was an artificial place. And their poetry is a little artificial : languid, over-decorated, and self-conscious. But it does achieve the beauty which is its object. Morris's clear-coloured medieval landscapes, with their belfried towns peopled by troops of heraldic figures, Rossetti's sultry Italian splendours, made melancholy by a brooding autumnal passion—these can still delight the eye of the imagination.

NEAR AVALON

A ship with shield before the sun,
Six maidens round the mast,
A red-gold crown on every one,
A green gown on the last.

The fluttering green banners there
Are wrought with ladies' heads most fair,
And a portraiture of Guenevere
The middle of each sail doth bear.

A ship with sails before the wind,
And round the helm six knights,
Their heaumes are on, whereby, half blind,
They pass by many sights.

William Morris

Associated with these poets was Swinburne. Unlike theirs, his was a lyrical talent, deriving from Shelley rather than Keats : and though he too was deliberately archaic in style, he was not so exclusively pre-Raphaelite. His dream world included elements taken from the Greeks and the Bible. Books rather than life were his inspiration. Indeed he had so little of his own to say, that his poetry is at times almost meaningless. But it too had beauty ; surging forth in a torrent of orchestral music, all a-shimmer with sumptuous words.

Swinburne, in so far as he had a philosophy, was a pessimist, tumultuously lamenting the vanity of all things human. Here he links on to the declared pessimists. In Edward FitzGerald's *Rubaiyat of Omar Khayyam*, a very free adaptation from the Persian, pessimism was combined with a keen sensibility to pleasure. FitzGerald is a most original writer, mingling an eighteenth century wit and precision, with a dreamy Oriental exoticism of mood. Since all ends in dust, is the burden of his song, let us enjoy ourselves while we can. Nowhere else in English is this ancient philosophy expressed so memorably as in his chiming, tolling stanzas.

Ah, my Beloved, fill the Cup that clears
Today of past Regrets and future Fears—
    Tomorrow ?—Why, Tomorrow I may be
Myself with Yesterday's Sev'n Thousand years.

Lo ! some we loved, the loveliest and best
That Time and Fate of all their Vintage prest,
    Have drunk their Cup a Round or two before,
And one by one crept silently to Rest.

And we, that now make merry in the Room
They left, and Summer dresses in new Bloom,
    Ourselves must we beneath the Couch of Earth
Descend, ourselves to make a Couch—for whom ?

Ah, make the most of what we yet may spend,
Before we too into the Dust descend ;
    Dust into Dust, and under Dust, to lie,
Sans Wine, sans Song, sans Singer, and—sans End ! . . .

From OMAR KHAYYAM

Equally beautiful, equally hopeless, are the lyrics of A. E. Housman, a Cambridge scholar, who came to maturity at the end of the century.

Thomas Hardy, o.m. 1840-1928
Drawing by William Strang, 1919

Here the setting is not Oriental but rural. He called himself the Shropshire lad ; and his pages are full of exquisite brief glimpses of the English landscape. But these only form an ironical background to a pessimism more intense than FitzGerald's.

> Into my heart an air that kills
>   From yon far country blows :
> What are those blue remembered hills,
>   What spires, what farms are those ?
>
> That is the land of lost content,
>   I see it shining plain,
> The happy highways where I went
>   And cannot come again.

Housman and FitzGerald are, for all their perfection, minor writers. Thomas Hardy is one of the great figures of English literature. We must read his novels to realise his full stature. His poems are often marred by a Browningesque roughness and quaintness. But, to a feeling for the countryside more intimate than Housman's, he joined an extraordinary nobility of spirit. Life to him was essentially tragic ; a grim battle, in which man was almost certainly defeated by Fate. Yet he faces it with a brave tender resignation, an unfailing compassion for helpless mortality, which somehow draws the sting from despair. Hardy's clumsy, plaintive strains have a mysterious power to soothe the heart, like the sight of the downland sky he loved so well.

THE END OF THE EPISODE

Indulge no more may we
In this sweet-bitter pastime :
The love-light shines the last time
Between you, Sweet, and me.

There shall remain no trace
Of what so closely tied us,
And blank as ere love eyed us
Will be our meeting-place.

The flowers and thymy air,
Will they now miss our coming ?
The bumbles thin their humming
To find we haunt not there ?

Though fervent was our vow,
Though ruddily ran our pleasure,
Bliss has fulfilled its measure,
And see its sentence now.

Ache deep ; but make no moans :
Smile out ; but still suffer
The paths of love are rougher
Than thoroughfares of stones.

Meanwhile, a few poets found security from the prevailing doubt, in the unchanging truths of religious faith. Coventry Patmore and Gerard Hopkins were Catholics. Both were original unequal writers, whose queer idiosyncrasies make them hard to appreciate at a first reading. Patmore was a follower of Donne, born two hundred years later, whose complex ingenious poetry strives to express a mystical vision mingling sensual and spiritual passion. Hopkins, a Jesuit priest, is difficult not for his thoughts but for his mode of expression. He was always experi-

EMILY BRONTË 1818-1848
Oil painting by Branwell Brontë

menting in language and metre ; at times so boldly as to be unintelligible.
His successful experiments, however, have a vivid astonishing splendour.

The one great Anglican poet of the period is easy to admire. Rossetti's
sister, Christina, expressed simple thoughts in simple language. But she
was an inspired genius, in whom an exquisite sense of art was charged
by a throbbing passion. Sometimes she sings of love, sometimes of religion;
but always with pathetic loveliness. Her modest achievement is one of
the most perfect in the whole of English literature.

A BIRTHDAY

My heart is like a singing bird
    Whose nest is in a watered shoot ;
My heart is like an apple-tree
    Whose boughs are bent with thickset fruit ;

95

My heart is like a rainbow shell
That paddles in a halcyon sea ;
My heart is gladder than all these
Because my love is come to me.

Christina Rossetti

Other poets with Christian beliefs are also memorable : Francis Thompson, sumptuous and impassioned, and the careful sensitive Alice Meynell.

Meanwhile a few other authors found confidence in life in creeds of their own. Emily Brontë, in a handful of verses, expressed a mysticism as fiery as Blake's ; the coloured, complicated poetry of George Meredith proclaimed a belief in the ultimate benevolence of nature ; Rudyard Kipling, famous also as a story-teller, made a religion of patriotism. His imaginative appreciation of England's romantic past, his triumphant belief in her imperial destiny, found expression in ringing strains that managed to make themselves heard far beyond the ordinary circles of readers of poetry, and sent their tunes lilting in the heads of Englishmen all over the world.

Finally two writers, living well into the twentieth century, brought Victorian poetry to a close in a fan-fare of triumphant music. Their careers run curiously parallel. Robert Bridges, starting as a song writer in a smooth, traditional manner appeared in his last work the *Testament of Beauty*, as a philosophic poet, intellectual in subject matter and writing in an austere, highly experimental style ; William Butler Yeats made his name as a sort of Irish Rosetti, the author of dreamy moon-lit poems set in a Celtic fairyland. In middle life he deliberately changed his style to become a poet of ideas, severe and rhetorical. Bridges and Yeats both founded their view of life on a belief in the absolute value of their art. They assert their conviction that beauty is its own justification. Here the likeness between them ends. Bridges has a thoroughly English talent combining a fastidious scholarly taste with a fresh birdlike sweetness. The beauty he worships is serene ; its classic temple stands in the rich smiling quiet of English park-land.

I love all beauteous things,
I seek and adore them ;
God hath no better praise,
And man in his hasty days
Is honoured for them.

I too will something make
And joy in the making ;
Altho' to-morrow it seem
Like the empty words of a dream
Remembered on waking.

ALEXANDER POPE 1688–1744
Oil painting attributed to Charles Jervas

ROBERT BRIDGES 1844–1930
Oil painting by Charles Furse

WILLIAM BUTLER YEATS 1861-1939
Charcoal drawing by J. S. Sargent

Very different is the gleaming shrine of Yeats's adoration, written
with the cabalistic symbols of some secret mystery, and shadowed by the
boughs of the Irish forest. For all the sophistication of his art, there is
something untamed in Yeats's inspiration; for all his mastery of the
English tongue, his genius is exotic.

A DREAM OF DEATH

I dreamed that one had died in a strange place
Near no accustomed hand;
And they had nailed the boards above her face
The peasants of that land,
And, wondering, planted by her solitude
A cypress and a yew:
I came, and wrote upon a cross of wood,
Man had no more to do:
She was more beautiful than thy first love,
This lady by the trees:
And gazed upon the mournful stars above,
And heard the mournful breeze.

97

RUPERT BROOKE 1887-1915
Posthumous drawing by J. Harvard Thomas

V

LONG before Bridges and Yeats died, poetry had entered on its modern phase. It is beyond the scope of this essay to try and estimate this. The writers of to-day have not been born into a happy age for poetry. The doubt and the despondency of the later nineteenth century, have been sharpened for them by the shock of world catastrophe. However, the poets have gone on writing; and though their work is fragmentary compared with that of their predecessors, it is full of originality and life. Individualistic and lyrical, it is still romantic in type. The Georgian poets, who flourished in the first twenty years of the century, were rural romantics. The most typical of them, Edward Thomas, Edmund Blunden and V. Sackville-West turned away from the unsympathetic atmosphere of industrial England to seek for peace in the homely charms of English country life. Contemporary with them appeared the passionate, disordered rhapsodies of D. H. Lawrence, the sculptured eloquence of Hillaire Belloc, the fresh songs of W. H. Davies, the direct appeal of Masefield's poetry and above all the elfin loveliness of Walter de la Mare.

THE SCRIBE

What lovely things
  Thy hand hath made
The smooth-plumed bird
  In its emerald shade,
The seed of the grass
  The speck of stone
Which the wayfaring ant
  Stirs—and hastes on !

Though I should sit
  By some tarn in thy hills,
Using its ink
  As the spirit wills
To write of Earth's wonders,
  Its live, willed things,
Flit would the ages
  On soundless wings
Ere unto Z

  My pen drew nigh ;
Leviathan told,
  And the honey-fly :
And still would remain
  My wit to try—
My worn reeds broken,
  The dark tarn dry,
All words forgotten—
  Thou, Lord, and I.

Walter de la Mare

These writers came to maturity before the war of 1914. They still retain something of the serenity of a former age. Even if they were dissatisfied with the world they knew, they felt confidence enough to build a world of their own. Those who felt the shock of the war when still quite young, found this impossible. During the war itself, England produced little poetry ; only some poignant verses of hope by Rupert Brooke and others, at the beginning, and at the end some poignant verses of despair by Wilfred Owen and others ; these were moving rather from their sincerity of feeling than their poetic excellence.

The bleak anti-climax of the peace brought forth a new school led by T. S. Eliot. These are romantics in full disillusionment, yearning vainly after ecstasy. Mr. Eliot is a Christian ; his younger successors, Mr. Auden and Mr. Spender, seem to look for salvation to a kind of Communism ; but both are so disheartened that neither the real world nor that of their dreams seems to give them any zest of inspiration. To express their frustrated mood they have evolved a new style, complex, intellectual and ironical, modern in diction, broken in rhythm.

What, at the time of the birth of Our Lord, at Christmastide,
Is there not peace upon earth, goodwill among men ?
The peace of this world is always uncertain, unless men keep the peace of God.
And war among men defiles this world, but death in the Lord renews it,
And the world must be cleaned in the winter, or we shall have only
A sour spring, a parched summer, an empty harvest.
Between Christmas and Easter what work shall be done ?
The ploughman shall go out in March and turn the same earth
He has turned before, the bird shall sing the same song.
When the leaf is out on the trees, when the elder and may
Burst over the stream, and the air is clear and high,
And voices trill at windows, and children tumble in front of the door,
What work shall have been done, what wrong
Shall the bird's song cover, the green tree cover, what wrong
Shall the fresh earth cover ? We wait, and the time is short
But waiting is long.

T. S. Eliot from MURDER IN THE CATHEDRAL

Such poetry is too obscure and too joyless ever to be widely popular. But at its best, it has a pungent fascination, softened by gleams of a wistful beauty. Dorothy Wellesley and W. J. Turner, in their imaginative and philosophical poetry, the Sitwells, Ruth Pitter in her religious verse, have not broken away from the main English tradition. They have contrived to set their modern thought to a music which is still rich with the overtones of past poetry.

Now once more war is sweeping the country. How far it will affect literature and in what direction, it is too early to say. But poetry seems by now so deeply rooted in the English nature, that it is impossible to believe it will ever be extinguished.

BRITISH DRAMATISTS

GRAHAM GREENE

ANYONE who goes into a Roman Catholic Church during the Holy Week services, can see for himself the origin of our drama : on Palm Sunday the priest knocks on the door of the church and demands to be admitted, the palms are borne along the aisle : on Good Friday the shrill voices of Judas and the High Priest break into the narrative of the Gospel : the progress to Calvary is made more real by human actors.

It seems a long road to have travelled—from this to the drunken ladies of Noel Coward's *Private Lives*, and one which can only lightly be sketched in so short a book as this. But there remains all the time—whether we are considering the latest Drayton-Hare farce or the enormous despair of *King Lear*—the sense of ritual. Perhaps the child is more aware of it than the grown man at the theatre : the chatter subdued as the overture begins, or else the three sudden raps like those of the priest at the church door : the regular rise and fall of the curtain between our world and theirs. To the child it little matters what happens upon the stage : the ritual is there—the magic : the maid who crosses the stage towards the ringing telephone as the curtain goes up has to the innocent eye the appearance of an acolyte moving from left to right before the altar.

Even though little evidence is available for the years between it is easy enough to conjecture the way in which the drama began. On one side of the narrow gap is the Mass with its dramatic re-enactment of the Last Supper : on the other the Mystery and Miracle Plays—incidents from the Old and the New Testaments, legends of saints acted often by priests, in the precincts of churches. Popularity drove these plays out of the church into the churchyard where the feet of the mob trampled over the graves. And so to save the graves they had to go further and become more secularised. Acted at fairs on movable scaffolds, forming part of the riotous medieval processions, played by jugglers and members of trade guilds, their subject-matter widened. Noah could be drunk in a market-place as he could not be in a church. And so when we look again towards the end of the fifteenth century we find the drama flourishing in nearly a hundred towns, religious still but sometimes twisting into odd Gothic humours. Four great cycles of Miracle Plays (known as the York, Towneley, Chester and Coventry) are still in existence, representing the whole biblical story from the Creation to the Ascension. Of the York cycle we have the order of the Pageant on Corpus Christi, 1415, with each guild assigned its part in the gigantic cycle of the Fall and the Redemption : the Tanners, the Plasterers, Cardmakers, Fitters, Coopers and Armourers, Glovers, Shipwrights, Fishmongers, Bookbinders, Hosiers, Spicers and Pewterers and Chandlers and Vintners—the list is only limited by man's needs. These plays grew, like a church, anonymously : we have reached the drama, but not yet the dramatist.

One reads these plays now for pedantry rather than for pleasure ; where humour or a kind of simple poetry creeps in, perhaps we value it too highly for the contrast : the scene in the Chester play of *Noah's Flood* when Noah's wife refuses to enter the ark :—

> "Yea, sir, sette up youer saile,
> And rowe fourth with evill haile,
> For withouten anye faiyle
>   I will not oute of this towne ;
> But I have my gossippes everichone,
> One foote further I will not gone :
> They shall not drowne, by Sante John !
>   And I may save their life."

the scene in *The Sacrifice of Isaac* when Abraham prepares to kill his "sweet sonne of grace" ; or most striking of all—like a comic gargoyle on a Cathedral roof—the *Secunda Pastorum* in the Towneley Plays when just before the Angels sing their *Gloria in Excelsis* we watch the shepherds search the house of Mak, the sheepstealer, and at last find the missing ewe wrapped in swaddling clothes—a bold caricature—lying in a cradle:

> "Gyf me lefe hym to kys, and lyft up the clowtt.
> What the deville is this ? he has a long snowte."

Alongside the Miracle Play grew up the Morality, of which the story was only the vehicle to illustrate the beauty of virtue and the ugliness of vice. This is the abstract theme of later drama robbed of the particular plot and particular characters—Macbeth appears only as Ambition and Iago as Deceit. It is the bones without the flesh, just as so often in twentieth century drama we have the flesh without the bones—characters who act a plot before us and have no significance at all outside the theatre, who are born when the curtain rises and die when it falls.

The Morality play reached its highest point with *Everyman*, composed before the end of the fifteenth century, a play of such permanent interest

MAN SURROUNDED BY THE VIRTUES RECEIVES THE MESSAGE FROM DEATH
Illumination from Thomas Chaundler's *Liber Apologeticus*

that it excludes from the attention of all but scholars its predecessors and contemporaries, just as the ordinary man's knowledge of Elizabethan drama is justifiably confined almost entirely to Shakespeare's plays. That it is founded on an original Dutch version is neither here nor there : it lives as poetry and the poetry is English. The plot is as bone-dry and unadorned as the verse : it belongs to the world of the Black Death and the theological argument. God sends Death to Everyman to summon him to judgment, and Everyman's cry, "O Death, thou comest when I had thee least in mynde," bare and precise and human, goes echoing through the century which separates him from Shakespeare to reappear in the more studied, more evocative, but hardly more telling Renaissance cry : "She should have died hereafter. There would have been a time for such a word"—all that fear of death's heavy responsibility which belongs to the Age of Faith and lay on Hamlet's will as much as Everyman's. Everyman tries in vain to bribe Death to delay : but Death is unbribable. He tries to wring out some hope of return. All he can procure is consent that he may take with him a friend on his journey.

And so Everyman goes first to Fellowship, and here under the abstract name we can see the dramatist beginning to evolve character—much as novelists of the eighteenth and nineteenth centuries hid a particular man under the abstract name—Mr. Allworthy, Sir Gregory Hardlines and the like. Bluff, cheerful, bogus Fellowship is not quite an abstraction as he greets Everyman : there is nothing he will not do for a friend : only let him name his grief : he will die for him : he will go to Hell for him, but the straight name of Death on his friend's lips freezes his promises.

> "Now, by God that all hathe bought,
> If deth were the messenger,
> For no man that is lyvynge todaye
> I will not go that lothe journaye,
> Not for the fader that bygote me."

There is no room to follow Everyman's course in detail : from Fellowship to Good Deeds :—

> "Here I lye, cold in the grounde,
> Thy synnes hath me sore bounde
> That I can not stire,"

and on to Knowledge who leads him to Confession, and so to the last sacrament and his farewell to Beauty and Strength, Discretion and the Five Wits, all except Good Deeds. The pilgrimage is conventional, but it is passionately described : it is theologically exact, because that exactitude seemed to the fifteenth century author to express the truth. It is the first English play that belongs to our living literature, and we have to wait nearly a hundred years for another.

In the interval something new emerges—the author.

'A SCENE FROM *VENICE PRESERVED* : A TRAGEDY BY THOMAS OTWAY
David Garrick as " Jaffier " and Mrs. Cibber as " Belvidera "
Oil painting by John Zoffany

BEN JONSON 1573(?)-1637
Oil painting by an unknown artist
By courtesy of the National Portrait Gallery

THESE first authors are not of great interest except historically, and that is because the theatre was still the fair and the market-place. To try to revive these plays in a different *milieu* would be like trying to revive on the great screen, before the huge auditorium of the modern cinema, some little reel of celluloid made for the nickelodeon. The theatre is a popular art, and we must not confuse the historical interest—confined to a few—with the dramatic interest. *Everyman* lives as poetry, and as a play, but these first experiments in secular drama, by men like Heywood and Bale, have not that much life in their dry bones : Folly, Hypocrisy, Good Deeds and the rest have been given names—they become Johan the Husband, Tyb the Wife, Sir Jhon the Priest, Neighbour Prattle. They have a rough humour, satire as blunt and heavy as a quarter-staff —that applies to Heywood. Bale introduced history—*Kynge Johan* and *Apius and Virginia*. It is the period of Henry and Mary, when religion is becoming confused with politics, and it is really safer to leave religion alone. Men who write plays have heads to lose and their bodies are as inflammable as others.

The New Learning too had arrived, and simple men, it may well be, were ceasing to write in these confusing times. The unknown authors of the early Miracles were not men of intelligence—they were men of feeling and men who had been taught rather than teachers. The moralities are like children's lessons. The new plays are ceasing to be popular ; they are written at Eton for Etonians, acted in colleges and in the Inns of Court, with Terence and Seneca for models, and the stage has become at last stationary—but not in a market-place (though it must be remembered that the mob could still see the old Miracles and Moralities—they were being acted here and there as late as when Hamlet took the stage, just as the Morality, if you look for it, still lingers to-day at the seaside in the Punch booth).

The drama had become separated from the people, and it will not really interest us again until the audience has once more become popular. We are interested in the dramatists of these days only as stations along a line, and we have to go a long way before the line curves and returns towards the market where we started.

So Heywood and Bale are important only as the rude precursors of George Gascoyne and Sackville and Norton, who in turn are only important because they lead us a little nearer to the day when, without warning, the greatest playwright the world has known broke on his age. Sackville and Norton, whose monstrous *Gorboduc* (1562) was an exact imitation of Seneca, mark a stage because they were the first to use dramatic blank verse. This new way of writing, the freedom from rhyme, the approach to realism made possible by the broken rhythm, released the dramatic imagination : the speed with which the drama developed from this point is comparable to the speed with which the film developed. How astonishing it is to think that Elizabeth, who listened one January night in 1562 to *Gorboduc* in the Inner Temple Hall, was able to listen forty years later to *Twelfth Night.* Hear the ghosts in that bombed, deserted hall intoning *Gorboduc* before the court :—

> "We then, alas, the ladies which that time
> Did there attend, seeing that heinous deed,
> And hearing him oft call the wretched name
> Of mother, and to cry to her for aid
> Whose direful hand gave him the mortal wound,
> Pitying—alas, (for nought else could we do),
> His ruthful end, ran to the woeful bed,
> Despoiled straight his breast, and all we might,
> Wiped in vain with napkins next at hand . . ."

The instrument had been invented, but who that night could have foretold these sounds from it ?

> "O, fellow, come, the song we had last night.
> Mark it, Cesario, it is old and plain ;
> The spinsters and the knitters in the sun
> And the free maids that weave their thread with bones
> Do use to chant it : it is silly sooth,
> And dallies with the innocence of love,
> Like the old age."

You cannot simply say that Shakespeare was a poet, and that Sackville and Norton were not : the difference to an audience was less subtle than that. These lines of Shakespeare's are *realistic :* they refer to the common known life, they have the uneven rhythm of speech and grammatically they are simple. How difficult by comparison are the involved periods of *Gorboduc.* The audience must often have found themselves hopelessly lost in the maze of those immense rhetorical sentences. They lie over the drama like the folds of a heavy toga impeding movement.

What filled those forty years ? One is inclined to answer simply, Marlowe, but of course there were others, hammering at that stiff formal medium, increasing the subject-matter of verse. Religion was better left alone for the time (and afterwards found itself left alone for good) so that Shakespeare only allowed himself occasional glancing lines (Hamlet's prayer, the papal nuncio rebuking Philip of France) which showed just the fin of the dangerous thoughts moving below the surface. We are still dealing more with the history of verse than of the stage : Kyd, remembered by scholars for *The Spanish Tragedie,* in which the blank verse was constructed with euphemisms as complicated as the dingy plot, but where the play began to lose the bogus dignity of the pseudo-Seneca ; Robert Greene who would hardly be remembered to-day if he had not sneered at the young Shakespeare as an "upstart crow," written a few

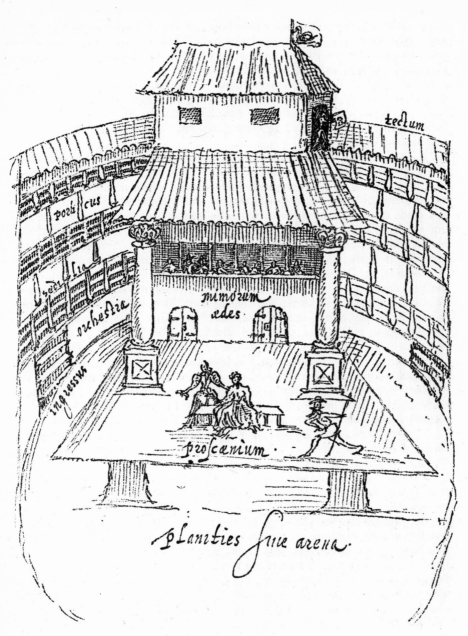

INTERIOR OF THE SWAN THEATRE IN 1596
Contemporary drawing by John de Witt

songs which please anthologists and drunk very deeply ; George Peel and Lyly—but they are too many to notice here, these men whose plays only survive in the memory of scholars and enthusiasts. To Greene alone perhaps is this judgment a little unfair : Greene with his idealised milk maids, cool-fingered, spiritual and content, who ranged the air above the dreary room, the alehouse and the stews which formed his actual scene—a scene more pleasing to scholars than to men who live those lives. But even Greene belongs more to a record of minor poetry than to a record of drama.

We are dealing in this book with dramatists and not with the mechanics of the stage : but it is essential to note in passing the changing *milieu*—from churchyard to market-place, from market-place to the great house-hold where the peer could watch the players without smelling the vulgar, and from the peer's household, with the support of their patron, into the inn yards. Then in 1576 came the blow which looked like attaching playwrights permanently to the household, when the Corporation of London forbade the performance of plays in public within the bounds for the sake of morality and hygiene. But this was answered in the same year with the first theatre, in Shoreditch, outside the city limits, and so for the first time we get the fixed stage, the management, the responsibility towards an audience, the profit-and-loss account—all those considerations which the dilettante regards as unseemly checks on the freedom of the artist, but which the artist knows to be the very mould of his technique and the challenge to his imagination. It is nothing to wonder at that it took less than thirty years then to produce *Hamlet*, but one may well speculate whether without the commercial theatre the dramatists would ever have risen higher than the learned imitations of Seneca or Terence, or the elaborate and poetic conceits of Lyly.

The result was not immediately seen—even Marlowe did not belong to *his* stage in the easy way that the miracle players belonged to theirs. Perhaps there is no dramatist more over-rated—and that because his plays are only read and seldom seen. Perhaps it would be wrong to say that *Tamburlaine* is as unactable as *Philip van Arteveld* because it has, in its day, been acted, but one detects no enthusiasm even in such classically-minded theatres as the Old Vic for trying the experiment again. Marlowe was a fine poet who can be seen at his best in his translations from Ovid : fine lustful realistic couplets which remind us of Donne's satires. Stray lines from *Dr. Faustus* and *Tamburlaine* have lodged in the popular memory : the general effect of his work is of a great gallery lit by the sun and lined with statues, hung with pictures, littered by valuable cabinets, tables, *objets d'art*, so many that they end in tedium: the vulgarity of renaissance riches, the over-enjoyment of life, and the concupiscence of a young man. He had immense potentialities which glimmer through the interminable boring rant of *Tamburlaine* and the broken-backed construction of

INSIDE THE RED BULL PLAYHOUSE, CLERKENWELL
Engraved frontispiece Kirkman's *Drolls*, 1672

THE GLOBE THEATRE, SOUTHWARK, c. 1612
Here most of Shakespeare's plays were performed between 1599-1613
Engraving from Wilkinson's *Theatrum Illustrata*

Dr. Faustus : in *Edward II* he came nearer to writing a fine play in which the occasional poetry was conditioned by the action and held in check by character. But he meddled too much in active life : the speculations which brought him a fine for blasphemy were really safer : he was stabbed not, as we used to learn, by a tavern-roisterer, but—as Dr. Hotson discovered a few years ago—by a political spy, leaving behind him at the age of twenty-nine a few fine torsos, some mutilated marble. It is always idle to speculate about a dead man's future : a man dies in the way he lives—and Marlowe's life and talent were both spectacular.

He is a telling contrast to his great successor—whom even Greene had sneered at. This is the sort of life we need for great achievement : so anonymous that even rumour runs off the smooth flanks like water : the man who simply works day in, day out, part of the theatre like the boards worn by actors' feet, protectively covered, with no ambition known to his fellows but the one we all can share—of a house and land and security in troubled times. The rumours of unhappy marriage, of a dark mistress and homosexual love, carry the biographer nowhere ; nobody who lives escapes a private agony : one can assume them in Shakespeare's case without, like a gossip-writer, fixing the wrong public name. The important thing is the plays, more important even than the poetry, for poetry

WILLIAM SHAKESPEARE, 1564-1616
Engraving by Martin Droeshout
Frontispiece to the first folio edition of 1623

alone cannot make a good play (or else Tennyson's *Queen Mary*, which contains some of the finest verse he wrote, would live upon the stage).

Obviously, the whole length of this book would be inadequate to deal with one of Shakespeare's plays ; let us in the pitiably small space allowed consider this first and greatest Man of the Theatre without looking at the poet. He had, of course, to learn—as no one after him, until we come to the prose Restoration play, had to learn again : he did the work for all. If *Edward II* was the height his predecessors reached, that was little enough for him to build on. Consider these points : how a play begins, how it proceeds, and how it ends. What did *Edward II* have to offer to the future then ? A good plain opening, it may be said, with Gaveston reading a letter from the King recalling him to England ; but from that point we proceed dryly and choppily by chronological stages—like *Little Arthur's History of England*—the meeting with the King, the quarrel with Coventry, the peer's anger, the banishment to Ireland, the recall again to England—

SCENE FROM *THE TAMING OF THE SHREW*
Engraving from the first illustrated edition of
Shakespeare, edited by Nicholas Rowe, 1709

all this compressed shapelessly into a single act which has no unity of itself, where no scene prepares you for the next, without the sense of destiny, the thread on which, rather than the passage of time, a play's scenes should be strung. And what is the play's end ? After the horrifying murder of Edward—in which Marlowe's dramatic genius reached its height and the violence of his spirit found for once perfect expression—we have a sorry little hustled postscript in which the young prince—who has hardly been established as a character—turns on the Queen and Mortimer and avenges his father's death. We feel cheated —rather as when the murderer in a detective story proves to be someone who only appears in the last chapter. And how did Marlowe use the chief handicap and—in the right hands—the chief asset of the Elizabethan stage—the absence of scenery ? Certainly he improved on *Gorboduc*, whose authors saw in this only an enforced and colourless unity. The scenes of *Tamburlaine*, unlimited by pasteboard sets and an expense-sheet, shifted boldly all over Asia : *Edward* moved here and there, to London and Warwickshire and Pontefract, but the shifts are never made visible to the audience. The only scene that writes itself on the inner eye is in the bare prison cell, the castle's sewer.

One disparages Marlowe only to throw up into greater relief the craftsmanship of Shakespeare : those first scenes which grip us like the Ancient Mariner's eye—the angry mutterings in the Venice streets, the sudden broil which brings Othello on the scene ("Keep up your bright swords for the dew will rust them") : the witches loitering on the road to Forres ; the heroes returning from the field of Troy and passing under Cressida's balcony. The endings : Othello's "base Indian" lament : Cleopatra's death : the fool's ironical song at the end of *Twelfth Night ;* the violence of Hamlet and the sudden close—"the rest is silence"; the verbal power which continually puts a scene before our eyes far more vividly than the later scene-painters could do it: the dark after-midnight castle where Duncan lies : the forest of Arden : the battlements of Elsinore.

We confuse the issue when we talk of Shakespeare's greatness as a poet : in the plays the poetry is rightness—that is nearly all : the *exact* expression of a mental state: the *exact* description of a scene. "Think, we had mothers," Troilus's bitter outburst is not poetry in any usually accepted meaning of the word—it is simply the right phrase at the right moment, a mathematical accuracy as if this astonishing man could measure his words against our nature in a balance sensitive to the fraction of a

SCENE FROM *A MIDSUMMER NIGHT'S DREAM*
Engraving from the first illustrated edition of Shakespeare, edited by Nicholas Rowe, 1709

milligramme. The effect it has on our minds is roughly similar to the effect of poetry, but the emphasis on the poetic content of the plays had a disastrous effect on the future—for it made poets think they were dramatists.

We have left out of account what the modern dramatist considers most important of all—character. Of course Shakespeare created characters—Falstaff, Macbeth, Cressida ; but was Hamlet a character, or Lear, or Iago—any more than Marlowe's Faustus ? They are mouthpieces for a mood, for an attitude to life, far more than characters, and it is doubtful whether in fact Shakespeare's plays depend on character at all. *Twelfth Night*, his most perfect play contains no character ; Viola, Olivia, the

Duke—they have just enough of our human nature to play their light
lyrical parody of human emotion: Aguecheek and Sir Toby and Malvolio—
these are fantasies not characters. In that lovely play all is surface. It
must be remembered that we are still within the period of the Morality:
they are being acted yet in the country districts: they had been absorbed
by Shakespeare, just as much as he absorbed the plays of Marlowe, and
the abstraction—the spirit of Revenge (Hamlet), of Jealousy (Othello),
of Ambition (Macbeth), of Ingratitude (Lear), of Passion (Anthony and
Cleopatra)—still rules the play. And rightly. Here is the watershed
between the morality and the play of character: the tension between
the two is perfectly kept: there is dialectical perfection. After Shakespeare,
character—which was to have its dramatic triumphs—won a too-costly
victory.

PERHAPS the most startling line of poetry in all our literature occurs
in one of Shakespeare's sonnets: "Desiring this man's scope and
that man's art." Whose scope could the man who wrote both *Twelfth
Night* and *Troilus and Cressida* have envied, and whose art? Perhaps
the writer who had made poetry realistic envied the conceits of Lyly
and Greene: perhaps the creator of Falstaff envied the stiff magnificent
dignity of Jonson. We are tempted to the opposite extreme: to be aware
only of silence after the burial in Stratford.

But that is unjust to Shakespeare. He had taught the craft of the theatre;
he had lifted the play on to a level which even without his genius was to
remain higher than the one he had found. We have only to compare
Jonson's *Sejanus* with the pre-Shakespearian historical plays to notice
the difference. The play is less flexible than, say, *Julius Caesar*, drama-
tically and rhythmically, but what an advance it is on *Edward II*. The
blank verse is a little stiff, but it is vivid with the sense of life observed
from almost the first lines :—

> "We have no shift of faces, no cleft tongues,
> No soft and glutinous bodies, that can stick
> Like snails on painted walls . . ."

In this, Jonson's first play beyond the prentice stage, we notice the
quality which reached its height in the great comedies—*Volpone* and
The Alchemist—the concrete common image—a kind of man-in-the-street
poetry :—

> ". . . which by asserting
> Hath more confirm'd us, than if heart'ning Jove
> Had, from his hundred statues, bid us strike,
> And at the stroke *click'd all his marble thumbs.*"

AN EIGHTEENTH CENTURY PERFORMANCE OF *HAMLET*
Oil painting by Francis Hayman, 1708-1776

An ex-bricklayer and a braggart who had fought in the Low Countries and killed his man in a duel, the tyrant of a literary group in a favourite inn, he was conscious of his art as no one but Shakespeare had been before him. He might have written Dryden's prefaces—except that his prose was not good enough : he did not believe in happy accidents or fine frenzies—Shakespeare seems all spirit beside his earthly sturdy talent. One admires the quality one lacks, and we know how Jonson admired Shakespeare, but Shakespeare may well have admired in Jonson the sense of huge enjoyment. The sensuality of Volpone or Sir Epicure Mammon is described by a man whom the world has treated well :—

"I will have all my beds blown up, not stuft :
Down is too hard : and then, mine oval room
Fill'd with such pictures as Tiberius took
From Elephantis, and dull Aretine
But coldly imitated. Then, my glasses
Cut in more subtle angles, to disperse
And multiply the figures, as I walk
Naked between my succubae . . ."

Compare this with those self-torturing lines out of *The Winter's Tale* (a comedy !) :—

". . . There have been,
Or I am much deceived, cuckolds e'er now ;
And many a man there is, even at this present,
Now while I speak this, holds his wife by th'arm,
That little thinks she has been sluiced in's absence,
And his pond fish't by his next neighbour, by
Sir Smile, his neighbour . . ."

"It is a bawdy planet, that will strike
Where 'tis predominant ; and 'tis powerful, think it,
From east, west, north and south ; be it concluded,
No barricado for a belly. . ."

Even to Falstaff Shakespeare gave sombre thoughts, his streaks of pathos ; none of Shakespeare's characters belongs to pure comedy—tragedy creeps in with Shylock, with the ageing Falstaff, with a fool's song : heartbreak is always near while "the worm feeds on the damask cheek" ; but the fate of Volpone does not worry us ; Jonson alone has presented on the stage the full rich enjoyment of life—this is his real achievement, not his theory of "humours" which the professors discuss at such length and which he himself considered so important. His range is narrow : nearly all his comedies—and all his best—turn on the humour of the gull and the astute rogue ; his verse has not the speed, the vigour, the irregularity of Shakespeare, but he remains the greatest reporter of his age.

Ralph. Speak what thou art, and how thou hast been used,
That I may give him condign punishment.
1 Knight. I am a knight—

ILLUSTRATION TO THE DRAMATIC WORKS OF BEAUMONT AND FLETCHER
Water colour by Michael Rooker, 1743-1801

T HE Elizabethan is usually regarded as the richest period of our
drama, but it is the Jacobean which saw the greatest plays: the best
of Shakespeare and Ben Jonson. Even the minor playwrights had
learned the lesson of the master, and none of the smaller Elizabethan fry
reached the level of Webster, Massinger, Beaumont and Fletcher,
Chapman, even Ford and Tourneur.

There is no space in a book of this size to deal at any length with
these authors individually. There was the difficult metaphysical treatment

117

of melodrama which makes Chapman, the author of the two plays of *Bussy D'Ambois* and *The Duke of Biron*, more interesting for the study than the stage, where clarity, directness, speed are necessary ; even in his own life, when the taste of the audience was so infinitely superior to that of our own day, he was a failure and could have written with more justice and quite as much pride as Jonson :—

> "Make not thyself a Page
> To that Strumpet the Stage,
> But sing high and aloofe,
> Safe from the Wolves black Jaw, and the dull Asses Hoofe."

Far more successful with the Jacobean audience were the romantic pair, Beaumont and Fletcher, who handed on the theme of Honour to Dryden and the Restoration tragedians in plays packed to absurdity with scruples ; even the best, *The Maid's Tragedy,* contains situations as grotesquely unreal as when Aspasia dresses in boy's clothes and incites her faithless lover to a duel so that she may die by his hands. Yet the plays are saved by a youthful lyricism as fresh as the Elizabethan and less conceited, with a charming sensuous sexuality which makes the marriage preparations in *The Maid's Tragedy* as free from offence as Spenser's *Epithalamium.* Of all these dramatists Webster stands alone by virtue of his one great play, *The Duchess of Malfi*, the only play of which it is possible to say that, owing nothing to Shakespeare, it yet stands on a level with the great tragedies. *The White Devil* had showed him to be a poet of some erratic genius : it would have left a memory of morbid and magnificent lines : we should have remembered him with Ford and Tourneur, a group who share a kind of dark horror, a violent moral anarchy which seems to have followed the Elizabethan age like a headache after a feast. Among these writers you are aware of no moral centre, no standard of moral criticism— your hero may be an incestuous murderer, the most moving lines may be put in the mouth of an adulteress who has plotted the murder of her husband. In *King Lear* the cruelty of the world may appal us, but some-where outside there is virtue : the seventeenth century is not eternity, and death is an escape and not an end. But in Tourneur and the earlier Webster we are in the company of men who would really seem to have been lost in the dark night of the soul if they had had enough religious sense to feel despair : the world is all there is, and the world is violent, mad, miserable and without point. The religious revolution had had its effect : this was the rough uneasy strait which led to the serene Angli-canism of Herbert and Vaughan, and to the sceptical doldrums of the eighteenth century : in between the old unquestioning faith and the new toleration lay an unhappy atheism, which has none of the youthful re-belliousness of Marlowe's :—

> "We are merely the stars' tennis balls, struck and bandied
> Which way please them."

118

INTERIOR OF THE DUKE'S THEATRE, LINCOLN'S INN FIELDS
A performance of Elkannah Settle's *Empress of Morocco*, in the reign of Charles II
Engraving by Richard Sawyer

That attitude carried to Tourneur's extreme cannot make a good play, though it can make great poetry. Put on the lowest grounds—an audience must know whom to clap and whom to hiss. Webster's Vittoria Corombona, conceived as a devil, is transformed by the poetry of the trial scene into a heroine—it is too confusing.

But Webster emerged. Bosolo, the self-tortured tool of the Duchess of Malfi's brothers, has the bitter voice of an exile who has not quite forgotten. In his despair he uses heavenly images :—

"What's this flesh ? a little crudded milk, fantastical puff paste. Our bodies are weaker than those paper prisons boys use to keep flies in ; more contemptible, since ours is to preserve earthworms. Didst thou ever see a lark in a cage ? Such is the soul in the body : this world is like her little turf of grass, and the Heav'n o'er our heads, like her looking glass, only gives us a miserable knowledge of the small compass of our prison."

119

An exile who has not quite forgotten, a prisoner who knows by his own fate that there is such a thing as liberty—that is why Webster is an incomparably finer dramatist than Tourneur. He emerges in his later play far enough from the darkened intellectual world to organise—Vittoria Corombona speaks with the voice of angels, but the Duchess of Malfi is on the side of the angels. And on the side too, of ordinary commonplace humanity. Nowhere among this group of dramatists—except fleetingly in Ford—will you find the note of recognisable everyday tenderness as you find it in Webster, in the love scene when the Duchess gently forces Antonio to declare his love. It is as if the dark Jacobean vapours are lifting, and almost anything might have been expected of Webster if he had not died. Alone of these men he left behind something essentially his : only a scholar could differentiate between untitled scraps of the other poets, but Webster's tone is unmistakable—the keen, economical, pointed oddity of the dialogue—whether in prose or verse—expressing the night side of life :—

"How tedious is a guilty conscience.
When I look into the fishpond in my garden,
Methinks I see a thing armed with a rake
That seems to strike at me."

In this one respect his power was greater than Shakespeare's. That enormous genius must be allowed his limitations ; even in his darkest period he was too sane, too conscious of his art, to express madness convincingly. The mad Lear is no more mad than Hamlet—he is only distraught, and Ophelia and her flowers is a pretty conceit that might have come from one of Greene's novels. Surrealism is an overworked and a dubious term, but an intellectual generation which has re-discovered Blake and wandered with Dedalus and Bloom through the Dublin night should be quick to recognise the quality of Webster :—

"Woe to the caroche that brought home my wife from the masque at three o'clock in the morning! It had a large feather bed in it."

The astonishing thing is not that Webster has so small a public to-day but that he once had so large a one, the great popular audiences of the playhouse—this was what going to the play meant then that to-day means watching a Van Druten, a St. John Ervine or a Dodie Smith.

WILLIAM CONGREVE 1670–1729
Oil painting by Sir Godfrey Kneller

OLIVER GOLDSMITH 1728–1774
Oil painting ; studio of Sir Joshua Reynolds

THE enormous tide ebbed, and it was nearly fifty years before the English theatre produced another man of genius; a few names are left on the beach for scholars to pore over—Shirley, known to everyone for his lyric, "The Glories of our Blood and State," from *Ajax and Ulysses ;* Suckling, whose *Ballad of a Wedding* is worth all his tedious blank verse plays ; and Sir William Davenant, a fine lyric writer but an indifferent playwright, though he claimed to be Shakespeare's bastard (is the story too well known to repeat here of the priest who met the child Davenant running up Oxford High Street towards the Turl where he lived, and asked him what was the hurry ? He replied that his godfather Shakespeare had come, to which the priest replied, "Why do you take the name of God in vain ?" The tale is Davenant's own).

The moon which drew the tide back was civil war, the triumph of the Puritans. The theatres had always had a precarious existence : now they stopped altogether. The Puritan spirit ruled the country as much as the town : there were no longer any bounds beyond which the theatre could migrate : the market place as a centre of enjoyment had ceased to exist and the day of the miracle play was at last done. Men began to write plays to be read only : the literary quality of dialogue became more important than the dramatic : life was extinguished between calf boards.

It is wrong to think of the years of the Civil War and the Protectorate as an interlude merely between two dramatic periods—the closing of the theatres had as permanent an effect on our literature as the beheading of a king had on our constitution. The theatre had begun by being popular, had become a "class" entertainment and then become popular again ; now it ceased to be anything but the recreation of the educated, the aristocratic, and later, when these two terms ceased to be synonymous, of the well-to-do. The people were to disappear—or to become a few rude voices from the gallery reported in the Press with disapproval after a First Night. Most of us have been present on some occasion of baffled dislike among the "Gods"— courtesy title like that given to Prime Ministers after the power has gone : the hisses and catcalls from the gallery are drowned by the claps from the stalls, who feel that the author in some mysterious way belongs to them.

And belong he does. The Puritans saw to that. Shakespeare had belonged to the people, catching for the first time in verse the accent of common speech, giving them the violent, universal tragedies they understood—Doll Tearsheet and the murderer's knife and the laughter of clowns, and of course so much more : Jonson, too, had belonged to them, with his broad realism and downright poetry. They had served the people and the people had moulded them. The frequenters of bear-baiting demanded vitality : men and women who had watched from their windows the awful ritual of the scaffold were ready for any depth of horror the playwright cared to measure.

121

MRS. PINCHWIFE IN
WYCHERLEY'S *COUNTRY WIFE*
From Bell's *British Theatre*, 1780

But when the play returned, it returned almost literally to the drawing-room. There are always ways of evading authority if men care enough, and men have always cared deeply for storytelling. Perhaps if a novelist of Fielding's stature had been alive then, the play would never have flared into brief life, but the long folio romances translated from the French and Spanish must always have been a rather poor substitute for something better. So Davenant brought the play cunningly back by way of a mixed entertainment given in private —something rather like a revue with satirical dialogue and a few songs and some music.

That private atmosphere remained. When the theatres reopened—for a long while there were only two of them—the public were almost as much excluded as they had been at Davenant's entertainments. Tragedies like Dryden's *The Conquest of Granada*, written on the Corneille model in heroic couplets, with their complex ideals of honour, their exaggerated unities, their exalted sentiments and complete lack of human passion, were for the educated who could judge the technical dexterity of the verse, for the enforced travellers of the Court who could appreciate the echoes of what they had heard on the Continent.

Little wonder that it was, in these court circles, a time for foreign fashions : England had given these men nothing more attractive than prison, exile, impoverishment and prudery. Tuke's blank verse romance, *The Adventure of Five Hours*, was the first great success of the new theatre —with the Court : the poor, in the theatrical eye, did not exist, and when the bourgeois began reluctantly to enter the playhouse it was to see himself mocked, for he was now of the losing party : the City had sided with Parliament, and the cuckolds and wanton city wives and leanshanked aldermen of Restoration drama represented a kind of civilised vengeance for the scaffold at Whitehall. Compare Jonson's prose comedy, *Bartholomew Fair*, with Shadwell's *Epsom Fair*, and you notice two things : a vast improvement in the prose and a narrowing in the scope. Jonson was writing about human nature for a public as wide as his subject : the Restoration dramatist with his infinitely more graceful instrument was fashioning an amusing bijou for the drawing-room—a witty and scandalous joke against an unpopular and rather stupid neighbour. That, of course, is to ignore Restoration tragedy, but except for a handful of plays by perhaps three authors it deserves to be ignored.

Comedy before the Restoration had been poetic, and the new comedy does on occasion reach the level of poetry. Dryden's *Marriage à la Mode*, Wycherley's *Country Wife*, Cowley's *Cutter of Coleman Street*, even "starched Johnie Crowne's" *Country Wit* and the best of Etherege build up a sea-coast of Bohemia where rakes talk with the tongues of poets. You can name these plays in the same sentence as *Twelfth Night ;* the sweet sound that breathes upon a bank of violets breathes just as sweetly through the curtains of the great four-poster. And yet something has disappeared for ever : Southwark and Bankside are no longer there. *The Country Wife,* the lovely nonsense tale of the man who spread the rumour of his own impotency so that all the husbands

CLEOPATRA
IN DRYDEN'S *ALL FOR LOVE*
Illustration from Bell's *British Theatre*, 1780

in town left the field open to him for grazing in, is perhaps the finest prose comedy in our language. But it was not only among the dull staid citizens of the Exchange that the subtle obscenities of Mr. Horner and Lady Fidget failed to find appreciation—the rough Elizabethan mob had had another name for "china," and something went out of our literature when society took over the theatres.

The social reign lasted roughly forty years—from the Restoration of Charles the Second to the death of Dryden, and it is dominated by that great unlovable coffee-house figure. Other men wrote single plays of greater genius, but Dryden organized his age ; he led it through the period of the heroic tragedy in couplets back to blank verse which was almost free of the Shakespearian echo, led it into the amusing parochial morass of Restoration comedy, then publicly apologised and washed his hands and led it out again towards respectability and Sheridan. And like Jonson—and unlike most of his contemporaries—he knew exactly what he was doing : his critical essays—the first example of really modern prose—blazed the way he had gone. He made the prose-play just as surely as Shakespeare made the poetic : his contemporaries may have mocked the long critical prefaces, but they accepted the standards of taste he laid down, and to a great extent we can accept them still. Aristotle dates more than Dryden. The theatre he left behind was the modern theatre even in its mechanics—the scenery, the shape of the stage. If we leave Shakespeare out of account there is no period of our dramatic literature equal to the Restoration. Pampered and artificial, appealing to the educated few, lacking in moral interest, it was yet superbly finished. Wycherley, Etherege, Aphra Behn, Sedley, even Crowne produced plays which would hold the stage now as securely as *The Importance of Being Earnest* if it were not for the conventions of modern production : these plays need acting in modern clothes far more than Shakespeare's : the monstrous wig, the elegant cane, the flutter of lace handkerchiefs disguise their speed and agility.

Always in the foreground is Dryden, the great Mogul : wringing poetry even out of heroic tragedy with its flattery of human nature : then contemptuously abandoning the forms he had himself established to men like Elkanah Settle, the political hack who ended his days as part of the dragon at Bartholomew Fair ; planting in *Marriage à la Mode* the seed which was to flower in *The Country Wife* : already detaching himself from the obscene convention by the time Jeremy Collier launched his attack on the immorality of the stage, and in *All for Love* and *Don Sebastian* writing the last tragedies in blank verse which were to hold the stage for longer than their age. He was, as I have said, the great organizer, and the dramatic period that followed the Jacobean needed organization. It had its own darkness and its own anarchy, a flippant instead of a poetic anarchy. It is impossible to separate life and literature. Dryden almost alone among the writers of his time was ruled by an idea—the idea of authority. There is no inconsistency in his praise of Cromwell and his welcome to Charles : William he never welcomed, for by that time he had found the source of his idea and become a Catholic. Among the lechers and stoics of his time he stands as a figure of astonishing sanity : he was never taken in. One remembers the lines in *Don Sebastian* which compare the tempting stoical ideal of suicide with the Christian :—

> "But we like sentries are obliged to stand
> In starless nights and wait th' appointed hour."

The idea did not always make for perfect plays. In *The Spanish Friar*, for instance, one is aware of more thought in the background than the thin plot will stand. He produced nothing so graceful or perfect in form as Wycherley (apart from *Marriage à la Mode* most of the comedies are trivial enough, though lightened by incomparable lyrics) ; he had not the vitality in comedy of the despised Shadwell (and perhaps that was one reason for fastening a caricature of that gross figure before the eye of posterity) ; he had not perhaps—with all his logic, precision and steady

JOHN DRYDEN 1631-1700
Oil painting by James Maubert

growth in religious conviction—the moral genius of poor Nathaniel Lee who died in Bedlam, author of *The Princess of Cleves*, a strange Jacobean echo, but his leadership of the stage could hardly be questioned even by his enemies—who lampooned him and on one occasion set hired bravos to cudgel him as he left his coffee-house. The only man posterity has oddly enough chosen to set beside him is Otway, who, like Lee, died young and miserably. *Venice Preserved*, its blank verse written with ponderous regularity, hardly justifies his reputation. Perhaps the caricature of Shaftesbury has helped to give the play a longer life : scholars often like a little lubricity as a change from detective stories. Otway deserves to

THEATRE IN TANKARD STREET, IPSWICH
Here Garrick made his first public appearance in 1741
Engraving, c. 1800, from Wilkinson's *Theatrum Illustrata*

be remembered better for *The Soldier's Fortune*, a prose comedy which ranks only just below Wycherley.

Into this by no means happy company of playwrights—engaged in ferocious internecine intrigues reflected in the satires of Dryden and Rochester—Jeremy Collier was to burst with his too successful diatribe. It was as if the sense of humour had died with Charles. There followed three years of a moral stupid monarchy stiff and stubborn with the knowledge of other men's mockery, and then the Dutchman whose private life was too dubious even for lampooning was to become with his neglected queen an emblem of middle-class respectability. Dryden, Otway, Wycherley, Etherege, Shadwell, Crowne, Sedley and Behn: these in certain plays reached the height of intellectual comedy—their successors with three exceptions were only shadows. The exceptions were Vanbrugh, Farquhar and Congreve.

Vanbrugh carried on the tradition of Shadwell and Crowne—in between building those immense blocks of stone which are like the magnificent tombs of domestic greatness. His plays are on the old pattern with stupid country knights born for cuckoldry: his personal contribution was a

THE 'SCREEN SCENE, FROM *A SCHOOL FOR SCANDAL*
A performance at Drury Lane Theatre, May 8, 1777
Contemporary Engraving

knowledge of life which went further than the Court, the Coffee-house, the New Exchange and the plays of his contemporaries—a breath of the active world and the wars in Flanders. As for Congreve, Dryden began the long tradition of overpraise. He had already handed on his laurels to several other poets before, in 1694, he wrote his lines, "To My Dear Friend, Mr. Congreve, on his Comedy called The Double Dealer" :—

> "In Him all Beauties of this Age we see ;
> Etherege his Courtship, Southern's Purity,
> The Satyre, Wit and Strength of Manly Wycherley,"

reaching the astonishing conclusion :—

> "Heav'n, that but once was Prodigal before,
> To Shakespeare gave as much ; she could not give him more."

The Way of the World, in which Congreve's thin and perfect talent neatly and beautifully expired "like the rose in aromatic pain," will always be the delight of the dilettante—it is the dizziest height to which an amateur author has ever climbed. Congreve, as we know from the famous meeting with Voltaire, considered himself a gentleman rather than an author ; that is why his plays remain only exquisitely worded imitations of rougher work. He contributed nothing new to the stage : the famous scene in which Millamant lays down her conditions for marriage was a polished repetition of innumerable similar scenes. Even those famous lines which describe the approach of Millamant remind us of other lines by a far greater poet—to Delilah :—

> "With all her bravery on, and tackle trim,
> Sails fill'd, and streamers waving . . ."

Poor despised Crowne, in *The Country Wit*, had provided as good situations : Shadwell had had more life, and Wycherley more stagecraft—Congreve, like the smooth schoolboy, stole the prize and remains in most people's eyes the pattern-writer of Restoration comedy.

Farquhar followed one of the fashions of his time in dying young, leaving, at the age of thirty, seven plays behind, of which *The Recruiting Officer* and *The Beaux, Stratagem* are the most successful. This was the last fling of real Restoration comedy before Sentiment completely won the day, and Farquhar has a touch of genuine feeling, of wider poetry, and of the hurly-burly of experience which his predecessors lacked. *The Beaux, Stratagem* is the kind of play which Fielding might have written if all his serious attention had not been given to the novel—the lovely opening in the sleepy inn with the bustle of the night coach, the unctuous innkeeper, the pretty daughter, the gentlemen of the road, and the gibbet and the horse-pistols in the background of the comedy—as if Tom Jones and Jonathan Wild had got between the same covers with the hilarity a little subdued at the approach of death (Farquhar was dying as he wrote). The satire is more human than Wycherley's, who was concerned with man only as a grotesque sexual animal, and the lyricism Etherege might have envied : above all there is a masculinity : "Give me a Man that keeps his Five Senses keen and bright as his Sword" ; the fortune hunter boasts when he pools his resources with his friend in pursuit of an heiress : "I am for venturing one of the hundreds if you will upon this Knight-Errantry ; but in case it should fail, we'll reserve the t'other to carry us to some Counterscarp, where we may die as we liv'd in a Blaze."

RICHARD BRINSLEY SHERIDAN 1751–1816
Pastel by John Russell, 1788
By courtesy of the Trustees of the National Portrait Gallery, London

OSCAR WILDE 1856–1900
Caricature by " Ape " from *Vanity Fair*, May 24th, 1884

SO long as Farquhar, Congreve and Vanbrugh lived, prose was still written for the stage with the wit and unexpectedness of poetry. When we hear of the dull-witted husband who "comes flounce into Bed, dead as a Salmon into a Fishmonger's Basket," we are still not so far from Shakespeare and Jonson. The sense of ritual has not been lost, for ritual is the representation of something real abstracted from any individual element. It is the common touch in the human portrait—Cromwell without the personal eccentricity of the warts. Lady Fidget, it is true, is more of a "character" than Lady Macbeth, but she is still sufficiently abstracted—silly charming Wantonness itself passes across the stage as in a Morality and not a particular woman. All good dramatic prose—or poetry—has this abstract quality, by which, of course, I do not mean a woolliness, a vagueness. On the contrary the abstract word is the most concrete. But now the great period has drawn to a close. You will notice how often the writers of comedy as well as of tragedy up to now have had as their main figures representations of the dark side of human nature— Volpone, Shylock, Mr. Horner. Now sentiment is going to creep in : the author is going to fall in love with his own creations, identify himself with them, flatter himself by endowing them with all kinds of winning traits, so that we shall no longer watch Avarice, Lust, Revenge, Folly meeting the kind of fate which satisfies our sense of destiny. The happy ending is here, and we shall listen to Addison winning moral approval with the empty words of Cato, or Goldsmith's Mr. Hardcastle uttering the smug sentiments which will endear the author to his audience : "I love everything that's old : old friends, old times, old manners, old books, old wine ; and I believe, Dorothy, you'll own I have been pretty fond of an old wife." A generation before sentiments like those could only have been uttered satirically. Now the author's personality has begun to shoulder his characters aside. We have reached the end of serious dramatic writing : only individual authors will break the general barrenness.

The high points of eighteenth century drama are usually regarded as these : *The School for Scandal, The Rivals, She Stoops to Conquer*. It must be admitted that Sheridan and Goldsmith have held the stage, if it is enough to secure year by year the compulsory attendance of school children at well-meaning matinees. The awful humours of the duel scene in *The Rivals*, Lady Teazle "m'ludding" and flirting a fan, the unconvincing villainies of Joseph Surface, the sentimentalities of Mr. Hardcastle, Mrs. Malaprop's repetitive errors—have they really delighted generations or is it only that they have been considered safe plays for young people—Restoration comedy without the sex ? Sheridan's style has the smooth unoriginal proficiency of a Parliamentary orator : Congreve lacks life but he sparkles beside his successor. There is no reason why Sheridan should have been thus preferred to such minor writers as Mrs. Centlivre—except that her humour was still a little dubious, or George

Colman, whose comedy, *The Jealous Wife*, does possess a certain tang—the atmosphere of stables and Smithfield inns : it was simply that Sheridan was a personality, and he traded himself successfully. Authors were no longer so anonymous that the researches of scholars unearth only a few bills, a doubtful signature, or an unimportant law suit.

As for Goldsmith, his success was assured as soon as the age of Nell Gwyn and Moll Davis was over. The bourgeois, who had been the butt of the theatre, ruled the stalls and boxes : respectability must be the hero now, and if a Lady Fidget were to appear at all she must be treated with solemn reprobation. Marriage is no longer the subject of a joke : it is the happy ending to which all plays tend. Typical of the period is Arthur Murphy's *The Way to Keep Him*, in which two husbands for five acts remain secretly in love with their own wives : these plays usually end with little tags—one cannot call them moral so much as conventional. "In my opinion," Murphy brings down the curtain, "were the business of this day to go abroad into the world, it would prove a very useful lesson : the men would see how their passions may carry them into the danger of wounding the bosom of a friend" (O, the shades of Mr. Horner !) "and the ladies would learn that, after the marriage rites are performed, they ought not to suffer their powers of pleasing to languish away, but should still remember to sacrifice to the Graces." It sounds more like the subject for a ladies' magazine article than a play. Compare that discreet admonitory curtain with the old comedy, with the fool singing, "For the rain it raineth every day." It was the period of blarney : Sheridan, Goldsmith, Murphy—what a lot of Irishmen from that time forth were to make a good living out of the easily pleased prosperous public of the English theatre. They all had a certain flair—Murphy could turn a phrase quite as adequately as Sheridan : here was the touch of wistful poetry—"Adieu for him the sidebox whisper, the soft assignation, and all the joys of freedom" : a certain wit—"She has touched the cash ; I can see the banknotes sparkling in her eyes," and an occasional piece of vivid and robust reporting :—

"Did I not go into Parliament to please you ? Did I not go down to the Borough of Smoke-and-Sot, and get drunk there for a whole month together ? Did I not get mobbed at the George and Vulture ? And pelted and horse-whipped the day before the election ? And was not I obliged to steal out of the town in a rabbit-cart ? And all this to be somebody as you call it ? Did not I stand up in the House to make a speech to show what an Orator you had married ? And did not I expose myself ? Did I know whether I stood upon my head or my heels for half an hour together ? And did not a great man from the Treasury Bench tell me never to speak again ?"

Indeed men like Murphy had a great deal of talent : they had not the dreadful melting tenderness of Goldsmith or the smoothness of Sheridan, but it is the plot now and not the theme that matters. The illustration

SCENE FROM *TWELFTH NIGHT*
Painted by William Hamilton for Boydell's 'Shakespeare Gallery'

DAVID GARRICK IN THE GREEN ROOM
Oil painting by William Hogarth, 1697-1764

of the idea has driven the idea itself out of the theatre. We are beginning to ask the question, "How can he get five acts out of that ?" A question which never troubled an earlier audience. It is a question which becomes increasingly troublesome the nearer we get to the persons of the play ; the less abstract the drama the more we identify ourselves with the drama. Jealousy and Passion can fill any number of acts, but the misadventures of George and Margaret cannot.

One man there was with a more robust talent, and that was Foot, the comic actor-playwright, who has been called, rather unwisely, the English Aristophanes. He cannot stand up to a term like that : racy and vigorous though his plays are, we have to use the historic sense to appreciate them, for they depend for their interest on personalities who are now buried in the footnotes of history. He did in the theatre what Rowlandson did in painting, but the paintings have outlived the plays.

The trouble was—we had been too fortunate in our drama. Not even France could boast the equal of our greatest names. With the works of Shakespeare, Jonson and Dryden to draw upon, managers found it

A Performance of *Othello* at the Regency Theatre, 1817
Engraving from Wilkinson's *Theatrum Illustrata*

unnecessary to encourage fresh talent. And of course it was much cheaper. Mr. W. D. Taylor has calculated that "of the thirteen parts Garrick chose to appear in during his farewell performances at the beginning of 1776, ten are from plays written before 1730," and the same critic has noted a secondary cause of decline : "The greatest geniuses of the century preferred the novel. Neither Defoe nor Richardson nor Smollet nor Sterne attempted the dramatic form." Though, in fact, Smollet did.

THE theatre was not to see a revival until new subject-matter attracted better brains. The old abstract drama had dealt with important things : with "the base Indian who threw a pearl away richer than all his tribe," with the lark in the cage and the soul in the body ; that had gone, perhaps for ever, and the theatre had become a kind of supplement to *The Ladies' Magazine*. The religious sense was at its lowest ebb, and the political did not exist as we know it to-day. Man's interests shrank like a rockpool in the hard bright sunlight of reason. Garrick rewrote Shakespeare. (So in a small way had Davenant and Dryden, but at least they were fellow-poets : Garrick was one of the new breed of theatrical business men—the actor-managers).

The new subject-matter therefore could not be abstract and poetic : it had to be realistic, but on a different plane of realism. It had to be important as a leading article may be important, deal with ideas important for the period if it could not deal with ideas important for all periods. Tom Robertson's *Caste*, produced in 1867, is usually held to mark the change. It is not a play which bears revival : stilted and melodramatic, it was conventional enough in everything but the one novelty, that it did state, though in primitive naïve terms, the economic and social facts : as its finest flower it was to seed the work of Pinero, Henry Arthur Jones, Galsworthy, dramatists whose plays have barely outlived their deaths.

It was the first self-seeding in the English theatre since the days of the Miracle play. Always before the seed had blown from abroad—as it was to do again at the end of the century. From Spain and France we had magnificently developed. In our own island we were shut in : there was not the intellectual room to breathe, and the absence of foreign influences in the greater part of the nineteenth century—due perhaps in part to Victorian complacency, for did not we lead the world in coal and steam and were not foreigners notoriously immoral ? —had an odd and interesting effect. The theatre may sometimes appear dead, but it cannot die, and the English theatre developed in the empty years strange freaks to hold the attention. Many of these were imported from the Continent, but you can hardly dignify them by the name of influences. Our greatest actors ranted about the stage listening to imaginary bells, or mounted the scaffold as Sidney Carton—"It is a far, far better thing . . ." It was as if a buried popular public were signalling desperately for release : as if we were on the verge of rediscovering through the crudest melodrama a popular poetry. But middle-class educated opinion was too strong.

This was the age when the producer came into his own. And the designer. Scenery had never been so important since the days of the seventeenth-century masque, but it was painfully realistic scenery. Soon we would be reading "Cigarettes by Abdullah. Vacuum cleaner in Act 2 by the Hoover Company." The Times Furnishing Company is on the horizon, and soon we would be reading of Miss So-and-so's dresses and who had made them. *Caste* had given quite a new turn to triviality.

There were attempts at better things as the century progressed— attempts which beat hopelessly against the realistic tide. There was Tennyson's *Queen Mary* and Browning's *Strafford*. But the poets were too long-winded now that they wrote to be read, and the actor-managers who produced their plays smothered their merits under the expensive costumes. Browning had a real sense of the stage. *Pippa Passes* shows what a dramatist he might have been if the audience had been there, for audiences get the dramatists they deserve (if only the critics who sneer

ARTHUR CECIL AS MR. POSKETT IN PINERO'S *THE MAGISTRATE*
Water colour by Graham Robertson

at the bear-baiting public of Shakespeare would remember that). The quick love scene between Ottima and Sebald the first dawn after they have done away with the old doting husband is worthy of the Jacobeans—Sebald's shuddering refusal of *red* wine and Ottima's cry when conscience and despair drive them to suicide : "Not to me, God—to him be merciful." Browning, living in Italy, was free from the prudery of his age : he could afford to be honest : and his dramatic verse has the magnificent voluptuousness of a better time—"Those morbid, olive, faultless shoulder-blades." Tennyson, too, in *Queen Mary*, nearly wrote a great play. But he was hemmed in by indifference : in that prosperous and realistic age you could not deal effectively with the subtlety and the cruelty of religion. *Queen Mary* was stifled in its conception by the worldly success of the Church of England.

But these plays were as much "sports" in the Victorian theatre as Yeats's in the Edwardian, or Flecker's *Hassan*, or Eliot's *Murder in the Cathedral* in our own. The three-act play was here : the drawing-room set, the library set, and after a few more years the bedroom set. Cigarette cases were being offered, and very soon now butlers and parlour-maids would be crossing the stage, as the curtain rose, to answer the telephone. The panelling in the library looks quite Tudor, the club is lifted straight from St. James's (and now that acting has become a respectable profession the actors can be lifted from there, too).

There was something new in this : the novelty of photography—which was also to be mistaken for an art. Technically the new writers were amazingly accomplished. The theatre had become very slipshod : the soliloquy, a very valuable convention, had become hopelessly debased, and the aside, for which there was never very much to be said, had multiplied to such an extent that almost half the play of a dramatist of Murphy's time was addressed to the audience. Pinero and Jones levelled the play up against everyday behaviour and snipped off the excrescences. Nowadays, these plays have almost an old-fashioned charm ; they join Mrs. Cameron's photographs among the period pieces, but that only goes to show how up-to-the-minute they were in their own day—up-to-the-minute even in their conventionalities. The sentimentality of *London Pride* may be a little overwhelming—but so is the sentimentality of Mr. Noel Coward's *Design for Living ;* we don't recognize sentimentality until it has dated a little. These writers, too, were daring : *The Second Mrs. Tanqueray*, melodramatic and sentimental though it seems now, marked an advance as great as *Caste :* sexual situations could now be presented seriously in prose if they avoided crudities likely to offend the Lord Chamberlain, just as many years later Galsworthy's *Silver Box* was to open the way to criticism of our institutions. This type of play was to reach its apotheosis in Mr. Granville-Barker's *Waste*, in which we are convincingly introduced to the private lives of Cabinet Ministers. Church disestablishment is discussed at a length that only a consummate craftsman could have made tolerable ; the theme is the social convention that enforces the resignation of a Member of Parliament who is co-respondent in a divorce suit : the title of course refers to the waste involved in the retirement of the one Minister capable of nursing through Parliament the Disestablishment Bill. Mr. Barker might have written a play about Parnell, but he chose deliberately the rather drab political issue, just as Henry James in his later novels chose ugly names for his heroines : above all there must be no fortuitous

SIR ARTHUR PINERO
Oil painting by Joseph Mordecai

GEORGE BERNARD SHAW
Oil painting by Augustus John
By courtesy of the Artist and the Fitzwilliam Museum, Cambridge

glamour to confuse the subject with the plot. No other play of the realistic school is so likely to survive the circumstances of its time. It is honest through and through, and it is without a trace of the sentimentality that betrayed Galsworthy.

There was, of course, bound sooner or later to be a reaction against this sober high-minded pattern. Dryden, it was said, found English prose brick and left it marble : these authors were certainly remaking it in rather ugly bricks like a workhouse wall. One bright spirit had evaded capture, leaving behind him, after he had died of drink and disease, one of the most perfect plays in our theatre. How beautifully free from any sense of period at all is Wilde's *Importance of Being Earnest*. In *Lady Windermere's Fan* he tried to play the game like his contemporaries, but he had not their sense of reality and the result was rather like an Academy problem picture, but in *The Importance* he shook off his age and soared as freely in the delirious air of nonsense as Edward Lear.

Meanwhile, with critics like Mr. Bernard Shaw and William Archer in the stalls, a certain depression over the North Sea was bound to strike our shores. Henry James mercilessly described the atmosphere of Ibsen's plays as "an odour of spiritual paraffin" ; the long Oslo winter and the light of oil lamps had helped to form these extraordinary plays in which town councillors and sanitary inspectors wrestled with their egos as ferociously as the Prince of Denmark in surroundings of appalling drabness. To audiences accustomed to Pinero these plays were inexpressibly odd and obscure : factions developed, with critics in opposing camps : the cause was not helped by Archer's creaking translations. *The Doll's House* had a comparatively easy passage : 'women's rights' was a subject even Pinero might have tackled, but *The Master Builder*, *The Wild Duck*— this mixture of poetic symbolism and realistic detail could not be understood by that generation. It was as strange to Shakespeare lovers as to Pinero "fans." And before they had really time to accept Ibsen a second northern depression reached our island, this time from Russia ; and the Stage Society produced Tchekhov.

But Pinero, Jones and, increasingly, Galsworthy, and later Maugham, remained the staple fare, though perhaps the general shaking-up by Ibsen and Tchekhov caused as near an approach to passionate approval and fanatical disapproval as the English public could express, and helped the success of two authors who stood right outside the realistic social convention—Shaw and Barrie. Ibsen had introduced intellectual discussion to the stage, and Shaw seized his opportunity ; though perhaps it is too fantastic to detect a resemblance between the frustrated hopes, the wistful dreams and the strangely natural behaviour of Tchekhov's characters and Barrie's fairy backgrounds, enchanted woods, and Never Neverlands.

It would be idle here to attempt to scratch the tough surface of Mr. Shaw's enormous world-wide reputation. With Wilde, Byron, Galsworthy and Edgar Wallace he is the representative of our literature on the Continent. Like Sterne, another Irishman, he plays the fool at enormous length, but without that little bitter core which lies hidden in *Tristram Shandy*. Ideas are often adopted for the sake of their paradoxes and discarded as soon as they cease to startle. He gives his audiences a sense of intellectual activity—but they often imagine they have exercised their brains when they have really done no more than strain their eyes at the startling convolutions of a tumbler.

Barrie was as ill at ease in the world as Shaw is confident. Favoured from the very start of his career by Fortune he remained a misfit. He invented a dream world of sexless wives who mothered and understood their husbands, of children who never grew up because they had never really been born. His plays are cloyingly sweet, but there had been no dramatic writer since the seventeenth century who knew his business so well. The opening act of *Dear Brutus* for example could not be bettered : from the opening line as the ladies drift in after dinner he holds you with his Ancient Mariner's eye. He wrote with ease and grace and he was a consummate craftsman : "Had you with these the same but brought a mind." But yet when all is said, he *had* enlarged the subject matter of our drama : he had improved its prose style : yet it is odd that his plays should have led nowhere.

One great dramatist was working in our century : one pictures him reading Flaubert in Paris, walking the boulevards to keep warm and save coal, learning the kind of seriousness which the French can teach better than any other nation : the intense seriousness of finding the right word and the right method whether you are writing farce or tragedy. This is the seriousness you do not find in Shaw or Barrie or Galsworthy—from whom pity for an unrealised lower-class drove out every consideration of style or form. But Synge exchanging the boulevards for the West Coast of Ireland, lying flat on the bedroom floor of his inn with his ear to a crack, recording the phrases of the peasantry with scrupulous accuracy, was as careful and serious an artist as Flaubert. He reminds one of "the chief inquisitor" in Browning's poem :—

> "He took such cognisance of men and things,
> If any beat a horse you felt he saw ;
> If any cursed a woman he took note ;
> Yet stared at nobody—they stared at him."

The Shadow in the Glen, The Riders to the Sea : these were the exquisite marginal drawings for the two great compositions, *The Well of the Saints* and *The Playboy of the Western World.* The last play caused a riot in the Dublin theatre where it was first presented—but no riot was ever caused in London. The excessive tolerance of that city (often amounting to indifference) allows it to accept everything without protest.

J. M. BARRIE
Drawing by W. T. Monnington, 1932

Indifference can almost have the air of charity; but you cannot live on indifference, and Synge had not the secret of his fellow Irishman to shake London audiences into attention—he would not have wanted the secret. His work was done for the work's sake; personality was something to be excluded at all costs. The only hostility he aroused was in such places as the *Punch* office: a few comic writers wrote sneering little parodies of the Irish manner as they had written little sneering parodies of the Russian manner. Parodies sometimes have effects their authors never dreamed of, and I remember that my own first introduction to Synge was a parody in *Punch* when I was about fourteen years old—I went about for days with the magic of the silly jest in my ears.

Synge died young and again there was no successor; even in Ireland every new playwright had to begin over again and conquer the enmity of the Irish people.

IN this short survey we have reached our own times, and it is a little invidious to hand out bouquets and poisoned chalices to contemporaries. But it is impossible not to notice the dead end. There are fine plays, but no single figure dominates and directs his age as Dryden and Jonson did. One cannot say the poetic drama shows no sign of life, when one has seen the success of *Murder in the Cathedral*. Somerset Maugham in *Our Betters* wrote perhaps the best social comedy of this century, and in *The Sacred Flame* he certainly wrote one of the worst dramas. Ronald Mackenzie in *Musical Chairs* made a magnificent beginning under Tchekhov's influence and was then killed in a motor accident. J. B. Priestley has tried to enlarge the contemporary subject matter with the help of Dunne, and you cannot say experiment is quite dead so long as Sean O'Casey and Denis Johnstone are writing. As for craftsmanship, Noel Coward has all his contemporaries beaten. He is the best craftsman since Barrie and unlike Barrie is able to disguise his sentimentality, coming into the open only occasionally in such pieces as *Cavalcade*. Only as the years pass and the contemporary idiom changes does his sentimentality begin to show, emerging as the dye washes off, like the colour of a stolen horse. One other dramatist I should like to include here, and that is Vernon Sylvaine, the author of *Women Aren't Angels* and other farces designed for the Robertson Hare, Alfred Drayton combination. These plays with their great technical skill and their very national humour—full of discarded trousers and men dressed up in their wives' clothes and jealous women and timid husbands—are much more serious in the aesthetic sense than such fake tragedies as *The Sacred Flame* and *Loyalties*, which are exclusively written for the stalls and the upper circle.

It is a "bitty" picture, the contemporary theatre—so many talented authors, so many plays of great competence and even of some seriousness, and yet surrounding every effort this sense of a huge public indifference. In that lies the chief distinction between the English and the American theatre : over here we write perhaps just as many good plays, but in New York they have a good audience. There is in the air an interest, an excitement—at any moment, you feel, the great dramatist may appear again because the audience is ready to receive him.

The economics of the London theatre have a great deal to do with this indifference : the huge theatre rents make managers unwilling to take risks, and like cinema companies they stick to the familiar pattern of entertainment (it is the small theatres—the Westminster, the Mercury, the Duchess and the Unity—which have been responsible for most of the experiments we have seen of late years). The rents, too, raise the price of seats, so that theatre-going becomes the privilege of an economic class and of middle age. The young and the poor may squeeze into the gallery, but the "Gods" are powerless to influence the entertainment far below them.

J. M. Synge
Wash drawing by J. B. Yeats

But the picture is not wholly dark : the "Old Vic" has kept Shakespeare before the people, the small theatres are there, and it is unlikely that the high rental of the West End will survive the war. The indifference of London to living art has been the indifference of a class, of the well-to-do and the professional man cut to pattern by his education. The theatre is bound up with the world's fate as it has always been : young, lyrical, conceited in the first Elizabethan theatre : dark with disillusionment and violence in the Jacobean ; clever and conscienceless and making hay while the sun shone in the interval between two revolutions ; moribund, living on the imagination of the past during the age of reason ; journalistic and humanitarian during the reign of Victoria ; confused and indecisive in our own times. . . . Now we are heading either for chaos of such long duration that the theatre will not survive our civilization, or a world so new and changed it may well be that in the theatre it will seem as though Elizabeth were on the throne again.

BRITISH HISTORIANS

E. L. WOODWARD

I

IT would be pleasant to begin this survey with a phrase about a certain "island" temperament manifesting itself over the centuries in the work of British historians. An "island" temperament. "English" is not an inclusive term : "British to a historian means primarily the island of Great Britain, to the northern limit of Roman domination, before the coming of the Anglo-Saxon and Scandinavian invaders. There is, however, no need to quarrel about terms. Bede (672-3—735) the earliest, and, in many respects the greatest of the "island" historians, wrote an *Ecclesiastical History of the English Nation*. This book was written in Latin, and at a time when the "English Nation" had no unified political existence. Bede himself was the subject of a Northumbrian king whose rule extended, across the later Anglo-Scottish border, from the Firth of Forth to the Humber. More than a thousand years later another *History of England* became a best-seller ; the author was David Hume, a Scotsman from Berwickshire. About half way in time between Bede and Hume, Gerald de Barri, a Welshman of Norman ancestry, compiled the first "full-length" geographical description of Ireland. The honours may therefore be taken as even.

To some extent, indeed, it is possible to notice a difference, age for age, between English (for short) and continental historians. Bede, once again, is typical of the average "English" scholar. A certain quietness of mind ; a strong visual imagination ; a clear style, not without poetic quality ; a shrewd, tolerant judgment ; greater interest in character and action than in ideas. Among the readers of these "English" historians perhaps one might find a stronger dislike of pedantry and "dry-as-dust" than is found in some other countries. Nevertheless, the field of English historical writing is too vast to be summed up in a few sentences, and the individuality of the writers too stubborn to be juggled into averages. Macaulay had not a "quiet manner"; Stubbs had little visual imagination. Carlyle's judgment was not "tolerant." Gibbon's style cannot be described as "poetic." Neither Hume nor Acton was uninterested in ideas.

Furthermore, as the centuries have passed, the balance and emphasis of historical studies and writing have changed so much that there might seem to be little in common between the medieval chroniclers, the encyclopedists of the eighteenth century, and the "economic-minded" historians of the present day. It is well to remember that, as there has always been some kind of special technique, so also has there been a distinction between historians whose main interest is in the establishment of fact, and historians who have concerned themselves with the significance of the facts thus established. A little more than a hundred years ago, Macaulay, in his large and vivid language, wrote of the "two hostile elements," reason and imagination, which had "never been known to form a perfect amalgamation" in history. "Of the two kinds of composition into which history has been thus divided, the one may be compared to a map, the other to a painted landscape. The picture, though it places the country before us, does not enable us to ascertain with accuracy the dimensions, the distances, and the angles. The map . . . presents no scene to the imagination; but it gives us exact information as to the bearings of the various points, and is a more useful companion to the traveller or the general than the painted landscape could be."

Is it possible, then, to divide British historians into "map-makers" and "landscape-painters"? During the last four centuries there have been successive waves of protest against the overweighting of detail in history, and successive demands for a distinction between fact and "significant" fact, but the definition of "significant fact" has varied from generation to generation, and the division between annalists and philosophical historians has never been clear-cut. One might add that Macaulay lived before the age of aerial photography, and that a good map is a more exciting thing than a bad landscape painting.

It is better to look for special marks of British historical writing in another direction. Historians in Great Britain have been interested in subjects which have also interested their European contemporaries. They have written in the language and style of their times; Latin, Norman French, Elizabethan English, English of the Augustan age or of the Romantic Revival. They have passed judgments according to the standards of their environment. They have also been influenced by the events of English history and by the slow accumulation of circumstances in which English habits and English ways of thought have taken their national form and particular shape.

The people of this island have no claim to any special endowment of moral virtue; their history does not shew an unbroken continuity, still

144

THE ELEPHANT SENT BY ST. LOUIS TO HENRY III IN 1255
Illumination from Matthew Paris's *Historia Major*

less a monopoly, in the moral exercise of political and economic power. Nevertheless, for the last three hundred years, their national experience has given to them a sense of limits, a belief in liberty and toleration, and a practical conviction that the misuse of power brings retribution in the temporal sphere. The transition from medieval to modern times in politics and religion, and in the general social order, was made with less violence and bloodshed in this island than in almost any other part of the western world. Great Britain has known a longer period of internal peace and freedom from invasion than any country on the European mainland. She has met, and defeated, tyrannies which have threatened or overwhelmed country after country. Her own insular situation and dependence upon sea power have taught her, after one bitter lesson in the eighteenth century, the dangers of provoking a great maritime coalition against her navy. This tale of fortunate accident could be prolonged to cover many other aspects of British national life. For example, the custom,

145

legally established, that the younger sons of the nobility rank as commoners has saved us from the deep cleavage between the *noblesse* and the third estate, which long barred the way to internal unity in France.

It is thus to be expected that British historians, who, by definition, are concerned with the past, would have learned the large lessons of British history. They learned these lessons at an early stage. It is sometimes thought that the "moral approach" to history, the notion that the abuse of power brings retribution in this world, is a particularly Victorian feature of political and historical thought. Yet this idea, which, incidentally, dominated the historical writing of the Greeks, is strongly developed in Milton. It is found also in the eighteenth century. The cool and sceptical Gibbon could write: "I shall not, I trust, be accused of superstition, but I must remark that, even in this world, the natural order of events will sometimes afford the strong appearance of moral retribution."

The "moral approach" to a study of the "natural order of events" has its dangers, although the historian may be well aware that moral ideas have a history. Take two minor instances. In the nineteenth century Stubbs was not the only historian whose belief in the bracing effect of representative institutions led him into too great an emphasis upon the importance of parliamentary assemblies in the English middle ages. Freeman misunderstood many features of the eleventh century because he saw the lineaments of Mr. Gladstone in the West Saxon Earl Godwin. Nevertheless, if the "moral approach" may lead to distorted and unhistorical judgments, it can also give to a historian sympathy and elevation in his treatment of the past. Froude, for example, was a man of strong prejudices on the side of protestantism. Yet, as a prelude to the religious struggle between catholics and protestants, Froude could write:

> "Here therefore we are to enter upon one of the grand scenes of history; a solemn battle fought to the death, yet fought without ferocity by the champions or rival principles. Heroic men had fallen, and were still fast falling for what was called heresy; and now those who had inflicted death on others were called upon to bear the same witness to their own sincerity. England became the theatre of a war between two armies of martyrs to be waged not upon the open field in open action, but on the stake and on the scaffold with the nobler weapons of passive endurance. . . . If we would understand the true spirit of the time we must regard Catholics and Protestants as gallant soldiers whose deaths, when they fall, are not painful but glorious, and whose devotion we are equally able to admire even where we cannot equally approve their cause."

The "moral approach" of English historians has led to self-criticism as well as to sympathy. English historians have condemned the treatment of Ireland by their fellow-countrymen in the eighteenth and nineteenth centuries far more severely than Prussian historians have dealt with the Prussian treatment of Poland since the time of Frederick the Great.

'KING EUGENIUS OF SCOTLAND CAUSES HIS ANCESTORS
HISTORIES TO BE WRITTEN'
Woodcut from Holinshed's *Chronicles*, 1577

II

THESE judgments upon the misuse of power have been made, for
the most part, by men who have had some practical experience of
affairs. In order to understand the tradition of British historical
writing it is necessary to remember that the "academic" historian, the
"professor of history" is a recent figure. There have been Historiographers
Royal (there is still a Historiographer Royal for Scotland), but in the
development of historical writing their office has counted no more than
the office of Poet Laureate in the development of English poetry. Until
1724, Great Britain had no professors of "modern" history. In this year
George II founded the Regius Chairs at Oxford and Cambridge. These
foundations had a practical purpose ; the training of diplomats. The
professors were expected to supervise the instruction of undergraduates
in modern languages. For a century the holders of the chairs were of
little importance in the growth of historical studies. As late as 1841
Thomas Arnold saw nothing incongruous in holding the chair of modern
history at Oxford (where, incidentally, he lectured on Roman history)
while he was headmaster of Rugby.

British historians have thus been learned scholars, but, until our
grandfathers' times, few have done their best work, or even any of their
work, as professors. This fact is important. Guizot once said that,

until he had taken part in government and administration, he had under-rated the genius of Napoleon. Clarendon put the same point of view more sharply :

"It is not a collection of records or an admission to the view and perusal of the most secret letters and acts of state that can enable a man to write a history, if there be an absence of that genius and spirit and soul of an historian which is contracted by the knowledge and course and method of business, and by conversation and familiarity in the inside of courts, and with the most active and eminent persons in the government."

The scope of history is wider to-day than in the seventeenth century. Familiarity with the inside of courts is no longer a necessary part of a historian's equipment. Some kind of practical experience is necessary, and it is remarkable how many of the greatest British historians have had this experience. Bede lived in the monastery of Jarrow at a time when the joint abbeys of Jarrow and Wearmouth were centres of northern culture. Matthew Paris, a monk in the important abbey of St. Alban's, was known personally to King Henry III and was sent on a mission of state to Norway. Sir Walter Raleigh, Clarendon and Macaulay were concerned with the most important affairs of state. Burnet was chaplain to William of Orange on his expedition to England, and throughout his life was active in public affairs. Hume went, as a minor but not obscure figure, on several diplomatic missions. Gibbon was a captain in the Hampshire Militia before he wrote his history, and a member of parliament (holding, for a time, a place under the Crown) while he was writing his earlier volumes ; he has told us that "the captain of the Hampshire Grenadiers was not useless to the historian of the Roman Empire."

In the nineteenth century, Grote was a banker, Arnold a headmaster, J. R. Green the vicar of a London parish ; Acton was busy with politics and journalism, Bryce with politics and diplomacy. A good many holders of academic chairs to-day acquired, twenty-five years ago, first hand experience of "the discipline and evolution of a modern battle." Finally it will not be forgotten that the historian of Marlborough is now Prime Minister of Great Britain.

One might extend this survey to the antiquaries in order to shew that, in Great Britain, the study of the past has not meant exclusion from present activities. The great Camden was in turn second master and headmaster of Westminster. Moreover, the collection of historical material and the writing of history have been encouraged or enjoined by kings and statesmen for practical reasons ; reasons one might say, of dignity of state as well as of policy. King Alfred ordered and took part in the translation of Bede's *Ecclesiastical History*. He was also responsible for the development, and, probably, for the first compilation of the *Anglo-Saxon Chronicle*, a record almost unique in Europe, and continued, after Alfred's time, until the twelfth century. Later, after many generations,

BEDE 672-3—735
Engraving from André Thevet's *Portraits et Vies des Hommes Illustres*, 1584

Archbishop Parker in Elizabeth's reign made a collection of manuscripts in order to establish the continuity of the Elizabethan church with the medieval past. This collection included the most important of the manuscripts available to-day for students of Alfred's chronicle.

Archbishop Parker's practical motives were shared by many of the historians and antiquaries of the seventeenth century. One of the typically English features of the civil and religious conflicts of this century was the appeal, not to abstract notions of right, but to historic precedents. Hence there were solid and immediate reasons for the investigation of the past, although these reasons did not of themselves lead to impartial writing. It is, however, dangerous to attribute any single motive to historians. The same writer may well combine disinterested curiosity with extreme partisanship; "the care of knowing causes," in the seventeenth century phrase of Thomas Hobbes, is as great as the pleasure of getting the last word in an argument. There is the simplest motive of all for the writing and study of history : the appeal of tragedy as a purging of the emotions of pity and terror.

> "Let us sit upon the ground
> And tell sad stories of the death of kings."

There is also a practical motive, not connected with political or ecclesiastical advocacy, but directly associated with personal conduct. Men have written histories because they have thought, not without justification, that, if history does not repeat itself, historical situations recur, and that directly useful lessons can be learned from the past. Sir Walter Raleigh believed that the purpose of history was "to teach by example of times past such wisdom as may guide our desires and actions." Nearly a century and a half later Lord Bolingbroke repeated this view in the epigram that history is "philosophy teaching by example." Once again, after an interval of more than a hundred years, S. R. Gardiner, the most careful and unprejudiced of historians, wrote that he wanted to convey "something better than information . . . It seems to me that, without any attempt at preaching, merely to explain how men acted towards one another, and the reason of their misunderstandings ought to teach us something for the conduct of our lives."

Acton's whole career shewed that he held this view, and that he too combined it with an absolute impartiality in scientific judgment. In our own time when "preaching," direct or indirect, is out of fashion, the "moral approach" to history, in the sense of a warning against private as well as public abuse of power, is implicit in the *saeva indignatio* with which scholars like Dr. and Mrs. Hammond have approached the social and economic history of the early nineteenth century.

Whatever the motives of historians, the field of historical curiosity has widened. There were more people in England during the lifetime of Oliver Cromwell than in the reign of Alfred ; they were doing a greater variety of things. There were many more millions in the nineteenth century ; they were doing an even greater variety of things. Moreover in the course of the generations the quality as well as the quantity of written records has increased. Before the age of printing few people in western society could read or write ; outside the learned professions there was not a vast amount of business for which reading and writing were essential. The continual increase in the complexity of affairs since the fourteenth and fifteenth centuries has brought a greater demand for accuracy in the records of public and private transactions. Consider for example, the task of balancing the national accounts in an age before the introduction of arabic numerals or the invention of double-entry book-keeping. In the twentieth century the accumulation of "known facts"—precisely, not approximately known facts—has set the historian a problem hardly known to earlier ages. The trouble now is not the finding of material, but the selection of "significant fact" from a mass of *data*.

ILLUMINATION FROM GEOFFREY DE MONMOUTH'S *HISTORY OF BRITAIN*
Early 14th century

III

IT is necessary to remember the limiting conditions of the time in dealing with the work of medieval historians. These historians were chroniclers. They wrote down the story of events; they took for granted the social and economic background. Many of the happenings which interested medieval men, and particularly, medieval churchmen, have little detailed interest to-day. Nevertheless, for those who will take trouble to get some knowledge of the background, and to read medieval chronicles in their proper context, there is plenty of excitement. The context is, however, remote ; the antique and, often, child-like setting in which the work was done sets barriers to unfamiliar readers. Until the thirteenth century medieval chronicles tend to be bare records strung together in poor Latin. Most of them were written in monasteries, for the good reason that there were few places outside the monasteries where historical study was possible. The interest, or rather, the bias of the chroniclers was often ecclesiastical in the narrowest sense ; respect for the rights of a particular monastic order, or for the property of one monastic house became the standard by which kings and even popes were judged. Nevertheless a monastery, and especially one of the greater monasteries situated on a much travelled road, was a good centre for historical writing, and the nearest medieval equivalent to a modern news agency. A large community, with widely scattered properties, and with interests touching and touched by affairs of state ; a community affiliated to other houses of a single order, and reaching across the seas to the court of Rome ; a guest-house receiving travellers of every rank and station, and collecting the talk of the realm.

Bede, like most men of genius, is the great exception to generalisations about the aridity of the early historians. Bede had a clear, logical, encyclopedic mind ; he knew how to control his material, and how to write. Incidentally, any one who dates a letter to-day is following Bede's method. Bede introduced, though he did not invent, the style of reckoning years from the year of the Incarnation. From Northumbria this calculation of "years of grace" was brought, probably by the Devonshire man Boniface, to the Frankish court, and thence to the papal Curia.

There were indeed other writers whose work deserves the title of history; for example, William of Malmesbury (c.1080-c.1143), a monk of Anglo-French descent who wisely modelled himself on Bede, or the Yorkshireman, William of Newburgh (d. c. 1198) whose political judgment and insight were unusual for his age. Matthew of Paris, English by birth, in spite of his designation, is the most interesting of the historians of the thirteenth century. Matthew Paris entered St. Alban's abbey in 1217. He went to Norway in 1248 as the bearer of a message from Louis IX of France (St. Louis) to King Haakon VI of Norway. The King of Norway invited him to reform the Benedictine abbey at Trondjhem. After carrying out this work, Matthew Paris went back to St. Alban's, and lived there until his death in 1259. St. Alban's already had a competent school of historians ; Matthew Paris continued their chronicle of events. He wrote in a pleasant, easy style, but he was less scrupulous than Bede, and not above tampering with the text of documents (including the text of Magna Carta). His interests were narrow and his judgments often those of a partisan, yet he was bold enough to write down criticisms of the king's policy. It is true that he did not intend these criticisms to see daylight ; he noted in the margin against the more doubtful passages of his work the Latin word *offendiculum ;* a little offence.

LONDINI,
Anno Domini 1571.

DETAIL FROM THE TITLE PAGE OF MATTHEW PARIS'S GREATER CHRONICLE
Edition of Archbishop Parker, 1571

O sculata oscula Lactement labuf impreffa. at
inter eadem iudicia repeantur inf...ncie
utpare uer' gr te fili' infi Alludver...cu
nevuf gr parie'ye di genie' imparet.

THE VIRGIN AND CHILD WITH MATTHEW PARIS KNEELING BELOW

Illumination by Matthew Paris from his Shorter History

By courtesy of the Trustees of the British Museum and the Walpole Society

EDWARD GIBBON 1737 - 1794
Oil painting by Henry Walton
By courtesy of the National Portrait Gallery

MATTHEW PARIS wrote in Latin because his readers expected serious history to be written in Latin. There were indeed in the later middle ages a number of rhyming chronicles in English, but these jingles can hardly be called histories, though they are neither more nor less readable than the first crabbed prose compilations in the English tongue. The English prose chronicles of the sixteenth century told the Elizabethans all that they knew about the earlier history of England and Scotland. Raphael Holinshed (d. c.1580), for example, one of the latest in a long sequence, gave Shakespeare the plots for most of his historical plays. Holinshed worked as a translator in the printing office of one Reginald Wolfe. Wolfe had already planned a universal history and cosmography; Holinshed helped him to carry out this enterprise. Wolfe died before the work was finished. Holinshed then limited it to a history of England, Scotland and Ireland.

The vernacular chroniclers were laymen. They wrote for a lay public. They were not irreligious laymen, uninterested in church affairs, but their interests, and those of the new class in English society which read their books, were not bound up with an oecumenical church. They wrote, also, in an age of rapid social and political change. Historians to-day are a little wary about the use of the term "renaissance." The middle ages were not a period of intellectual stagnation; there were at least two "revivals of learning" between 800 and 1300. The so-called "new learning" of the fifteenth and sixteenth centuries was not altogether new, even as learning. In any case, the reception of the new ideas was slow and uneven; one might describe the seventeenth century as a period of greater intellectual importance and originality than the Tudor period.

On the other hand there is much truth in the view that the age between the death of Richard III and the accession of James I saw a general widening of secular intellectual interests, and the establishment of a new class in a central and dominating position in English society. Medieval conditions were not unfavourable to speculative and artistic genius, but there is a quality about men like Sir Thomas More and Sir Walter Raleigh which had been almost unknown in western Europe since the end of the Roman peace. These men were not "modern"; they were the grandsons and great-grandsons of medieval men. Nevertheless, for better or worse, our own "modern" ideas, our secular outlook, our scientific culture reach back directly to the years in which Greek and Latin authors were read in a new way, and scholars and artists recovered a lost continuity with the ancient world.

The significance of this age can be seen in English historical writing. Sir Thomas More wrote a *History of King Richard III*. This work is not a piece of modern historical research, but it is nearer in style, in de-

MACBETH AND THE THREE WITCHES
Woodcut from Holinshed's *Chronicles of England, Scotlande and Irelande,* 1577

lineation of character, and in maturity of judgment to a work of the present age than to a medieval chronicle. Consider this summary of the character of Richard III :

"Free was hee called of dyspense, and sommewhat above his power liberall. With large giftes hee get him unstedfaste frendeshippe, for which hee was fain to pil and spoyle in other places, and get him stedfast hatred. Hee was close and secrete, a deepe dissimuler, lowlye of countenaunce, arrogant of heart, outwardly coumpinable where he inwardely hated, not letting [*i.e.* hesitating] to kisse whome he thought to kyll, dispitious and cruell, not for evill will alway, but after for ambition, and either for the surete and encrease of his estate. Frende and foo was muche what indifferent where his advauntage grew. He spared no man's deathe whose life withstoode his purpose."

Here is the Richard III whom Shakespeare put into his play, but the man was already drawn for him.

"History hath triumphed over time." This sentence in Sir Walter Raleigh's *History of the World* sums up at once the magnificence and the secular outlook of the Elizabethan age. Raleigh's words have a tragic meaning because the *History of the World* was written while the author was detained in the Tower under sentence of high treason. Others, possibly Ben Jonson, helped him in certain parts of the book, but the whole work bears the impression of a man who, above all others, added grace to everything which he touched. Raleigh planned to write a general history until the island of Great Britain began to take an important part in world affairs ; thenceforward the book would concentrate upon the history of England, though Raleigh intended to allow himself digressions or, in his military language, "sallies." He began with the Creation ; one of his "sallies" discusses, with much learning and practical observation from his own travels, whether the tree of knowledge was the Indian fig-tree, and whether Adam and Eve clothed themselves with the commodious leaves of this tree.

Raleigh had always been a great reader ; he had taken a trunk of books with him on every voyage. Obviously, even with his learning and reading he could not compile, at second hand, a history of the world from the beginning of historical legends ; he never reached the Christian era. In any case, his book was in danger of suppression because James I thought him "too saucy" in his treatment of princes. James was touchy on this subject, but Raleigh went a little far for the age when he wrote of Henry VIII that "if all the pictures and patterns of a merciless prince were lost in the world, they might all again be painted to the life out of the story of this king."

To the moſte hygh and

vertuous Princeſſe, MARY by the grace of GOD, quene of *Englande, Spayne, Fraunce, both Sicilles, Ierufalem, and Ireland, defendour of the fayth, Archeducheſſe of Auſtria, Ducheſſe of Burgondy, Myllayne, and Brabant, Counteſſe of Haſpurge, Flaunders, and Tyroll, her highneſſe moſte humble and obedient fubiect, VVyllyam Raſtell feriant at lawe, wiſſheth health, wealth, honour, and felicitie, worldely and euerlaſtyngly.*

DEDICATION TO QUEEN MARY I
From Thomas More's *Works*, 1557

V

RALEIGH'S history shews, incidentally, two features of the age which are reflected in most of the contemporary historical works; an interest in oceanic exploration and in the study of English antiquities. Here again the novelty lies as much in the approach to the subject as in the content of the works. There were travel-books and studies of ancient lore and traditions in the middle ages, but there is far more than a difference in date of publication between Geoffrey of Monmouth's twelfth century *History of British Kings* and Sir Henry Spelman's work on the Councils of the English Church or between the compilation of tall stories put together under the title of Sir John Mandeville's *Travels* and Hakluyt's *Voyages and Discoveries*.

Richard Hakluyt (1553-1616) was a scholar whose interest in geography and sea-voyages began with his first sight of a map of the world. He lectured for a time on geography at Oxford, and was for five years chaplain to the English Ambassador in Paris, but the greatest of his works was written while he was rector of a Suffolk parish.

His three volume work (the full title is *The Principal Navigations, Voyages, Traffiques and Discoveries of the English Nation made by Sea or over Land to the Remote and Farthest Distant Quarters of the Earth*) describes in a discursive way more than two hundred voyages. Although Hakluyt took a good many seamen's stories on trust, he also added to his collection numbers of documents, charters, letters of privilege and the like. Moreover he had a patriotic intention in writing his book. He wanted England to be the greatest sea power in the world; he was providing the "significant facts" which might help towards the attainment of this end. Hakluyt had "heard in speech, and read in books other nations miraculously extolled for their discoveries and notable enterprises by sea, but the English of all others for their sluggish security, and continual neglect of the like attempts." His book is an answer to this charge, whether made against his countrymen in times past or in his own age. The answer is summed up in the proud sentences of his "Epistle Dedicatorie":

"Which of the kings of this land before her Majesty, had theyr banners ever seene in the Caspian sea ? which of them hath ever dealt with the Emperor of Persia, as her Majesty heth done, and obteined for her merchants large and loving privileges ? who ever saw before this regiment, an English Ligier in the stately porch of the Grand Signor at Constantinople ? who ever found English Consuls and Agents at Tripolis in Syria, at Aleppo, at Babylon, at Balsara, and which is more, whoever heard of Englishmen at Goa before now ? what English shippes did heeretofore ever anker in the mighty river of Plate ? passe and repasse the unpassable (in former opinion) straight of Magellan, range along the coast of Chili . . . travers the mighty bredth of the South sea, . . . enter into alliance, amity, and traffike with the princes of the

TITLE PAGE OF RALEIGH'S *HISTORY OF THE WORLD*
First edition, 1614

Moluccaes, and the Isle of Java, double the famous Cape of Bona Speranza, . . . and last of al returne home most richly laden with the commodities of China, as the subjects of this now florishing monarchy have done ?"

John Stow, one of the antiquaries of the age, wrote that "the searching and unsatisfied spirits of the English" had led them to these voyages of discovery. It might be said that there were similar motives in the minds of the antiquaries themselves, but these men had another reason at least for the collection of historical material. The dissolution of the monasteries had brought the dispersal of many great and small libraries. The content of medieval knowledge was as much out of fashion as the theology of the eighteenth and early nineteenth centuries is out of fashion to-day. The old books and manuscripts were often thrown away as so much rubbish ; John Bale (1495-1563), a Carmelite friar who turned protestant, and became bishop of Ossory, described the attitude of many (though not of all) of those who acquired monastic buildings :

> "A number of them which purchased these superstitious mansions reserved of those library books some to serve their jakes, some to scour their candlesticks, and some to rub their boots, and some they sold to the grocers and soapsellers, and some they sent overseas to the bookbinders, not in small numbers, but at times whole ships full. Yea, the universities are not all clear in this detestable fact."

The monastic buildings were in many cases treated as badly as the manuscripts. It is therefore to the honour of the antiquaries of the later sixteenth and seventeenth centuries that they did what they could to leave a record of the visible monuments of medieval England. One of the earliest of these antiquaries, John Leland (c. 1505-1552) was chaplain, librarian, and antiquary to Henry VIII. Calais was at this time within the king's realm, and therefore within the territorial boundaries of Henry's "great alteration in the state ecclesiastical." The king gave Leland the living of Poppeling near Calais, but allowed him to appoint a deputy while he made a six years' tour of England. Leland's *Itinerary* (which was not printed until 1710) was the result of this "laboriouse Journey and Serche for England's Antiquities." One of Leland's letters throws an interesting light on the continuity of national habits. Leland asked that the books from the monastic libraries should be preserved in the King's Library. This measure "would be a great profit to students and honour to this nation ; whereas now the Germans, perceiving our desidiousness and negligence, do send daily young scholars hither, that spoileth them [*i.e.* the books], and cutteth them out of Libraries, returning home and putting them abroad as monuments of their own country."

John Stow (c. 1525-1605), a London tailor, also made journeys on foot over many parts of England in order to examine historical manuscripts. As far as his purse allowed, he bought old books and manuscripts to save

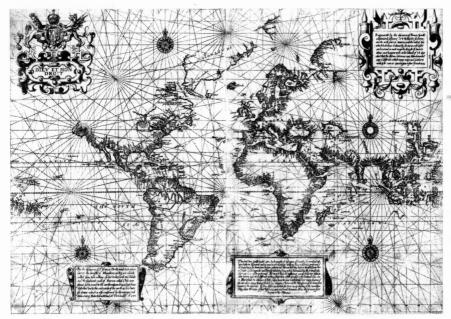

them from destruction. Archbishop Parker helped him with patronage and money; after Parker's death, Stow's resources were smaller, yet he gave up all his time to research and writing. He published a *Survey of London* in 1598. It is to the discredit of the "new learning" that, in his old age, Stow had to ask for a royal license to "repair to churches, or other places, to receive the gratuities and charitable benevolence of well-disposed people," and that, notwithstanding, he died in want.

Stow's younger contemporary William Camden (1551-1623), was more fortunate in his circumstances, though his great work *Britannia* was written while he was a schoolmaster. He travelled a good deal in the school holidays, visiting ancient sites and monuments. In 1597 he was given one of the heralds' offices, and was thus more free to spend time on antiquarian research.

Leland, Stow, and Camden were interested mainly in the materials of history: manuscripts, buildings, archaeological remains, ancient sites. Sir Henry Spelman, a Norfolk gentleman, was one of the first scholars to study, in an ordered way, the early history of English institutions. Leland had taught himself Anglo-Saxon. Spelman made investigations into the language, and published a glossary of obsolete terms in the laws of England.

VI

THESE antiquaries began an age of massive learning, which, as ever, was not free from pedantry and "collector's mania." The reaction of the ordinary reader in favour of "significant fact" goes back to the sixteenth century. Sir Philip Sidney in his *Apologie for Poetrie* (c. 1581) sets out the claims of a poet, a moral philosopher and a historian. The historian is introduced in unflattering terms as "loden with old mouse-eaten records, authorising himselfe (for the most part) upon other histories, whose greatest authorities are built upon the notable foundation of Hearesay, . . . better acquainted with a thousand yeeres a goe than with the present age : and yet better knowing how this world goeth then how his own wit runneth : curious for antiquities, and inquisitive of novelties, a wonder to young folkes, and a tyrant in table talke."

Although the demand for something more than a *précis* of "mouse-eaten records" was met slowly, the seventeenth century produced at least two short works of synthesis by writers of genius. One of the two is Bacon's *History of the Reign of King Henry VII*. Bacon remarked wisely and deeply on the study and writing of history in his *Advancement of Learning*. His short biography is not more than a compilation, but it is written in Bacon's laconic and masterful style, and ends with a portrait of the king which later research has done little to change. For example :

> "The less Bloud hee drew, the more he tooke of Treasure. And (as some construed it) hee was the more sparing in the One that hee might bee the more pressing in the Other ; for both would have beene intolerable."

Or, again, one sentence sums up this grim sovereign :

> "For his Pleasures, there is no Newes of them."

Milton's *History of Britain, that Part especially now called England ; continued to the Norman Conquest* is the first account of England before 1066 put together by a great artist. Milton was more critical than the Elizabethan compilers. He set little store on the early writers through whose work "the indistinct noise of many Battels and Devastations of many Kingdoms, overrun and lost, hath come to our Eares." He thought it useless to give too much time to the "Civil Broils" of the eighth century, and made no secret of his contempt for the "antiquitarians" who took "pleasure to be all thir lifetime in raketing the Foundations of old Abbies and Cathedrals" :

> "I am sensible how wearisom it may likely be to read of so many bare and reasonless Actions, so many names of Kings one after another, acting little more than mute persons in a Scene : what would it be to have inserted the long Bead-Roll of Archbishops, Bishops, Abbots, Abbesses, and thir doeings . . . swelling my Authors each to a voluminous body, by me studiously omitted ; and left as thir propriety, who have a mind to write the Ecclesiastical matters of

Hic oculos similes vultusq̃ hic ora tueri
Poteris, nec vltra hæc artifex quiuit manus.
ANNALES ipsum, celebrisq̃ BRITANNIA monstrant
Perenniora saxo et ære μνήματα.
Quisquis et Historiæ Cathedram hanc conscenderit, esto
Benignitatis vsq̃ monumentum Loquax.

DEGOREVS WHEAR PRI.
HIST. PR.P.E. POSVT.

WILLIAM CAMDEN 1551-1623
Oil painting by Gheeraedts (?)

those Ages ; neither do I care to wrincle the smoothness of History with rugged names of places unknown, better harped at in *Camden* and other Chorographers."

Milton's history is worth reading because Milton wrote it. The greatest historical work of the seventeenth century, was, however, a record, not of the remote and legendary past, but of contemporary events. Bacon had suggested that the "writing of Lives" should be more frequent. Clarendon's *History of the Rebellion and Civil Wars in England* is an auto-biography on a grand scale. Edward Hyde, Earl of Clarendon, was the son of a country gentleman of fair standing. He made his way at the bar and soon became a figure in the literary and political society of London.

At the outbreak of the civil war Hyde joined Charles I. He went into exile with Charles II, and before the Restoration, became the King's Lord Chancellor. From the Restoration in 1660 until 1667 he was the King's chief minister. After his fall from power he lived in France. Here he finished the history which he had begun in an earlier exile. The *History* is indeed a composite work. Clarendon began to write in 1646 ; he had not intended to publish his book. He was writing only for the King, and for a few chosen statesmen in order that they might learn the mistakes which had lost the royalist cause, and the policy by which the kingdom could be regained for the monarchy.

For twenty years Clarendon's book was unfinished. When he went into exile in 1667 he could not take his papers with him. Therefore he decided once again to write a history of his time, and to write it for his family as an autobiography. In 1671 his son was allowed to visit him, and to bring him his papers. Clarendon then resolved that, after all, he would write a history which in due time might be published. For this purpose he combined the earlier private history with the autobiography, and added the necessary connecting chapters.

The great achievement of Clarendon is not in narrative (though his descriptions are vivid and interesting) but in the full portraiture of character. Clarendon was a partisan, yet he could be just, according to his time, to his enemies. In his own way he was just to Oliver Cromwell :

"Without doubt no Man with more wickedness ever attempted anything . . . yet wickedness as great as his could never have accomplished those designs without the assistance of a great Spirit, an admirable circumspection, and sagacity, and a most magnanimous resolution. . . . In a word, as he was guilty of many Crimes against which Damnation is denounced, and for which Hell-fire is prepared, so he had some good qualities which have caused the Memory of some Men in all Ages to be celebrated ; and he will be looked upon by Posterity as a brave, wicked Man."

On the other hand Clarendon was not blind to the faults of Charles I :

"His Kingly Virtues had some mixture and allay that hindred them from shining in full Lustre, and from producing those fruits they should have been attended with . . . He was very fearless in his Person ; but, in his riper years, not very Enterprising. He had an excellent understanding, but was not confident enough of it. . . To conclude, He was the worthiest Gentleman, the best Master, the best Friend, the best Husband, the best Father, and the best Christian that the Age in which he lived produced. And if he were not the greatest King, if he were without some parts and qualities which have made some Kings great and happy, no other Prince was ever unhappy who was possessed of half his Virtues and Endowments, and so much without any kind of Vice."

The noblest of Clarendon's portraits is that of Lord Falkland who was killed in the first battle of Newbury. Falkland was only 33 at the time

TRIAL OF CHARLES I, 1649
Engraving

of his death. Until the outbreak of the civil war "his condition of life was so happy that it was hardly capable of improvement." His house at Great Tew, within riding distance of Oxford, was a centre of learning and wit ; his friends thought as highly of his judgment as of his ability. Falkland supported the king, but could not support him with the simple loyalty of a soldier like Sir Edmund Verney who summed up his attitude in the words : "I have eaten the king's bread, and served him now thirty years, and I will not do so base a thing as to desert him."

To Falkland's more subtle and reflecting mind the mere fact of civil war was a matter of deep melancholy. "From the entrance into this unnatural War his natural chearfulness and vivacity grew clouded, and a kind of sadness and dejection of spirit stole upon him, which he had never been used to." In the morning of his last battle "as allways upon action, he was very chearful," but, as the months had passed, he had become strangely morose and severe.

> "When there was any Overture or hope of Peace, he would be more erect and vigorous, and exceedingly solicitous to press anything which he thought might promote it ; and, sitting among his friends, often after a deep silence, and frequent sighs, would, with a shrill and sad accent, ingeminate the word *Peace, Peace ;* and would passionately profess 'that the very agony of the War, and the view of the calamities and desolation the kingdom did, and must endure, took his sleep from him, and would shortly break his heart.' This made some think, or pretend to think 'that he was so much enamoured on Peace that he would have been glad that the king should have bought it at any price,' which was a most unreasonable Calumny."

There were men on each side in the civil war who hated violence, and yet agreed with Falkland that peace could not be "bought at any price." On the parliamentary side the best contemporary history illustrating the ideas of the puritans was written by a woman. Mrs. Lucy Hutchinson, daughter of Sir Allan Apsley, Lieutenant of the Tower, wrote a life of her husband, Colonel Hutchinson. She wrote only for her own family, and her book was not published until 1806. For readers in the early nineteenth century Mrs. Hutchinson shewed the puritans in a new light. Hitherto, for all their private virtues, they had been regarded as philistines and boors, with Milton as a curious exception. Mrs. Hutchinson was something of a *grande dame*, and the circle in which she moved was very far from that of the non-conformist society of an English provincial town in the early years of the nineteenth century. Modern research has brought into the foreground of history many other private papers and memoirs of the period of the civil war, but, for a modern reader, Mrs. Hutchinson's book is probably more interesting than other and longer works of a more political or polemical kind.

Gilbert Burnet, the last of the contemporary historians of the seventeenth century (Pepys and Evelyn were diarists, not historians) was, like

Clarendon, though on a lesser scale, an actor in the events which he described. Burnet was born in Edinburgh, and graduated in Aberdeen. He was for a time professor of divinity at Glasgow, but settled in London in 1674. Here he gained a reputation as a preacher, and here also he published the first two volumes of his *History of the Reformation of the Church of England*. Burnet might have had a bishopric, if he had cared for court favour, and if he had not written a strong letter of remonstrance to the king on his "sinful pleasures" as well as on the evils of his government. After the accession of James II, Burnet, who had already travelled abroad, lived at the Hague, and became one of the principal advisers of William of Orange. William rewarded him in due course with the bishopric of Salisbury. In his later years Burnet wrote a *History of My Own Time*. The first volume of this work was not published until 1724; the second volume appeared ten years later. Burnet's times were then out of fashion, and the history was not well received. It is true that Burnet was self-important, prejudiced, and a little gullible about facts, yet he tried to be fair and accurate. Nevertheless his way of writing did not please the age. Swift, who disliked Burnet's politics, said of the book that he had "never read so ill a style." A modern generation is more likely to be satisfied with Burnet's quick and plain-spoken English, and less likely to feel offence at his political partisanship.

VII

IF the age of Pope and Swift was too sophisticated to enjoy Burnet, the learned tomes of the antiquaries were equally out of fashion. There had not been wanting a succession of scholars to continue the work of Leland, Camden, and Spelman. Sir William Dugdale (1605-1686) had begun during the Protectorate the publication of the English monastic charters, and had also written a book on the *Antiquities of Warwickshire*. Thomas Madox (1666-1727) wrote a learned history of the Exchequer. Thomas Rymer (1641-1713) historiographer to William III, put together, with the help of Robert Sanderson, a collection in twenty volumes of English treaties. Rymer was more successful as a collector of historical material than as a dramatist and dramatic critic. His *Foedera* survived as a standard work of reference. His historical play, *Edgar*, has been forgotten, and his *Tragedies of the Last Age Considered* will be remembered, if at all, for his unfavourable judgment upon the plays of Shakespeare.

Rymer's absurd literary judgment explains a good deal of the neglect, and indeed contempt, in which these scholars were regarded by their more brilliant if less learned contemporaries. English medieval scholarship of the late seventeenth and early eighteenth centuries has not been rescued from this undeserved contempt until our own generation. The scholars of the time (they included at least one woman : Elizabeth Elstob, who wrote an Anglo-Saxon grammar) did much to develop the methods of critical study, or, one might say, the method of history as a science. Their learning was, in a literal sense, monumental. They had an obstinacy, and often a noble passion, for truth ; they knew that the truth about the past cannot be found without hard and often dull work. They also knew that a great deal of the "history" written by men of letters is pleasant reading, but nearer to fiction than to "significant fact." Dr. Johnson, who knew the meaning of scholarship, once put this point in the presence of Gibbon :

> "We must consider how very little history there is : I mean real authentick history. That certain kings reigned, and certain battles were fought we can depend upon is true : but all the colouring, all the philosophy of history is conjecture."

If the critical methods laid down by these scholars had not been under-valued in England, if the material which they collected had been put to use, there would have been no need for Englishmen to learn over again from Germans the scientific treatment of texts. Even so, the antiquaries set an example in the study of local history in which England was pre-eminent in the eighteenth century. (An observer wishing to correlate the development of learning with contemporary social conditions would notice that county history had a special appeal to county families.) Unfortunately these scholars and antiquaries were, for the most part, tiresome, unprac-tical, pernickety men, without much skill in writing, or ability to see the wood for the trees. They frightened away the ordinary reader ; they bored the finished and elegant writers of the age even more than the table talk of their predecessors had bored Sir Philip Sidney.

This boredom was repaid by a cool and, at times, impudent disdain. Lord Bolingbroke, in his *Letters on the Study and Use of History* (1735), reviewed the utility and achievements of the patient servants of scholarship and research as a landed magnate might have reviewed the lesser figures of his household establishment. He admitted that it was difficult "to avow a thorough contempt for the whole business of these learned lives" ; the obligation to such persons, in every branch of scholarship, would be greater "if they were in general able to do anything better, and submitted to this drudgery for the sake of the public." Lord Bolingbroke recommended a "temperate curiosity" about the past :

> "Some [histories] are to be read, some are to be studied, and some may be neglected entirely, not only without detriment, but with advantage. Some are the proper objects of one man's curiosity, some of another's, and some of all men's ; but all history is not an object of curiosity for any man. He who improperly, wantonly, and absurdly makes it so, indulges a sort of canine ap-petite ; the curiosity of the one, like the hunger of the other devours ravenously and without distinction, whatever falls in its way."

WILLIAM DUGDALE 1605-1686
Frontispiece to Dugdale's *History of St. Paul's Cathedral in London*, 1658

The generation to which Lord Bolingbroke belonged was unlikely to produce a great historian. Furthermore, while in the seventeenth century there were practical reasons for searching the political and ecclesiastical annals of the past, in the middle years of the eighteenth century the establishment of state and church seemed fairly secure. In any case, until Burke once again appealed to history against the claims of an abstract political philosophy, the easy and comfortable doctrines of Locke satisfied men's minds. There was no need to dig up precedents from the years of "gothic" barbarism. Indeed, as Lord Chesterfield told his son, "much time would be ill-employed in a minute attention" to the history of the five or six centuries after Charlemagne.

Nevertheless, all English history, if not all history, remained "an object of curiosity" to the reading public, and, in the middle and later years of the eighteenth century, there was an increasing demand for "complete" histories of Great Britain. Once more the economic and social changes of the age were bringing new classes of readers, and greater opportunity for reading. Houses were better heated in winter, candles gave a brighter and steadier light. Chairs and living rooms were more comfortable, libraries more humane. Books could be printed more cheaply, sold and advertised more widely as communications improved, and newspapers had a larger circulation.

The scholars of "intemperate curiosity," who would not play down to the public, cared nothing for this great new market. Hence the demand for complete histories was met at first by writers whose knowledge was unequal to their task. One of the earliest forerunners of the modern popular history was Carte's four-volume *History of England to 1654*. Thomas Carte had the misfortune to lose most of his subscribers after the appearance of his first volume in 1747 because he made the mistake of saying that he had met someone who had been cured of the "king's evil" by the Old Pretender. In any event, Carte was little more than a hard-working compiler who would have lost his market to any competitor of first-class ability.

This market was taken by two Scotsmen, David Hume (1711-1776) and William Robertson (1721-1793). A third Scotsman, Tobias Smollet, better known as the author of *Roderick Random* and *Humphrey Clinker*, also wrote a *Complete History of England ;* other Scots collaborated with an Englishman, George Sale, and a Frenchman, Georges Psalmanazar, in the production of a *Universal History* of gigantic dimensions. Sale was a remarkable man ; a Kentish solicitor with a real interest in oriental scholarship. He published a translation of the Koran in 1734, and took part in the revision of the Arabic New Testament produced by the Society for the Promotion of Christian Knowledge. Psalmanazar was a more flamboyant figure who deceived the learned world for some time by pretending to be a native of Formosa ; he backed his claim by an invented Formosan alphabet and grammar. After his fraud had been exposed, he became very pious and won the respect of Dr. Johnson. The *Universal History* was not the only work of its kind. A similar venture, on a smaller scale, was launched with a preface by Oliver Goldsmith, for which the writer was paid the sum of three guineas.

Fifty or more volumes of world history suited some tastes in this age of encyclopedias. Other readers wanted less dispendious tomes, and were more curious about England than about the rest of the world. For this more limited demand Goldsmith himself wrote a four-volume history of England. The book would not be worth remembering if Goldsmith had not been the author, and if he had not disarmed criticism by the charming apology that he had written "not to add to historical knowledge, but to contract it."

'THE BURGHERS OF CALAIS'

A typical 19th century historical illustration

From Darton's Children's Picture Series

THOMAS BABINGTON MACAULAY, 1800 - 1859
Oil painting by Sir Francis Grant
By courtesy of the National Portrait Gallery

VIII

DAVID HUME turned to history almost by chance, and after the greater part of his philosophical work had been done. He had applied without success for philosophical chairs at Edinburgh and Glasgow. In 1752 he was appointed Keeper of the Advocates Library at Edinburgh. Here he decided to make use of his access to original and secondary historical sources : that is to say, sources already in print. Hume did not propose to bother himself with manuscripts and other unprinted sources. Within two years he produced a first volume of a *History of England*. The volume covered the reigns of James I and Charles I. (It is of interest that, in the nineteenth century S. R. Gardiner spent about thirty years in dealing with the same period.) Hume's first volume was not a popular success. The author was so much disappointed that he thought of leaving Scotland, changing his name, and settling in France. The outbreak of war with France made this plan impracticable. Hume therefore went on with his book. The sale of the second volume justified the addition of two volumes on the Tudors and two on the earlier period from Julius Caesar to the accession of Henry VII.

These volumes had an immense number of readers. Hume set a new standard of historical writing. He raised history to a philosophical plane, and clarified it of an excess of detail. He wrote in an easy, flowing style, although Dr. Johnson (not forgetting his dislike of Scotsmen) complained that the structure of his sentences was French. Lord Bolingbroke and other writers of his time had inclined to reduce history to a case book for statesmen or a manual of examples for young men about to take part in affairs. Hume knew the difference between "fact" and "significant fact" ; he also knew that the significance of history lay in the widest interpretation of human action rather than in any discreet series of "lessons." Hume's own interpretation was indeed very far from complete. He followed his age in a dislike of "enthusiasm," and in a preference for settled government, even though it might be arbitrary government. He cared more for order than for liberty, and was not much interested in "improvement." He overlooked almost entirely the importance of religion. A friend gives the reason : "Early in life he had conceived an antipathy to the Calvinistic divines." Nevertheless, in spite of his superficiality and his cocksureness, Hume does give his readers an idea of the unity of history, at all events in the sense of a cyclical progress in human affairs. A cyclical progress ; there was no finality about it, no long-sustained achievement. In Hume's own words, "there is a point of depression as well as of exaltation, from which human affairs naturally return in a contrary direction, and beyond which they seldom pass, either in their advancement or decline." All the more reason, therefore, to be gratified that one had the good fortune to be born into an advanced and civilised epoch like the eighteenth century.

Hume was a great historical writer, but he was not a great historian. His "significant" facts were not always accurate facts. He took his material almost entirely from the secondary sources in his library, and owed a good deal to the industry of the unlucky Mr. Carte. Hume's "intellect was perhaps too active and original to submit with sufficient patience to the preparatory toils and long-suspended judgment of a historian." So wrote a critic in the next generation. One might say, perhaps, more shortly, that Hume did not take enough trouble.

William Robertson was one of the Calvinistic divines whom Hume, in general, disliked. Robertson published in 1759 a *History of Scotland during the Reigns of Queen Mary and of King James VI till his Accession to the Crown of England*. This book also became an immediate success, and, for his next historical work, a *History of the Reign of Charles V*, Robertson received the princely and unprecedented sum of £4,500. He then turned to subjects outside Europe, and produced a *History of America* and a *Historical Disquisition on Ancient India*. The range of Robertson's work also shews its limitations.

On the other hand, Robertson's merits were like those of Hume, though on a lesser scale. A lucid, even, prose style, burdened, in Robertson's case, with too many heavy Latinisms; an "elegant" arrangement of fact; suitable philosophical reflections. The facts were taken at second hand; the reflections were a little commonplace, and most modern readers would agree with Cowper's description of the style as "pomp and strut."

The influence of Hume and Robertson can be seen in the writings of a host of lesser imitators who gave the public what the public wanted, and did well out of their work. Robert Henry (1718-1790) deserves to be remembered where others are forgotten because he was one of the earliest historians to write a "social history." Dr. Johnson once said that he wished much "to see one branch of history well done, that is, the history of manners, of common life." Hume had included in his work a small survey on these lines. Henry's *History of England on a New Plan* limited the narrative of political history to one section in each of his six volumes. The other sections dealt with the constitution and laws, religion, learning, the arts, and the state of manners.

These writers of popular works, attesting an astonishing demand, were eclipsed by the genius of Edward Gibbon. Gibbon was born in Putney in the year 1737. His *Autobiography* describes with *aplomb* the main facts about his life. He may have dramatised his decision to write the history of the decline and fall of the city of Rome when he says that he made up his mind on the subject as he "sat musing on the Capitol, while the barefooted fryars were chanting their litanies in the temple of Jupiter." The setting fits exactly with his summary of his own work; "I have described the triumph of barbarism and of religion."

MEXICAN HISTORICAL PICTOGRAPH
Frontispiece to William Robertson's *History of America*, 1777

The choice of subject, which Gibbon soon expanded to include the fall
of the Roman Empire, may well be called a decision of the whole man.
Gibbon had indeed always been interested in historical subjects, and had
long been considering a theme upon which to write a *magnum opus*. The
growth of Swiss liberties, a biography of Sir Walter Raleigh, a comparison,
on Plutarchian lines, between the Emperor Titus and King Henry V had
been among these projects. Gibbon actually wrote a short work on the
liberties of Switzerland : the biography of Sir Walter Raleigh would have
been a curious affair, but it was never even begun. Even after his decision
to take the immense theme of the Roman Empire, Gibbon waited before
engaging upon his subject. He did not begin to write until about 1772 ;
his first volume appeared in 1776, his last in 1788.

The Decline and Fall of the Roman Empire is unique not merely in
English historical writing, but in the historical writing of any country.

171

No work of such length has maintained its popularity for so long a time. As a modern critic has pointed out, Gibbon's book is "constantly re-published with notes and additions as though it were an original authority." No history can survive, except as a source of material for experts, unless it is also a work of art. The *Decline and Fall* is a great work of art ; it is not a work of the purest or noblest art, since Gibbon was an unheroic figure living in an unheroic age. Nevertheless, if he were incapable of great emotion, Gibbon was a master of "passionless impartiality" towards all men and things below the heroic level. This mastery is one of the main sources of his power. He was not an original thinker; his scholarship was not extraordinary, though it is significant that he was among the few "literary" historians who did not underrate the work of the antiquaries. He acknowledged his debt to others, and, in particular, to the French historian Tillemont. He failed—the failure was universal long after Gibbon's death—to do justice to the services rendered to civilisation by the Byzantine Empire. He knew little about the western middle ages. "The triumph of barbarism and religion" ignores the existence of countervailing facts over which modern scholars have spent years of investigation. It ignores equally the triumph of Chartres Cathedral, of the philosophy of St. Thomas, and of the *Divine Comedy*. Finally, the lack of nobility in Gibbon's work is a little too obvious, and there is something repellent about his *obscénité érudite et froide*. When all this has been said, Gibbon's achievement remains in the forefront of English historical writing. For the first time in any European language a single work, covering a period of more than a thousand years, was carried through from beginning to end without ever losing itself in digressions and side issues. Nothing is redundant or inconsistent ; every chapter and every page fit perfectly into the general scheme. No great ship was ever launched more smoothly. Hume had judged events in a long sequence, and had lifted their narration to a higher level. Gibbon had a finer visual imagination as well as a greater care for accuracy of fact. He wrote in a mandarin style, inimitable, uniform, heavy, artificial ; yet the repetition of the same cadences, the same measurement of words, the same antithesis of sentences does not become wearisome. The book can be read ; the book is read, and, centuries hence, readers will continue to savour Gibbon as they savour Dr. Johnson.

IX

GIBBON died in 1794. For nearly twenty years after his death almost the only historical work of importance published in England was Sharon Turner's *History of England from the earliest period to the Norman Conquest*. Sharon Turner was a lawyer by profession. He settled in 1795 in the neighbourhood of the British Museum because

THE CAPITOL FROM THE SIDE OF THE CENTRAL STEPS
Engraving by Piranesi, dated 1776

he wanted to be near to the manuscripts in the library. It is significant, though not surprising, that Sharon Turner's work has been forgotten by the general public, and that little attention was ever paid to it except by other scholars. A generation later Palgrave's *Rise and Progress of the English Commonwealth* hardly met with a better fate. Palgrave's book did not extend beyond the rise of the commonwealth; even this story was left incomplete, though in a later work Palgrave reached the Norman Conquest. These books were not widely read because they were in fact unreadable. The public, as always, wanted history; the scholars gave them historical research.

As Sir Walter Scott pointed out in the preface to the 1829 edition of the Waverley novels, "when the author addresses himself exclusively to the Antiquary, he must be content to be dismissed by the general reader with the comment of Mungo, in the *Padlock*, on the Mauritanian music, 'What signifies me hear, if me no understand ?' "

At first sight the situation appears to be similar to that of the early eighteenth century. There were, however, several changes of such magnitude that an analogy between the two periods is misleading. In one respect it is possible to find continuity. In the early nineteenth century, as in the age of Lord Bolingbroke, the universities gave little thought to the history of England or, for that matter, to the modern history of Europe. This neglect was more striking, and, for a time, more serious because the universities on the continent of Europe, and particularly in Germany, were paying notable attention to historical studies ; though here again it must be remembered that the main impulse to the study of national history came from outside academic circles. The development of these studies in Germany was due in part to political motives, but there was a solid basis of scholarship upon which this political superstructure could be built. German scholars had done remarkable work in the field of philology, in the editing of texts, and in the study of law. This work was directed at first to classical texts and to ancient history ; the new methods were soon extended to other spheres. This extension, in turn, was partly, though not wholly, the result of the Romantic Revival. The first stages of the Romantic Revival were literary ; a search for new forms and new subjects at a time when the so-called classical modes of the eighteenth century were becoming stale, cold, and hackneyed. The search for the glamour of "far-off things" was most easily satisfied by the richness and colour of medieval centuries ; once looked at in and for themselves, these centuries became a source of positive intellectual interest, and not merely of emotional excitement. A cynic might add that the medieval centuries could be contemplated with greater detachment after their practical discomforts had been forgotten, and the ground was no longer cumbered with the débris of medieval institutions and customs which had once served a purpose, but continued to survive only as dangerous anachronisms in a changed political world.

For Germans in particular, the study of the middle ages provided a political as well as a literary inspiration. The medieval empire was the archetype of German unity, and, it might be added, of German secular domination over large areas of Europe. What Germans had once achieved, they could achieve again ; German superiority, lost or submerged in the political and religious wars after the reformation, might be reasserted. There were no such political motives in Great Britain, where the antiquarian scholarship of three centuries had failed to arouse more than a faint interest in medieval history. Sir Walter Scott touched the work of these antiquaries with his genius, but the study of medieval history on the grand scale was not undertaken in Great Britain until the Germans had transformed the character of historical work in every field.

During the nineteenth century it was indeed customary to exaggerate the uniqueness of German scholarship. The authority of Lord Acton has been given to the view that England had nothing to teach Germany, and Germans everything to teach Englishmen in historical method. Acton went to Germany as a young man at a time when the German schools of history were at the height of their fame. He knew little about the detailed work done by the English antiquaries, and to his death, never realised the value of this work in departments of knowledge to which, in spite of his vast learning, he was a stranger.

Nevertheless Acton was right in the sense that the gap between the antiquaries and the historians in Great Britain was not bridged in the early nineteenth century, and that the English historians of this time learned most of their critical methods from Germany. They might have learned these methods from France, where the foundation of the Ecole des Chartres in 1821 continued in secular hands the splendid traditions of scholarship set by the French Benedictines of the eighteenth century. The generation in England which followed the Napoleonic wars was, however, readier to take lessons from Germans than from Frenchmen.

The slowness with which educated opinion in Great Britain demanded the highest standards in historical methods can be seen in the history of the keeping of the national records. A Record Commission was created in London as early as 1801, a quarter of a century before the appearance of the German collection *Monumenta Germaniae historica*. The Commission was filled with important personages who knew nothing about the editing of documents. Neither the Society of Antiquaries nor the universities interested themselves in the matter ; hence little good work was done until, in 1830, Harris Nicolas, the editor of Nelson's letters, published a protest against the carelessness with which the records were treated. After the Reform Act of 1832 there was a change for the better. The Public Record Office was established in 1838 ; a new Record Commission which included experts, began a series of publications *in extenso* or in the form of abridgements or "calendars." The appointment of a Historical Manuscripts Commission in 1869 has led to similar provision for the care of manuscripts in private hands.

Meanwhile, and again outside the universities, English writers had begun to apply the new apparatus of scholarship to historical work intended for an ever widening public. Lingard's *History of England*, the first of these new books, began to appear in 1819. Lingard was a Catholic priest whose purpose in writing was to convince Englishmen, by a careful exposition of historical fact, that they held wrong views about the Catholic Church. He pleased neither Catholic nor Protestant controversialists, but the quietness, honesty, and high competence of his work gave it a place which it kept throughout the greater part of last century as a standard general history.

For some time after the appearance of Lingard's first volume the new interpretation of ancient history begun by Niebuhr (a Holsteiner who took service in Prussia) became the main interest of a generation of Englishmen trained in classical scholarship. Arnold's *History of Rome* and Thirlwall's *History of Greece* were written under this influence ; Grote also acknowledged the "inestimable aid of German erudition." Grote's *History of Greece*, which eclipsed Thirlwall's book in popularity, is of particular interest as the only historical work of importance (other than James Mill's *History of India under British Rule*) produced by the English philosophical radicals of the early nineteenth century. Arnold and Thirlwall were men of strong personality and strong political views, but they kept their politics out of sight in their histories. Grote never concealed his intention of writing a defence of Greek democracy ; the defence might have been more satisfactory if it had been based upon a real understanding of the fundamental differences between democratic government in the ancient and modern worlds. Grote was a learned but not an interesting historian ; it is not easy to account for the popularity of his book over many years except on the simple (though remarkable) ground that, since Grote's time, no English historian has attempted a full-length general history of the great age of Greece.

X

GROTE'S political bias takes on a mild appearance before the cock-sureness of Hallam and Macaulay. On the whole Hallam was more imperturbably certain of himself. Macaulay could monopolise a conversation by sheer brilliance ; a friend once described Hallam as a "perfect boa-constrictor in argument." It is also doubtful whether Macaulay ever committed himself to a judgment as sublime as Hallam's assertion that the whigs had "a natural tendency to political improvement, the tories a natural aversion to it." Hallams's *Constitutional History of England from the accession of Henry VII to the death of George II* was written on this thesis. Hallam has been called a hanging judge ; his verdicts are usually too severe and often deserve the attacks which Southey made on them in the *Quarterly Review*. Moreover, although he took the greatest pains over his work, Hallam was not a scholar in the sense in which Palgrave or von Ranke were scholars. Modern research has upset a good deal of the evidence upon which his over-confident interpretations were based.

Hallam's influence was very great, and, for a circle of readers whose taste was not over-exacting and to whom boredom came less easily than to Lord Bolingbroke, the *Constitutional History* was an ideal exposition of a polity in which freedom slowly broadened down from precedent to precedent, and did not broaden too far or too fast. There is some charm in the fact that this heavy-handed work, which Queen Elizabeth would have torn up in anger and Charles II would have thrown away out of *ennui*, was studied with earnestness by the youthful Victoria and Albert.

If Macaulay was less "goddam" about the whigs as such, he was even more satisfied with his own age. It is therefore easy to call him a "cultured philistine." It is easier and sillier to say that he was merely a *bourgeois* writing for *bourgeois*. In 1848, after the publication of the first and second volumes of his history, Macaulay received a vote of thanks from a working men's club for "having written a history which working men can understand." The late Sir Charles Firth, in his excellent *Commentary on*

THOMAS CARLYLE 1795 - 1881
Oil painting by J. McNeil Whistler
By courtesy of the Medici Society

E. A. FREEMAN 1823 - 1892
Oil painting by Hubert Vos, 1889
By courtesy of the President and Fellows of Trinity College, Oxford

Macaulay's History, said the same thing from a different angle : "Macaulay never wrote an obscure sentence in his life, and this may seem a very small merit unless we remember of how few writers we could say the same." Macaulay himself is even more illuminating about his style : "My manner is, I think, and the world thinks, on the whole a good one ; but it is very near to a bad manner indeed, and those characteristics of my style which are most easily copied are the most questionable."

Carlyle, who "did not much like happy men," made the absurd comment that "four hundred editions of the *History*" could not lend it any permanent value. Macaulay had obvious limitations. He was not a deep thinker ; like Gibbon, he failed to understand the significance of many of the noblest activities of mankind. As a writer, he had an astonishing power of description, but little sense of design. The scale upon which he began to write a history of England from the Restoration to the death of George IV might well have been too large for any man; too large perhaps, even for a man of Macaulay's genius who had been free to give the greater part of his life to study. Macaulay was forty-eight in the year in which the *History* began to appear. He had been called to the Bar in 1826 and had already started his long series of essays for the *Edinburgh Review*. He was elected to parliament in 1830 and, in 1833, appointed a member of the Supreme Council of India. He spent three and a half years in India ; during this time he laid the foundations of the Indian educational system and composed, almost single-handed, codes of criminal law and criminal procedure. He continued to sit in parliament on his return to England and for a time held office. Macaulay had talked in "printed words" from the age of three, yet, with his many interests, and with a liking for ordinary social life, the task of reading all the material for his subject was overwhelming. In spite of these difficulties Macaulay finished his third and fourth volumes. If he had lived fifteen years longer, he might have achieved the impossible, and completed at least half of his task.

The catalogue of Macaulay's faults might be extended. In a final count they would be reckoned as light weight in comparison with his immense and solid genius. He was master of the first-hand authorities which he used. He made fewer mistakes of detail in a volume than many of his critics in a single chapter. Dislike of his robustness is sometimes a sign of weakness of nerve on the part of his readers. Macaulay was not necessarily wrong because he believed in whig principles ; few people who know the facts would question his assumption that, for ninety out of a hundred of the inhabitants of Great Britain, the early Victorian age was a better time than the reigns of James II or William and Mary. As for Macaulay's "lack of elevation," human life is lived, and may be studied, at different levels. Macaulay never claimed to write the history of thought or action at the highest levels, but this does not mean that all history should be written as from the mountain tops, or that Macaulay is necessarily superficial because he did not see England in the age of the Revolution *sub specie aeternitatis* as Wordsworth once saw London from Westminster Bridge.

For different reasons Carlyle may also be called a great historian. Carlyle shared with Macaulay, and indeed with all historians of genius, the power of losing himself in his work until, in the paradox of artistic creation, the work became impersonal and universal. Take, for example, Carlyle's account of the night before the battle of Dunbar :

> "And so the soldiers stand to their arms, or lie within reach of their arms all night. . . The night is wild and wet ; 2nd September meaning 12th by our calendar ; the Harvest Moon wades deep among clouds of sleet and hail. Whoever hath a heart for prayer, let him pray now, for the wrestle of death is at hand. Thus they pass the night. . . We English have some tents ; the Scots have none. The hoarse sea moans bodeful, swinging low and heavy against whinstone bays ; the sea and the tempests are abroad ; all else asleep but we— and there is one that rides on the wings of the wind."

This paragraph breaks all the rules of prose rhythm and composition which lesser writers, if they are prudent, will take care to observe. In any case it is an odd paragraph to find in an edition of a historical text. Yet there must be thousands of Englishmen who, like myself, came upon it in boyhood, and ever afterwards, at sight of the harvest moon, think of Cromwell's army on a wild September night in 1650.

Carlyle did not begin to write history until his fortieth year. Perhaps he never wrote history ; the *French Revolution* is nearer to Hardy's *Dynasts* than to a prose record of political events. Carlyle, in fact, did not care much for "policy." He was interested in people and, above all, in problems of right and wrong ; so much interested in right and wrong and in the assertion of personality that he began to confuse power with right. His book on Frederick the Great suffered from this confusion and therefore exasperates modern English readers. For all his recklessness of judgment Carlyle took immense pains over his work. He was never "ravenous" for facts ; he admitted, or rather, declaimed, that the duty of reading masses of inartistic material was a weariness. He described the sources for the Cromwellian period as "a waste continent of cinders" and the German historians of Frederick as "dark, chaotic dullards." In spite of all, he found his way through cinder heaps and chaos, and gave an interpretation which needs correction in detail but is still valid in the large both for Cromwell and for many of the chief actors of the French Revolution.

XI

THE careers of four men, Freeman, Froude, Green, and Stubbs, who dominate English historical writing for a generation after 1860, shew the transition to the modern age of the professional or "professorial" historian. Although three of the four held the Regius chair at Oxford,

J. A. FROUDE 1818-1894
Chalk drawing by Samuel Lawrence, 1863

their main work was done elsewhere, and they learned little of historical method from the university. Freeman's *History of the Norman Conquest* loses nothing as a story from his enthusiasm for the Anglo-Saxons. On the other hand his interpretation of the Conquest was defective because he worked almost entirely upon printed records which he could use in his Somerset country house.

Froude also did most of his writing at country houses in Wales and Devonshire, but he armed himself with material from Spanish as well as English archives. Froude wrote at even greater length than Freeman ; his *History of England from the Fall of Wolsey to the Defeat of the Spanish Armada* fills twelve volumes. These volumes were bitterly attacked. To some extent Froude laid himself open to severe criticism. Newman and Carlyle, the two main influences in Froude's life, hardly set him examples of steadiness of opinion or of judgments unclouded by emotion. Froude's later friendship with Kingsley (whose sister-in-law he married) did little to correct his faults. His critics accused him of gross carelessness as well as of bias. In some respects Froude was careless, but he was compelled to do much of his archival research in circumstances which made accurate copying almost impossible. It may be said that he has cleared himself of the most damaging "technical" charges. His bias is beyond defence. His interpretation of documents, his likes and dislikes, or rather, his loves and hates are often absurd. The late Sir Adolphus Ward once pointed out that the "list of animals to whom Mary, Queen of Scots, is in turn compared in Froude's History is that of a small menagerie." This wilfulness in painting heroes or villains according to his tastes has lost Froude a position to which otherwise he is fully entitled. His work might have been a classic for generations, if his readers had not been left to wonder all the time whether they were not following a *tour de force* of the most sustained and magnificent kind.

The readers of Stubbs' sober and learned pages are spared any such doubts. Although Stubbs saw the middle ages through the distorting atmosphere of his own time, he was never a partisan. His scholarship was rather of the magisterial kind which deserves and obtains confidence. Stubbs learned Anglo-Saxon at school and began to read medieval documents in the court house of his native town of Knaresborough. The greatest of his books, the *Constitutional History of England*, was published between 1873 and 1878 ; that is to say, after he had done much work in editing the Rolls series of English chronicles, and before his time was occupied by the administration of the large diocese of Oxford. Stubbs wrote for scholars and students and, for them, he remains a master. He set the lines of research for half a century ; even to-day no one would think of attempting serious investigation into the medieval history of England without first reading everything which Stubbs has written on the subject.

John Richard Green was less epic in style than Freeman and less dispassionate in manner than Stubbs, though both Freeman and Stubbs admired his work, and did their best to help him. Freeman, in fact, put all his rough energy into the support of "Johnny Green." Green did not need much "boost." His *Short History of the English People* (1874) was an immediate success. The title was as fortunate as the date of publication. In the period between the second and third reform acts of the nineteenth century, and a few years after the passing of Forster's Education Act, there was a public waiting for a history, not of the English kings, but of the commons of the realm. Green's title was not, however, just a bait ; the public was given a work of art. Green had been a clergyman in the East end of London from 1860 to 1869 ; he had written a number of "middles" for the *Saturday Review*, mainly on historical subjects. He left his parish in 1869 for the librarianship of Lambeth (a post from which many contributions of value have been made to English historical studies) at a time when he was threatened with consumption. Green died at Menton in his forty-sixth year ; before his death he had written a longer version of his *Short History*. The longer version was not better than the earlier work, and it is doubtful whether Green could have improved on it.

The *Short History* owed much of its vividness to the rare conjuncture of knowledge and emotion under which it was written. The book was Green's protest against the drabness and poverty of Victorian London ; a historian's protest, as William Morris's *Dream of John Ball* was the protest of a master-craftsman. The book was thus the first of its kind in England (Carlyle's *Past and Present* was more of a pamphlet than a history) to be written under the influence of a new and wider conception of social justice. Arnold Toynbee's *Lectures on the Industrial Revolution* (1884) were written from a similar impulse. The two books shew the change in opinion since Hallam and Macaulay ; a change which has led, in our own time, and again following the demand of a new class of reader, to the close and specialised study of economic history. This study had indeed begun from the side of the economists and statisticians before the "political" historians paid detailed attention to it. The first two volumes of J. E. Thorold Rogers' *History of Agriculture and Prices* appeared in 1866 ; a generation earlier J. R. Porter's *Progress of the Nation* had shewn the difference between the new "statistical approach" and the itineraries and surveys of the age of Leland and Stow, or even of the period of Arthur Young.

The other historians of this remarkable age of scholarship and writing also bring one to the eve of the twentieth century. Lecky's greatest work *A History of England in the Eighteenth Century* (1878-90), was written in a colder mood than Green's *Short History*, but once again the book shews in a curious way the turn in interest towards the history of ideas and of social and economic movements, and the mood of opinion in Great Britain during this long age of peace ; it is almost impossible to imagine that a German historian, writing within a decade after Bismarck's three wars, would have dismissed the battle of Blenheim in a sentence. On the other hand, Lecky's book is, like Spencer Walpole's *History of Twenty-Five Years*, a record of change for the better; greater liberty of mind, a softening of manners, a more sensitive public conscience.

Lecky and Walpole were interested mainly in the British Isles, or at all events, in the development of civilisation in Europe. Seeley was the first English historian to feel something of Hakluyt's exultation in the majesty of English power. Seeley's *Expansion of England in the Eighteenth Century* belongs to the new age of imperialism. In some measure Seeley's enthusiasm was unfortunate. He was too didactic and too much of a partisan to be the founder of a school of historians of the British Empire. Hence the subject was neglected for several decades, and has not been rescued until our own time from political controversy. One branch indeed has never been treated satisfactorily ; since Mill's time no history of India under British rule (with the exception of Lyall's *Rise and Expansion of the British dominion in India*) has done justice to the interest of the subject.

XII

THE foundation of the *English Historical Review* in 1886, with Creighton as editor, may be taken as the beginning of the modern epoch in which short historical studies of the first rank have ceased to find a place in quarterly or monthly journals, and the accumulation and specialised treatment of historical material have set almost as many problems as they have solved. Freeman once complained that "history has no technical terms" to frighten incompetent writers from writing historical books. In the twentieth century one might complain that history has too many technical terms, and that the old gap between the antiquaries and the historians has widened again after a recession in the mid-Victorian era.

The gap has become wider in many respects. It is wider in life as well as in learning. With the increased *tempo* of social and political change, and with the rapid movement of the population, the average man—now a townsman—tends to be a *déraciné*, cut off from the past of his own people and country. Few people in the large cities of England even know where their great-grandparents are buried. It is harder to visualise the past when you do not live in it as the English and Scots of earlier centuries lived among institutions of church and state which linked together the generations. In the sphere of learning, the problem is equally difficult. As more is known about earlier periods, the "marginal area" of knowledge, upon which research tends to be concentrated, becomes withdrawn from the field of vision of the ordinary reader. A detailed investigation into the economic life of the fifteenth century or into the finances of the Stuart kings is bound to involve terms and assumptions with which experts alone are familiar. Fifty years ago F. W. Maitland wrote on the history of English law and institutions with great brilliance and lucidity, yet it is not easy for a layman to follow Maitland's arguments, or to realise the full significance of his work in the interpretation of medieval England. The real question, however, is not whether all historical work is of equal interest or even of equal intelligibility to the public at large. The public is interested in the results, not in the processes of the ascertainment of significant fact. There have been historians in recent times (the late Professor Bury of Cambridge was one of them) who have been ready, in theory, though not in their own work, to allow history to become an esoteric science. The wisest contemporary historians have refused to accept this view. Sir Charles Firth was by common consent, one of the most learned men of his time. He was also one of the most accomplished and interesting writers. In his *Commentary on Macaulay's History*, Firth discussed Bury's view that "to clothe the story of human society in a literary dress is not more the part of a historian as an historian, than it is the part of an astronomer to present in an artistic shape the story of the stars." Firth's comment was given with his usual Yorkshire good sense : "After all, when a man puts his pen to paper and proceeds to print the result, he is attempting to convey his ideas to some other man. He presupposes the existence of a reader. It is therefore essential that he should arrange his ideas clearly, that he should state them so that they may be understood, and express them so that they may leave a lasting impression on the mind of the person to whom they are addressed. If he fails to achieve this, he has done only half of his work."

It would be invidious to attempt an inclusive list of names as evidence that most "professorial" historians of to-day agree with Sir Charles Firth, but one might take three examples as typical of the scholarship of three universities of Oxford, Cambridge and London : Pollard's *Henry VIII*, Trevelyan's *England under Queen Anne*, and Powicke's *The Christian Life in the Middle Ages*. Furthermore, the historians of our own time have not only known how to combine good scholarship with good writing ; they have also done much to develop a technique of co-operative work which goes a long way towards solving the problem of the isolation of the specialist in his separate sphere. The progress made during the last thirty years in the co-ordination of the work of individual scholars may be seen by a comparison between the earliest and the latest of the Cambridge series of general histories.

One might also notice that, since 1914, British historians have realised more clearly that the writing of history need not be confined to the remoter centuries. There has indeed been a return to the seventeenth-century fashion of writing contemporary history. This revival of interest in the day before yesterday has been due partly to demands made upon historians by the public. The historians have been able to meet the demand because to-day there is much greater material than a hundred years ago for writing the history of the immediate past on a scientific basis. In the seventeenth century "conversation and familiarity in the inside of courts" were necessary for a historian who wished to write a history of his own time ; to-day there are few aspects of recent history outside the sphere of foreign policy which are not fully documented. The greater part of the material for the study of social and economic history is to be found in sources available to students within a year or two of the events concerned.

Historians in the last two decades have been set more difficult problems than the elucidation of events which are still within living memory. The reading public asks for a final interpretation of history, and for an answer to the question why civilisations rise and fall. Is there, as Hume thought, a tidal movement in human affairs and nothing more than this tidal ebb and flow ? Is there no hope of stability or of unmixed achievement in the temporal sphere or can it be said that, in spite of ages of regression towards barbarism, historians are able to bring evidence of progress towards a desirable end ?

To these questions British historians are not very ready to give an answer, and, in general, the answers which are given are not put forward by the most learned or the most profound scholars. In the preface to his *History of Europe* H. A. L. Fisher wrote that he had no ultimate philosophy of history. Such a view does not imply scepticism, or even lack of belief in the possibility of a final synthesis. The difficulty at present is that the *data* are insufficient. To a historian the history of the world of man is a very short history. The years of the astronomers and the geologists reach beyond a historian's reckoning ; a small fraction only of these vast epochs is covered by the period during which man, with knowledge of the wheel, of fire, of pottery, and of edged tools, has set out to be master of his environment. Within this fragment of time, the history of lettered and civilised man fills an even smaller space. It is therefore not remarkable that a satisfactory clue has yet to be found to the meaning of the strange acts of the strangest of living creatures. Bede tells the story of the Northumbrian thane who compared the life of man on earth, in relation to the unknown immensity of time, to a moment in which a bird might fly into the warmth of a hall in winter, and then be lost to sight again in the storms—*de hieme in hiemem regrediens*. Of this short space of time men had knowledge; they knew nothing of what had gone before, nothing of what might follow after.

British historians are not necessarily without "the care of knowing causes" if they refuse to commit themselves to any more definite judgment upon the pattern of history and the meaning of human existence.

ENGLISH
DIARIES AND JOURNALS

KATE O'BRIEN

LET me begin with the hard saying that the best English diaries have been written by bores. It will be the purpose of ensuing pages so to illustrate, explain and modify this statement as, I hope, to remove its sting ; but for clarity's sake I must start from it as set down above, for I believe it to be a basic truth about the greatest diarists. A bore has been excellently defined as 'a person who mentions everything.' 'L'art d'ennuyer c'est de tout dire,' and face to face with us, across the fireplace or the dining table, the exponent of this art is very nearly intolerable ; but at the remove which lies between a writer and a reader, when the 'everything', printed not spoken, is in our power, to be taken or left as we feel inclined, and when distance, time, have given it patina and perspective, he who in life might have been our plague becomes our entertainer, and sometimes more than that—a light, a lamp, a gentle, accidental resurrector for a while of what had been cold and dead.

And it is of course probable, indeed almost certain, that in life this diarist, this entertainer, was *not* a bore, that he escaped the Nemesis of his temperament by the grace of being a diarist; for it is unlikely that a man who noted down in ink everything he saw, heard or otherwise experienced each day over a period of years should have had the vitality or indeed the time to recount himself to his contemporaries *verbatim* as he does to us. So their escape is our gain ; and his adaptation to script of his perpetual need to pettifog and annotate translates the latter into positive merit, and in some cases makes posterity and history immeasurably the debtors of a few eccentric or fussy or over-cautious men who, but for the chance that they scribbled rather than chattered, might have remained for ever obscure to us—just departed bores, mercifully stemmed in the irresponsive grave from their habit of 'running on'.

A good diary is not necessarily literature ; for of its nature it must be free of most of the disciplines and tests of a work of art. Vision, imagination, passion, fancy, invention, scholarship, detachment, and the steely restraints and consciously selected embellishments of form and of design—none of these has a vital place in diary-writing. They break in, it is true, or may do so; but that they are not essential to a diarist or part of his talent is at once his advantage and his peril—his advantage if, apart from them, he possesses enough of the attributes his task *may* demand, for so, merely by pleasing himself and evading all the pains of art, he will come to wear a laurel as evergreen as Pepys'; his peril, too, because any piece of writing, diary or what you will, can only manage to live and get itself read by projecting somehow that illusion of life and truth which is the function of literature. So the diarist might be in a dilemma were he self-conscious along these lines, or posterity-conscious. But he need not worry, very likely; for his impulse—to set down everything—proves his vitality. And vitality, the first and the only unfakeable element of literature, is what he needs above all else for getting read hereafter. Let him be alive, and rock-set on reproducing for us the daily pattern made by his own liveliness—an odd necessity, you may say, in any really lively person, but that is irrelevant—and ten to one you will get a good diary. History and its ironies, the eternal nostalgia of readers and their simple curiosity—all will do for his pages what the creative artist would have had to do for them himself; and out of a minimum of effort and a maximum of self-indulgence, something which is almost a work of art may be observed to grow, to have grown.

In the simplicity therefore with which the typical English diarist sets out to capture on paper the busy to and fro of his earthly span lies the threat of his being by nature a bore. For, if we except journals kept in special circumstances—as for instance in the course of perilous explorations such as Captain Scott's, or say Wesley's enormous and businesslike record of his missions—there is something a touch complacent and niggling in the design. And it is true that so far as we know almost no really great man has been in the normal course of his life a consistent diary-keeper. André Gide is a curious exception, and we must hope that he is still industriously and resolutely proving the rule—for our future enlightenment and delight. And we shall never know what journals and notebooks many of the great have had the wit, or the folly, to throw into the fire. But, as the records stand and as the diaries have come down to us, they are provedly not a form of self-expression which has appealed to the richly endowed. They are the medium of secondary types, as a rule—the outlet of the modest, the orderly and, sometimes, the complacent.

And they are none the worse for that. Indeed, paradoxically, their greatness, or more accurately, their great value lies now in their littleness, their concern with the passing day and the particular—the price of a dish of Tongue and Udder, the effect of a rhubarb purge, the writing of a postcard. Diarists have found such matters worth the setting down—

which means that had they not set them down they would have pestered their contemporaries with them—and been bores of the kind we all know, who labour the obvious, and teach grandmother to suck eggs.

Trivia of custom, of gossip or of comment could not of themselves, of course, sustain a diary, or give it importance ; but the diarist's necessity of writing them down places them, willy-nilly, in relation to large things and gives them as it were their function of accent or balance in the composition of a period ; time itself heightens this function ; and in the greater diaries the writer, managing to relate his very self to his notes and his doings, managing actually to express his own life, however modest or however brilliant, in just proportion to his time, does arrive, even if haphazardly, at creating one kind of work of art. So we may fall upon the irony of the little man of little talent and less ambition accomplishing, in conspiracy with time, such strokes of illumination, of irony or of sheer, true life as the great imaginative ones have always had to wrestle for in uncertainty and pain, and with all their faculties on the stretch. Thus it is, perhaps, when Nancy Woodforde writes down, as dully and smugly as possible, on Friday Sept. 28th, 1792, in a Norfolk parsonage : 'Mr and Mrs Custance sent us a brace of partridges. Dreadful times in France. Many are fled for refuge here.' That placid entry shows us as neatly as it could be done how wide and green and safely misted were then as for a long time afterwards the miles that lay between historic inevitabilities and that constant of rural England, the provincial lady. And when Francis Kilvert writes, on March 7th, 1873 : 'As I walked home across the meadows the sun was sinking low. In the clear beautiful evening a bird-hunting boy with a light heart was singing at the top of his voice across the fields. I only caught snatches of the verses. It seemed to be a love-song, and he repeated the same lines again and again. When he had ended his song the boy relieved his feelings by a shout and then sang "Saturday Night is soon a-coming" '—we have a particular spring evening, its sound, its stillness, its essence, related—by a boy's voice across a field—to a hundred such evenings we have known. For that is one thing the diary at its best, can do—not merely inform us about life, but, by chance fusion of some inner or outer facet of it with what we also know or feel, make us recognise it.

If I seem arbitrary in the pages that follow, I hope I shall be forgiven ; for I take my task to be the pleasant one of discussing my own preferences and dislikes among diarists, rather then gravely and detachedly to compose a concise history of the diary. I shall skip, I shall ignore ; perhaps, should any such glance my way, I shall get into trouble with a scholar or two ; and indeed it might save time for some readers were I forthwith to put my cards on the table and, since what I am about to write will be no more than a record of personal taste, confess at once my chief reaction to the most celebrated of all diaries ? But no—let us begin at the beginning, and hold as nearly as we can to the only order it is practicable to impose on so brief a sketch of a vastly diversified minor art—a loosely chronological one. Let us for simplicity's sake review English diarists and their diaries century by century, as they come.

The English Diary proper seems to have made its first appearance in the seventeenth century. Sir William Dugdale, an industrious Warwickshire gentleman, who laboured all his long life at works of antiquarianism and of heraldry and fought for Charles I in the Civil War, kept a journal during the latter forty-five of his eighty-two years of life which, dull, dry and broken as it is, the merest jotting indeed—'Queene impeached of Treason. Two regiment of foote came from York to Newark.' 'Two sunnes appeared this day.' 'King Charles the 2nd departed this life, about noon.' —does build up, slow stroke by stroke, a portrait of a man. A dull man, unremarkable, inarticulate, hide-bound, yet one faithful alike to his duties and to his interests, having unity in him, and with his conventions tempered by a carefully ordered individualism. In fact, from dry, modest notes never intended for publication, notes localised and made small by the writer's phlegmatic temperament even when they touch on large events, we get a reliable portrait—neither inspired nor grossly out of drawing, but merely faithful—of the English country gentleman as he has persisted through three hundred years. Domestic and orderly as well as conventional and idiosyncratic—for Sir William's very last note is simply this : 'Payd Elizabeth Taylor for her Quarter's Wages, now ended, and she going away from us . . .' It is an entry we are to read again and again through the diaries of three hundred years. But Sir William also left us this hearsay note, for January 30th, 1649 : 'The King beheaded at the gate of Whitehalle . . . His head was thrown downe by him yt tooke it up ; bruised ye face. His haire cut of. Souldiers dipped their swords in his blood. Base language uppon his dead body.'

When very near the end of his life this modest diarist crossed with a greater, and thus got his name recorded in such a full and broad-flung journal as he could never have attempted. For May 21st, 1685, John Evelyn begins his entry: 'I dined at my Lord Privy Seal's, with Sir William Dugdale, Garter King-at-Arms, author of the *Monasticon* and other learned works ; he told me he was 82 years of age and had his sight and memory perfect . . .'

John Evelyn was a man so gifted, so prosperous, so balanced, so long-lived, so popular, so sane and so naturally self-confident that the average human being may be forgiven if he turns from the bright prospect with something like a shudder. 'A strain of innocent gaiety and refined enjoyment marks Evelyn's life from first to last,' says one commentator. 'Innocent gaiety' is an attractive phrase, but it is open to the neutral reader of

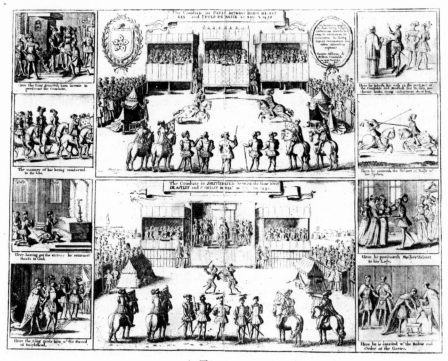

A TOURNAMENT

Engraving from William Dugdale's *Antiquities of Warwickshire*.   Second Edition, 1730

the great journal to question its accuracy in description of the gentlemanly shrewdness, the balanced worldliness, which dominate John Evelyn's every page.   For my own part, while conceding the 'refined enjoyment,' of which there is a remarkable plenty, I withhold the former tribute as too free and luminous for what it praises.   It is captious, maybe, to quarrel however mildly with eighty-five years lived so gracefully, on a high level of learning, taste, piety, good temper and tolerance—yet one cannot but feel that Evelyn's life opened more sweetly and freely, and in greater spiritual and individual promise, than he later understood, or looked for. In 1641, when he was twenty-one, he began the diary which he was to keep with fidelity during sixty-four full and exemplary years ; but in the opening pages he sketches in briefly his birth and parentage, and the scenes and major events of his childhood ; and from these first passages we get hints of carelessness, of temperamental eccentricities and difficulties in the boy which were to disappear from the worldly, balanced record of the man—'I was now . . . put to nurse to one Peter, a neighbour's wife and

189

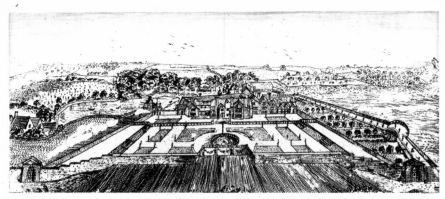

WOTTON IN SURREY, THE HOUSE OF GEORGE EVELYN
Engraving by John Evelyn

tenant, of a good, comely, brown, wholesome complexion, and in a most sweet place towards the hills, flanked with wood and refreshed with streams; the affection to which kind of solitude I sucked in with my very milk.' True, in part ; and becoming a great gardener and horticulturist, he remained always attracted to the more civilised beauties of rural life, and even protested sometimes his yearning for 'recess,' as in a letter to Cowley : '. . . . should think myself more happy than crowned heads were I, as you, the arbiter of mine own life, and could break from those gilded toys . . .' But no man has ever been more than Evelyn the arbiter of his own life, and all his writings calmly set out his polite but obstinate pre-occupation with the 'gilded toys.'

As a schoolboy, he begged off Eton, being 'unreasonably terrified with the report of the severe discipline there,' and was schooled, very indifferently, in Wotton village and at Lewes, taking 'so extraordinary a fancy to drawing and designing that I could never after wean my inclinations from it, to the expense of much precious time . . .' At Oxford he seems, by his own account, to have wasted his time, save that he 'began to look upon the rudiments of music, in which I afterwards arrived to some formal knowledge' ; and in the Middle Temple he was plainly bored with the law, 'that impolished study.' So that when, in his 21st year, he lost his father, he felt a great anxiety and chill in bereavement, and described himself as being at that time 'of a raw, vain, uncertain and very unwary inclination . . . who now thought of nothing but the pursuit of vanity, and the confused imaginations of young men.'

Such he was then, in the year of his own majority and of the beginning of Charles the First's bitter struggle against Parliament. When we place these simple and interesting admissions beside what we know of his unusual natural talents, the quickness and ease of his mind, the diversity

JOHN EVELYN, 1620-1706
Engraving by Swaine

and excellence of his interests, and when we add that he was rich, free, well-born and honourable, it can be agreed that he was a young man of immense potentialities. Anything might come of the alliance of so many positive endowments with the temperamental diffidences, vanities, curiosities and 'confused imaginations' to which their possessor has confessed. We recall, when we survey the brilliant, dangerous sum of this young man, William Windham, of whose intermittent diary-keeping we shall have occasion to speak later on. But Windham, always conscious of frustration and of the seeds of failure in himself, would have understood, in application to his own soul, Shelley's line about 'the contagion of the world's slow stain'; whereas Evelyn so conditioned and governed himself that it is probable that the relation of such a phrase to his bright and safe maturing would have struck him as sheer nonsense.

Yet the contagion of the world, of his own concern for the world and for having the best of it, did somehow blight his life, making it neatly perfect, like the gardens he cherished, instead of free and incalculable, as it could have been. He took a curious decision in 1642-43—curious, that is, for the man who two hundred years later was to be celebrated in *John Inglesant* as the flower of the Cavalier type. Here it is, in his own words: 'The 12th November was the Battle of Brentford, surprisingly fought; and to the great consternation of the City, had his Majesty (as it was believed he would) pursued his advantage. I came in with my horse and arms just at the retreat; but was not permitted to stay longer than the 15th, by reason of the army marching to Gloucester; which would have left both me and my brothers exposed to ruin, without any advantage to his Majesty. . . . on the 10th (December) returned to Wotton, nobody knowing of my having been in his Majesty's army . . . 12th July, I sent my black menage horse and furniture with a friend to his Majesty, at Oxford. 23rd, The Covenant being pressed, I absented myself; but, finding it impossible to evade the doing very unhandsome things . . . October the 2nd I obtained a license of his Majesty, dated at Oxford and signed by the King, to travel again.' Thus in November 1643, aged twenty-three and unencumbered, he left England, and stayed away for four years. He returned, a newly married man, but leaving his wife in Paris, in September 1647, 'to settle my affairs'; stayed for eighteen months, settled into Sayes Court in Deptford, bought and sold manors and works of art, sat for his portrait, studied chemistry, and kept his ear well to the ground in the political scene. 'I got privately into the council of the rebel army at Whitehalle, where I heard horrid villainies.' 'The villainy of the rebels proceeding now so far as to try, condemn and murder our excellent King . . . struck me with such horror that I kept the day of his martyrdom a fast, and would not be present at that execrable wickedness . . .' Six months after the King's execution Evelyn rejoined his wife in Paris, and except for one brief trip home in 1650, stayed abroad until the spring of 1652. He then settled at Deptford, and arranged for his wife to come to England, being advised by his friends 'to compound with the soldiers.' Whence may be said to have begun the full flow of that settled, correct, domestic, scholarly, social and altogether perfect life, which was to run without heat or quarrel and with scarcely a sorrow, scarcely an anxiety, into the beginning of the reign of Anne.

He had decided, at twenty-three, on caution, and on attending to his own interests. Not, so far as we can discover, out of intellectual contempt for the mess his country was in, and not out of lack of interest in the general situation—but simply for selfish reasons. Perhaps he was right. In any case, his decision served him well, and no one ever sought to penalise his curious tepidity. 'He must have conducted himself with uncommon prudence, and address,' writes his first editor, William Bray, in 1818, 'for he had personal friends in the Court of Cromwell at the same time that he was corresponding with his father-in-law, Sir Richard Browne, the ambassador of King Charles II at Paris . . . His manners we may presume to have been most agreeable; for his company was sought by the greatest

The Navy Office London

By courtesy of the Parker Gallery, London

THE NAVY OFFICE, CRUTCHED FRIARS, LONDON, WHERE PEPYS HAD HIS OFFICE

Coloured engraving published by T. Taylor, 1714

NANCY WOODFORDE

Chalk drawing by Samuel Woodforde

By courtesy of Dr. R. E. H. Woodforde

men . . . He was happy in a wife of congenial disposition with his own, of an enlightened mind . . . though he remained a decided Royalist, he managed so well as to have intimate friends even amongst those nearly connected with Cromwell; and to this we may attribute his being able to avoid taking the Covenant, which he says he never did take . . .'

Tolerance and tact are excellent things, but it is impossible not to regret the excess of them which we find in Evelyn, and their alliance to self-interest; for passion, that warmth in a man which, even in his mistakes, may make him the friend of his fellowmen and a part of their humanity, could have been nobly mettled by all the gifts which Evelyn preferred to harness to decorum and to social ease. He might have been a leader of his age; he was instead one of its most fixed and untarnished decorations. He wrote a great deal, on politics, on Jesuitism, on the Navy, on Sculpture, on Engraving, on Forestry, Agriculture, and Horticulture. He was linguist, scientist, and amateur of the arts. He helped to found the Royal Society; and after the Restoration he sat on various Royal Commissions. In all these undertakings he excelled, as also in his duties as husband, father and landowner; and he lived and died a devout, untroubled Christian. All this, and very much more, we learn from his vast diary, which is an incomparably informative, full picture of a society and an era. It gives us everything that the observant Evelyn saw and touched upon in eighty-five years—except the passions, the urgencies, the doubts, despairs and sins of men, or of one man. The external symptoms of these elements may be touched upon, but only to be banked down by conventional pieties or—when for instance he describes the Fire of London, so admirably, so vividly—with a detachment that is just a shade too cold, too touched with carefulness. '. . . blessing and adoring the distinguishing mercy of God to me and mine, who, in the midst of all this ruin, was like Lot, in my little zoar, safe and sound.' 'Still, the plague continuing in our parish, I could not, without danger, adventure to our church.' 'This night was acted my Lord Broghill's tragedy, called *Mustapha*, before their Majesties at Court, at which I was present . . . I was invited by my Lord Chamberlain . . . though in my mind I did not approve of any such pastime in a time of such judgments and calamities.'

He was too great a man to be so priggish and careful; too intellectually gifted to hunt so consistently with the hares while he ran with the hounds. But he has left us a splendid panorama, crowded but clear, of a time in English history which was packed with events, with troubles and with development. As a man, measured by his own powers and opportunities, he is disappointing; but as a diarist he is invaluable.

His friend, Samuel Pepys, a distinguished public servant, kept a diary too—though only for nine years, instead of sixty-five; and this diary which, it seems clear enough, was never intended for any other eyes besides its writer's, has become the most famous in the world. Everyone knows about it, and most people have read it, or read in it. Pepys began to keep it on 1st Jan., 1660, when he was twenty-seven years old, and just about to be appointed a Clerk of the Acts in the Navy Office; he was a married man, having in 1655 espoused a young lady of Huguenot extraction; he was of gentle birth and had been educated at St Paul's and at Cambridge; he was industrious, lively, talented, and had influential friends; his major desires were to get on in life, to do his work dutifully, and to enjoy himself. Trouble with his eyes compelled him to abandon his diary at the end of May, 1669. He died in 1703, at the age of seventy. In the course of his public life he was Clerk of the Privy Seal, Secretary to the Admiralty, Member of Parliament, President of the Royal Society and Master of Trinity House. Once, because of his loyalty to his chief, the Duke of York, he was charged with implication in the Papist Plot, and sent to prison. He was the friend of Dryden, of Evelyn and of many distinguished persons. He was interested in literature and in the theatre; particularly he was interested in music, and was generous and kind to musicians. He liked to dress well, to eat well and to be in on the talk of the town; he liked to dally with women, and to live contentedly with his wife, to control her extravagances, and to see her pretty and happy. He worried about money; he took an interest in his house and its decoration; he collected a library, gave musical parties and was sociable; he fussed about his health, and every 26th March he piously celebrated his having been successfully 'cut for the stone' on that day in 1658; he worked very hard and was trustworthy and scrupulous, staying at his post in London, for instance, all through the panic of the Great Plague. He was, in short, the type, the prototype of the English higher Civil Servant—and he appears to have succeeded better than many such in gratifying his natural ambitions, public and private.

The Diary proves and supports the external story. It does so by the paradoxical method of turning it upside down, or inside out and revealing to us that the basic man on whom this other, this watchful, educated, diplomatic, honest, anxious keeper-up of appearances, is founded is in fact that other's antithesis—naïve, ignorant, reckless, shy, a taker of the silliest risks, a bewildered victim of himself, the creature of his petty impulses, a man forever in danger from his own instabilities and inconsistencies. What could be more interesting, consoling or alarming for any of us to read? Who is there who has not shuddered to imagine some sudden impossible revelation to the world of his actual self—not the self of this very high or that inexpressibly low moment, but the true small self that frets and chugs along relentlessly, in time with our outward gestures and grimaces? The self *we* know, but which, while we alternately inflate and enjoy it, or miserably writhe against its monstrous embrace, we are at least determined no one else shall come within miles of knowing? Pepys has, as nearly as any man ever, brought off this dreadful, unnatural feat—of

SAMUEL PEPYS, 1632-1703
Oil painting by John Hayls, 1664

presenting his whole self, stark naked, quite defenceless, to his fellowmen. No wonder he is an immortal. He has done it very well too—working his whole self, all he is, all his most pitiful and true *minutiae*, into a bright, close, restless picture of London and Court Society during a time that was unusually vivid and loose, unusually dangerous, exciting and worth observation. The story he tells is packed with characters and stories, overflowing with plums for historian and gossip—but he is his own central theme, and he does not mislay himself. Naïve, chattering, and childishly fussed to catch in everything, he gives us, as we say, the works. '. . . My mind, God forgive me, too much running upon what I can *ferais avec la femme de Bagwell demain . . .*' So on, so on; Krupp and Pierce and Mercer and The. Turner and poor Deb; and all the small sins, ailments and sensations of the common day; all the humiliations of our wretched, silly flesh. 'Here I did *ce que je voudrais avec* her most freely, and it having cost me 2s. in wine and cake upon her, I away sick of her impudence, and by coach to my Lord Brunker's.' It is an astonishing and, in the full and serious meaning of the word, a shocking achievement.

Perhaps it is somewhat *too* shocking. For my own part, I have never liked Pepys' diary ; I have found that a very little of it goes a mighty long way, and at that leaves me bored. To have dared so much for so tiny a result ; to empty out breast, brain and entrails, and have so wretchedly little to show for the awful violence ; to be, after all and with all said, nothing better or worse than fussy, kindly, nervous, lecherous, dirty, self-pitying and respectable ! To be in fact inside, after all the drama of confession, exactly what the outside advertised—no more and no less ! That is Pepys—as no doubt it is all of us. And if so, there is the strength and merit of his diary. Yet one must be forgiven for not liking it. It is amusing, but not amusing enough ; it is honest, but too pedestrianly ; it is realistic, but on themes which are too tiny and too recurrent. It bears about it an *insect* quality ; it fidgets the nerves and conscience to no purpose. And it is, for all its pieties, devoid of spiritual pain. It is without light and it is somehow ignoble. In fact I might easily call it a very depressing work. But history and the world are against me—and it is the most famous, the most read and perhaps the best loved of all known diaries.

It is curious that these two most famous of all English diaries remained unpublished until more than a century after the deaths of their authors, and then appeared within seven years of each other : Evelyn's—by permission of the Evelyn family, and edited by William Bray—in 1818 ; Pepys' in 1825 under the editorship of Lord Braybrooke. Pepys had indeed taken careful measures against easy publication. He wrote his diary in a mixture of shorthand—Shelton's system—and a misleading confusion of foreign words and invented jargon. The manuscript was among his books, which he bequeathed to Magdalene College, Cambridge—and English literature owes one of its most curious and famous possessions to the extraordinarily patient research of an undergraduate of Cambridge called John Smith, who deciphered the text between 1819 and 1822. When it was published in 1825 it naturally caused a vast sensation—and, like Evelyn's Diary, threw floods of light upon seventeenth century society.

Men of the world, Evelyn and Pepys ; and their records, though decently strewn with Christian sentiments, portray a society of worldlings, of men and women committed to personal pleasure and personal success. But parallel with their long, complacent lives lived in the glittering capital ran another—spent at first in English villages and country towns, and later either in prisons or on long, difficult journeys in Holland and Germany, in America and the West Indies ; and not 'steeple-counting,' as Evelyn might have said, but in pursuit of souls, in spread of grace. George Fox, a weaver's son and the first of the Quakers, was born in Leicestershire in

1624, and died in London in 1681. His *Great Journal* is little read now, I imagine—save by members of the faith he founded; and indeed for the uninitiated layman it makes uneasy, unattractive reading. It is crude, naïve and often turgid; it repeats and overstresses, and labours with too pugnacious simplicity experiences and trains of mystical thought which cannot be conveyed by so much positiveness. But it is impossible to open it anywhere and read a page or two without feeling the pure force of the man behind it, the spiritual generosity, the sheer missionary good-will. It is the textbook of a life dominated by zeal for the good, and by natural understanding of goodness; it is the record of one who quite simply *applied* mysticism to daily life and was perfectly content to suffer for this peculiarity, and to go on preaching its necessity in all times and places, to his last breath. The Journal is an important spiritual work not because it possesses any high literary merit, but because it is passionately sincere and generous, and is the first record of the humble, difficult and often desperate beginnings of a faith which was to become a great social force, and one of the brightest, steadiest lamps which religion has ever lighted upon earth.

OAK TREES UNDER WHICH GEORGE FOX PREACHED THE GOSPEL
View of Flushing, Long Island, North America
Lithograph by Motte after Milbert

THE REVEREND JAMES WOODFORDE, 1740-1803
Oil painting by Samuel Woodforde

No collector of English diaries can escape the Woodforde family. It is probable that between 1600 and 1820 there can hardly have been a day on which one Woodforde or another did not note down what he ate for dinner or what the weather was like, or that the harvest was carried, or that the tailor overcharged him for mending a waistcoat. They were a respectable Northamptonshire and Somerset family of parsons, soldiers, sailors and country gentlemen—and almost all had the diary-hobby, even that one of them, the second or third Samuel Woodforde who stepped so so far out of their tradition as to become a painter, and an R.A. In 1932 a twentieth-century member of the family, Miss Dorothy Heighes Woodforde, published a volume of extracts from what appears to be a great mass of journals—which indicates that between them the Woodfordes have assembled an enormously full and detailed record of English country life over a period of about two hundred and fifty years. It seems that the diaries of Samuel the Academician are merely dull notes of commissions undertaken and people met—and I gather from references to him in Farington's Diaries that he was a dry stick of a man, of no particular charm or talent ; but such pages as I have read from certain other Members of the family have got a kind of slow, comfortable reality in them, and a gentle, unexacting variation of colour and theme, suggestive of English landscape, and carrying the conservative, traditional, place-bound quality, and if you like, charm of English country-house life. Menus, recipes, small scandals, small journeys ; exchange of neighbourly courtesies and acrimonies ; little kindnesses, little tasks ; an earache, an inoculation ; the text of a sermon, a 'scene' of some kind in church ; sixpence won at cards, or a maidservant's dismissal ; a snowstorm, a ripening of cucumbers, a rumour from the wars in France ; the garden, the weather, the walk before dinner—always these three—the garden, the weather . . . it is England that they give us, the Woodfordes ; one particular England, the one they knew and counted on and took for granted as their especial right and pleasure always. And they wrote it down, Nancy, Robert, Samuel, James, with that careful literalness, that adherence to presented facts and unconsciousness of lurking ideas, which has always been the staple of conversation in houses such as theirs ; they give us English country-house life, its very accent and idiom, exactly as the English upper class has evolved and cherished it.

And one Woodforde took the family's hobby a very long way, and made it famous in his own person. The Reverend James Woodforde, born in Somerset in 1740, and Rector of Weston Longeville in Norfolk from 1776 to 1803, the year of his death, began his diary when he was eighteen and kept it up faithfully for the remaining forty-five years of his natural span. *The Diary of A Country Parson*, published in five volumes by the Oxford University Press, became celebrated at its first bow, and is nowadays known and loved by very many readers. 'Reading the Diary of the Reverend James Woodforde is like embarking on a long voyage down a very tranquil stream,' says his editor, Mr J. B. Beresford. 'There is no grand or exciting scenery ; there are no rapids, *nor is there any ultimate expectation of the sea.*' The italics are mine. The five volumes are quite unbeatably non-expectant ; they present as steadily as possible the obvious comings and goings, worries, kindnesses and duties, family and social obligations and pleasures of a typical unpretentious and respectable parson. Nothing more ; but all is set down with a faithful intimacy, and with that repetitiveness which is unavoidable in so close and long a record—so that reading of life in the Weston parsonage—first with troublesome nephew Bill for second string, and later with diary-keeping niece Nancy—becomes after a volume or so the same thing as living there. And it is not altogether dull. There are touches of scandal and fuss ; there are parties—an astonishingly catastrophic one on September 16th, 1777 ; there is a great deal of food and drink ; there are the excitements of the rhubarb purge : 'Sister Clarke, Nancy, Sam and myself all took it into our heads to take a good dose of Rhubarb going to bed . . .' ; and there are outbreaks of horseplay. 'Mrs Davie and Nancy made me up an Apple Pye Bed last night.' 'I took Mrs Davie's garter to-night and kept it. I gave her my pair of garters and I am to have her other to-morrow.' The parson was over forty at this time. 'There are green fields on either side,' says Mr Beresford, in further description of this diary, 'and trees, and a very pleasant murmuring of water . . .' True enough. It catches all the quiet of its place ; it is a benevolent, placid record of habits and customs, unruffled by any hint of mind, or of a private life in the breast.

The Reverend William Cole, of Blechely, Waterbeach and Milton Parsonages, was less suave of temperament than Mr Woodforde ; indeed malicious, contentious, eccentric and with a fair span of tastes and interests —as might be expected of a friend and correspondent of Horace Walpole. His life ran from 1714 to 1782 ; but his diaries, as they have been given to us by Constable, edited by Mr F. G. Stokes and introduced by Miss Helen Waddell, cover only the years 1765 to 1770, when he was in his earlier fifties. The first of these diaries deals with a sojourn in Paris in 1765, whilst Walpole was living there ; the remainder are of country parsonage life, and thick with detail of characters, happenings and humours —to say nothing of details of farm and garden, of food and drink, of health, domestic managements and the expenditure of money. All sharply seasoned with the Reverend William's authoritativeness, guile and acrimony, as well as some pungent reflections on Church and general affairs. He was a meticulous, fussy bachelor, very domesticated and with individual taste. He packs his journals with all these interests, and although the details are wearisome, and there are too many names, too many small disputes, too many capital letters, and too much eccentricity in his prose style, for some tastes—he is undoubtedly an oddity, and has left himself and his scene alive and rich and contributory behind him, for the occasional pleasure of the curious and the nostalgic.

And while the unhurried lives of these divines plodded forward— 'wrote . . . to send a porter to Mr Walpole's for my French china and Pastilles which he bought for me at Paris,' says Mr Cole ; and 'A very comical dull day with us all. Sister Clarke very low. In the evening Sam spoke in favour of the Methodists, rather too much I think,' says Mr Woodforde—Methodism, having long flooded out from Oxford's Holy Club and 'our little society in Fetter Lane,' was sweeping up and down the island, preaching the grace of God without pause or compromise, and indeed by 1770 having established 'The Lord our Righteousness'— newly, formidably, as an uncrushable social force—in Scotland, in Ireland and in New England. John Wesley, born in a Lincolnshire rectory in 1703, had taken Holy Orders and been made a fellow of Lincoln College, Oxford before Rev. James Woodforde was born, and while Mr Cole was

JOHN WESLEY, 1703-1791
Oil painting by Nathaniel Hone, 1766

still at Eton ; and as he wasted no time in developing and exercising his missionary vocation, before the latter were middle-aged men the Methodist societies and meetings were a constant part of English life and English news—a controversy, an anxiety, but beyond question a passionate, true force, from which the respect of honest men could not be withheld, and which was impervious to the malignancies of prejudice. And if anyone wonders why a simple, scriptural apostolate, an unblushing appeal to goodness and the sources of grace, could so effectively and rapidly disturb alike the lazy privilege, the sceptic rationalism and the dark, lost ignorance of eighteenth century England, he has only to acquaint himself even a little, by a volume or so of his writing, with John Wesley. And the easiest and truest way to do this is to read a part, or the whole, of his great Journal.

We find there all the chief things that this remarkable man was : the energy, the passion, the organising power, the foresight, the adaptability, the courage and the trenchant, economical eloquence—all of which had share in his missionary success. As a record of sheer, unbroken industry alone it defeats most known biographies, and it paints a very remarkable portrait of a man complicated by a great endowment of attributes— emotional, hard-headed, domineering, intellectual, even sceptical, and brave ; a conservative reformer, a reactionary radical, an arrogant, self-confident saint—all co-ordinated by singleness of purpose, so that a very human man becomes a supernatural force, to transform the lives and hearts of millions.

The story the Journal tells is enormous ; because it is businesslike and thorough and covers the oft-repeated labour of sixty years, it is some-times dull country for the modern reader, and sometimes, since we cannot, merely by reading of this extraordinary apostolate, find Wesley's 'peace with God,' we can only read in astonished acceptance the scripturally phrased descriptions of conversion. 'Then God began to make bare his arm in an extraordinary manner. Those who were strangers to God felt as it were a sword in their bones, constraining them to roar aloud.' Nor can we feel at ease, at our remove from the fresh impulse, when we read of little children that 'sometimes one, sometimes more, prayed aloud ; sometimes a cry went up from them all, till five or six of them, who were in doubts before, saw the light of God's countenance.' But perhaps we can a little measure what we do not understand or feel at home with in Wesley's Journal by those parts of it that we can apprehend : the honesty, the courage, the mercy and the sheer love of men that bind it together ; the trenchancy of the unaffected prose ; the intelligence of the diarist's comments on his very catholic reading—and, above all, the generous bitterness, the truth, shrewdness and mercy of his observation of life as he finds it : 'Our eyes and ears may convince us there is not a less happy body of men in all England than the country farmers. In general their life is supremely dull, and it is usually unhappy too.' There is plenty of such non-sentimental comment all through the volumes ; highly dis-turbing to the lazy and the comfortable—as John Wesley compelled his Methodism to be.

Two intellectuals of the eighteenth century wrote diaries which are alike in that each reveals an aspect of its writer's temperament which the rest of his life either concealed or hardly suggests to us. In 1761, when Edward Gibbon was twenty-four and serving as a Captain in the South Hampshire Militia he began a diary, which he kept with fair regu-larity during three years. The latter part of it, from his arrival in Paris in January 1763 until he reached Rome in May 1764—when it ceased—

VIEW OF PARIS AS GIBBON SAW IT IN 1763
Sepia drawing by Georges Michel

is written in French. It is not a very full, deep or elaborate journal, but it gives an interesting account of his reading and the directions of his thought at a time when he had not yet made up his mind about future work ; also it throws some light on the difficulties placed in the way of a temperament such as Gibbon's—scholarly, ironic, non-combative and of indifferent physical health—by the affectionate interference and domination of an ambitious father, whose only child he was ; and chiefly it is entertaining in that it offers us an unexpected picture—amusing, tolerant and altogether to his credit—of the historian of the Roman Empire in training as a British soldier. As one reads of the scrupulous pains he took with his duties, of how loyally he cared for the prestige and the comfort of his men, of how honestly he gave his attention to the incongruous life—with only a very occasional mild grumble, 'tired of companions who had neither the knowledge of scholars nor the manners of gentlemen'—one is reminded of many young men of his mental colour, who are to-day in like case with Gibbon, though risking much more than he was asked to risk ; not geniuses all, indeed, though one among them may be—but like him impressively gracious and scrupulous in accepting a distasteful occupation and adapting themselves to it. 'I exercised the Battalion for the fourth time, officers and eighteen rounds. These field days were of some service both to men and officers. I am sure they were the greatest to me.' 'We had a field day . . . Tho' I had not exercised them so long yet I found myself very clear and I believe I made no mistakes.' Horace Walpole might lead the wits in scepticism about these volunteers, in a vein which our Home Guard has nowadays learnt to take at its traditional worth : 'John in the rear will be firing his piece into the Backside of his friend Tom in the Front . . .' and the young man, Edward Gibbon, could be humorous too, though more subtly, about his own and his neighbours' soldiering—but while he was at it—mud, route-marches, drinking, noise, regimental disputes and all—he gave it a dutiful, even a genial, attention. And leaving it, summing up the pros and cons of the experience, he says : 'But what I value most is the knowledge it has given me of mankind in general, and of my own country in particular . . . the sum of all is that I am glad the Militia has been, and glad that it is no more.'

William Windham was so versatile, so extravagantly endowed—in birth, possessions, education and friends as well as in personal abilities and graces—that it is surprising to find his career stop short of total success, but perhaps not so surprising that his diaries reveal him as a restless, unhappy man, distrustful of himself, constantly perplexed and at a loss. Yet in his lifetime the world does not seem to have been allowed to know the latter side of the medal ; for when the diaries were published in 1866—more than fifty years after his death — Lord Rosebery observed of them that they dealt 'an almost mortal blow to his reputation.' A comment difficult to understand. Surely when a man has all the gifts, such total absence of smugness as made Windham unhappy and unstable may be allowed to be, though difficult, the ultimate grace ?

He was born in 1750, heir of a distinguished Norfolk name and estate. In youth at Eton and Oxford he excelled in everything, only too easily. In politics he began as a Whig, *protégé* of Fox, and spent a few months in Ireland as Secretary to the Lord Lieutenant in 1783. In 1787 he was, with Burke and Sheridan, a manager of the impeachment of Warren Hastings. At the outbreak of the French Revolution he followed Pitt, and was Secretary for War in 1794, holding office until 1801. He returned to the War Office in 1806, in the 'Ministry of All The Talents.' He died, aged sixty, in 1810. His versatility made friends for him everywhere—among Cabinet Ministers, Oxford dons, actresses, race-horse owners and women of fashion. He read Greek like a scholar, and was exceptionally endowed for mathematical studies ; he loved prize-fights ; he made a perilous ascent in a balloon ; he interested himself in country matters and the business of his estate ; he was a constant student of Shakespeare, and a close friend and critic of Mrs Siddons ; he was devoted to Burke and admired by Fanny Burney ; he loved Dr Johnson with devotion. He was successful with women, and—the diaries make it clear—he found the exactions of sexual love a major cause of restlessness and dissatisfaction. He had love-affairs, but the most constant and uneasy was with Mrs Byng,

IN THE LAKES

Water colour by J. Varley, 1778 - 1842

BENJAMIN HAYDON 1786 - 1846
Pencil and red chalk drawing by G. H. Harlow, 1816
By courtesy of Sir Robert Witt

WILLIAM WINDHAM, 1750-1810
Oil painting by Sir Joshua Reynolds

wife of the Hon. John Byng, afterwards Viscount Torrington. After many years of restless, uncertain intrigue with her, their feeling resolved into friendship, and late in life he married her younger sister, Cecilia Forrest, who had long been devoted to him. The marriage was childless, and appears to have been happy.

The journals make dry and somewhat tired comment on all the emotions, friendships, ambitions, projects and disappointments of a full life. They are revelatory only of Windham's dissatisfaction with himself, and into that they do not plunge wholeheartedly. They ring wearily for the most part ; there is nothing in them to resolve the enigma of his life, or expose its heart—but they do deepen and underline it, adding a grace of sadness and second thoughts to a personal history which might otherwise seem monotonously brilliant.

We will depart from the eighteenth century under the nimble, bright escort of Fanny Burney. She breaks new ground. For one thing, she is the first English *woman* of any significance—*pace* the Woodforde ladies—who has left us a diary. For another, she leads us, a little unfairly, towards a suspicion which later increases somewhat, that women make more refreshing, more effective diarists than men. Be that as it may, you may have your Pepys and Evelyn and, with both hands, the pettifogging parsons—except Rev. Francis Kilvert—if you will leave me Fanny Burney ; all the uneven, over-written seventy years of her industrious and spirited jotting-down.

She was born in 1752 and she died in 1840 ; she began to keep her diary in 1768, when she was sixteen, and she made her last entry in it on 5th March 1839, when she was eighty-seven. 'I broke off, and an incapable unwillingness seized my pen,' that last note begins—and we feel the old lady's petulant surprise. Incapable unwillingness had not normally been her trouble with a pen. Indeed her *Juvenile Journal*, covering the years before she published *Evelina* and 'Addressed to a Certain Miss Nobody' is torrentially, excessively facile—and at times too facetious and coy for present-day taste. But when she romps overmuch, we can remind ourselves that she is very young, at least during the first four or five hundred pages, and also that a great deal of the clatter is in fact sheer talent that has not yet perceived or taken hold of itself. And perhaps the final impression left with us when we reach 5th March 1839 is that—for all her success, for all the brilliance and fun and fame, and though she will always hold a place in English letters—the gifted creature never measured her own powers, never extended or wrestled with them, and thus never became the writer she was born to be. Her first success surprised and enchanted her—and she seems to have gone on being surprised, enchanted and a touch amateurish to the end.

Most people know the outline of her life. She was one of the large family of Dr Charles Burney, musician and historian of music, and she spent a free and happy girlhood in London, educating herself at random and enjoying the brilliant, varied society of her father's friends—musical, theatrical, intellectual and merely fashionable. She surprised her world, and her family, with *Evelina* when she was twenty-six, becoming famous at a blow, and becoming moreover Dr Johnson's 'Fannikin' and his 'little Burney.' Reynolds, Burke, Windham, Sheridan became her friends ; Mrs Thrale took her up, and she met Mrs Montague and all the 'Blues' ; Madame de Genlis sought her out on her first visit to England, and wooed her friendship ; and the aged Mrs Delany patronised her — with the unfortunate result that the foolish Fanny, after having repeated the *Evelina* success with *Cecilia*, found herself, at the age of thirty-three and when a famous woman of letters, installed as Second Mistress of the Robes to Queen Charlotte, the dull wife of George III. 'And now began a slavery of five years,' says Macaulay, and '. . . we are utterly at a loss to conceive how any human being could endure such a life, while there remained a

THE GARRICKS ENTERTAINING DR. JOHNSON
Oil painting by Johann Zoffany, 1725-1810

vacant garret in Grub Street, a crossing in want of a sweeper, a parish workhouse or a parish vault.' Without being quite so extravagantly at a loss, we marvel too—especially as we read the diarist's brilliantly revelatory account of life as Queen Charlotte's attendant. It was an absurd appointment, and it broke Miss Burney's health and she had to be released from it. Thereafter she fell into the society of some *émigrés* from the French Revolution and in 1793, at the age of forty-one, she married the penniless Chevalier d'Arblay and settled down with him in a cottage in Surrey, to live on her court pension of £100 a year. They had one child, a son, and they were very happy. The diaries are in nothing better than in their restrained, true portrayal of her marital peace, and the sweetness and gaiety with which they recount the baby years of her child, and her delight in him. From 1801 to 1810 she lived in France, her husband's fortunes being somewhat restored under Napoleon; she brought her son back to England in the latter year, and rejoined her husband in France in 1814. She was in Brussels in 1815, and her diaries contain a famous account of June of that year, and the thunders and repercussions of Waterloo. Thereafter her husband settled in England again, until his death in 1818. Her son, who became a clergyman, died unmarried in 1837. Between her marriage and her death she did much literary work—some unsuccessful plays, a novel, *Camilla*, and an unreadable novel called *The Wanderer*, for which she is said to have received £7,000 ; also *Memoirs of Dr. Burney* and some pamphlets—as well as the never neglected diaries.

It is well she did not neglect them, for they are the best of her, and her chief claim on immortality. They are so much better than most diaries because they are imaginative, free and subjective ; they are, in fact, the work of a *writer*, which most diaries are not. Miss Burney does not stick to the facts of each day in the sense of merely setting them down ; she uses them, expands them, enjoys herself with them, and lets us take all those details for granted which she does not select as essential to her vein of narrative. She gives us conversations—with Mrs Thrale, with Windham, with George III, with Talleyrand, or with her little son—not *verbatim* or in any kind of shorthand but as her imagination and her brilliant memory feel them when they echo in her afterwards—so that they are truer than truth and, without strain or apparent falsification, achieve a richness, a certainty of character and a sequence and pace which in fact they almost certainly did not have, but which the artist rightly felt they merited.

As we read, and taste the variety of her experiences and the power, understanding and charm which she brought to bear on all she encountered, we cannot but wonder why she never took herself in hand and became a great novelist, as great as Jane Austen. She seems to have had all the needed natural abilities ; and she had besides a wide knowledge of life and the world, she had the goodwill of all the best minds of her day, she had health and long life and a great zest for writing. Yet she never mastered these advantages and soared to genius on them.

The reason may lie with her benevolent and rather foolish father. Not in any of his conscious acts—for though it clearly was silly of him to persuade her, with Mrs Delany, into becoming a Mistress of the Robes, we do not go all the way with Macaulay in his shocked tirades against the Doctor for this ill-judged piece of snobbery and worldly hopefulness—for Fanny was, after all, thirty-one then and famous, and had twice resoundingly proved her ability to succeed in letters ; she could have decided for herself against an undertaking which, the diaries make clear, she viewed with uneasy fear. 'I have always and uniformly had a horror of a life of attendance and dependence . . . Could I but save myself from a lasting bond ? ' However, she did not save herself ; and this major occasion is only the full declaration of a curious docility that ran all through her life, often weakening or tarnishing its merits.

I trace this to her father—and not to any fault of his, but to his unconscious, potent influence on her. She loved him very much, and he was in childhood and girlhood the source and inspirer of all that ease and fun

FANNY BURNEY, 1752-1840
Oil painting by E. F. Burney

and pleasant learning and talented go-as-you-please in which she and her sisters were so happy. The love, the confidence he bred in Fanny would seem to have trained her into a marked dependence on the elderly, and a curious need to be loved by them, and to take their directions. She loved her father; and also in girlhood she loved the elderly Mr Samuel Crisp of Chessington, 'Daddy' Crisp, for whom with her sister Susan all the early diaries were written. 'My papa always mentions him by the name of my *Flame*. Indeed he is not mistaken—himself is the only man on earth I prefer to him.' She loved Dr Johnson with veneration for the last years of his life, and sought his company constantly, though she was only in her twenties; she was for a time during Dr Johnson's life the slave of the already elderly Mrs Thrale; she adored the venerable and boring Mrs Delany; she persuaded herself that she adored the 'sweet Queen' Charlotte, and similarly that she had a great affection for poor George III at his maddest and feeblest; and when at last she loved a man enough to marry him, he too was elderly, in his middle fifties. All these people, from elderly to aged, were at different periods the dominating influences in her life; they advised her, they moulded her, and she seemingly found it impossible ever to doubt their wisdom, be sceptical about them, or give them, however privately, a disrespectful or a rebellious thought. They intimidated her, though she did not perceive it, for she needed, in some obscure way, their elderly authority; she needed, in every important relationship, to find an element of her first strong filial devotion. And all these influences, while they made her happy and flattered her and gave her a sense of safety, not only led her away from her more forceful and self-reliant parts, in which she might have found the true ore of her talent, but also turned her back from adventures in friendship which might have helped her to that end. For constantly in the diaries we are disappointed by fits of prudery and caution which can only have been induced by the shocked gossip of the old, and must have arisen from the docile need to 'please papa' in everything—as when she nonsensically took Dr Johnson's cue and ended her friendship with Mrs Thrale because the latter chose to marry Mr Piozzi; and later in life abandoned in turn her friends Madame de Genlis and Madame de Stael—simply because of *rumours* about their private lives and while protesting her personal sense of loss and her admiration of the ladies' talents. Such parochialism and docility to the views of the cautious sit ill with her wit, her keen interest in character and her general liveliness and *verve*. But they run all through the bright fibre of her life, and seem to spring from that early, first desire to be everything her father most admired. All the rest of life had to be dovetailed into that essential.

'November 11th, Wednesday. Baked bread and giblet pie—put books in order—mended stockings. Put aside dearest C.'s letters, and now at about seven o'clock we are all sitting by a nice fire. Wm. with his book and a candle, and Mary writing to Sara.' It is 1801, we are at Grasmere,

QUEEN VICTORIA'S FIRST PRIVY COUNCIL
Detail showing Greville at the extreme left
Oil painting by Sir David Wilkie, 1785-1841

and Dorothy Wordsworth is making her gentle note of the day. And it
is hardly necessary for us to interrupt her, or do more than name her
here among our English diarists—for the publication in 1941 of all her
Journals, under the editorship of Mr E. de Selincourt, created such a

happy new *réclame* for her and was received with such universal pleasure that she certainly stands in no further need of commendation. And I observe this all the more contentedly since I have to admit—making, so far as I know, a minority of one—that the *Journals* disappoint me taken as a whole, and when considered in relation to the personality we know their writer to have been. All except the *Grasmere Journal* (1800-1803) and the brief *Alfoxden Journal*, which in their kind—though not the kind we might have longed for—are perfect; and parts of the *Journal Of A Tour In The Isle Of Man* (1828), which in spite of premonitory shadows here and there of sadness and ill-health contains much of the simple, lyrically-touched realism, the fastidious, clear selectiveness which distinguish so especially the Grasmere pages.

But though we could not spare any one of her exquisitely measured strokes of simple observation—'Wytheburn looked very wintry, but yet there was a foxglove blossoming by the roadside—' knowing Dorothy Wordsworth somewhat from the loves and friendships she won and kept—from Coleridge, from the Lambs, from Crabb Robinson, from all her brother's admirers, and from the adored brother himself—we want from her in her writings more of that 'meddling intellect' that William inveighed against; we want her thoughts as well as her observations, and when she 'walked with Coleridge,' when 'William and I strolled in the wood,' when 'we had a sweet and tender conversation' we desire exasperatedly to know a little at least of what was said. There is too much suppression everywhere in Dorothy Wordsworth of what clearly must have been a most distinguished and original mind; too much daily practice of that 'wise passiveness' which William invoked, but—we surmise, for all his sister's passionate care of his legend—did not easily command. Curiously, we might think after reading her *Journals* that Dorothy is, by temperament, that ideal poet of the Preface to *Lyrical Ballads* whom William believed himself to be. But she did not write verse, and she undertook to be William's angel—so egoism and intellectual restlessness were subjugated by responsibilty and by love; and she is so loyal, so discreet that we are never allowed to guess at any possible second thoughts. Her glinting, delicate sense of humour, which she uses sparingly, is never allowed to hurt William or anyone else—although his humourlessness, his quality of seeming to have been born an old man, must often have puzzled, not to say wearied, a companion so girlishly, though fastidiously, willing to be amused. The poet was, when he travelled abroad, prone to make scenes—and though Dorothy records these as justified, she cannot quite keep humourous uneasiness at bay. 'Mary and I walked on ahead . . .' and 'Wm. refused to give more than the sum agreed for—the man grew impertinent—and William desired the Magistrate might be summoned—a woful resource!' Such gleams relieve the repetitive descriptions of scenery which abound in *A Tour Of The Continent* (1820); but there are

QUEEN VICTORIA AT OSBORNE, 1865

Oil painting by Sir Edwin Landseer

By courtesy of the Royal Geographical Society, London

MOUNT EREBUS FROM HUT POINT

Water colour by Dr. E. A. Wilson drawn on the Second Scott Expedition, 1911 - 1913

not enough of them, and there is far too much guide-book observation. Love made her too discreet. No one could wish her to be crudely expansive about, for instance, the trip she took with William to Calais in August 1802, to visit Annette and his daughter Caroline, before his marriage to Mary Hutchinson—but is it unnatural to be surprised that the circumstances induced no greater depth of comment, no closer or more individual reflections than she made on any other of their journeys?

Still, she has left us the small, imperishable beauties of the *Grasmere Journal*, its constant loveliness heightened by sweet, plain touches. '. . . I sate half an hour afraid to pass a cow. The cow looked at me and I looked at the cow, and whenever I stirred the cow gave over eating.' 'The Lake of Rydale calm, Jupiter behind, Jupiter at least *we* call him, but William says we always call the largest star Jupiter.' '. . . at last I eased my heart by weeping—nervous blubbering, says William. It is not so.'

Between 1809 and 1811 an eccentric poor governess lived at a house called Dove's Nest on Windermere. 'There are many characters here worth observation,' she wrote in her diary, or letter-book. 'S. Coleridge, the conductor of a new and valued publication entitled "The Friend," resides only a few miles hence.' But she never mentions the Wordsworths, with whom Coleridge was then living at Allan Bank; and though she occasionally records going to Grasmere church on Sunday she does not seem to have known that a great poet lived so near her. Her employers, the wild and frantic Pedders who led her a terrible dance, would not have been sympathetic to William or to 'dearest C.'—so the remarkable and forthright Miss Weeton, brushing just wide of a chance of mention in Miss Wordsworth's diaries, did well, and rather better, to keep her own.

She was an obscure, unlucky woman, born in Upholland, Lancashire, in 1777, and brought up in great poverty by her widowed mother who kept a little dame school, and handed it on to her daughter. Miss Weeton forged out from it in exasperation in her thirties and became a governess, scraped an independent living one way and another, was trapped by a brother, for his own ends, into a wretched marriage, stormed out of that, fought a long, wild battle for the custody of her one child—won the battle, established herself as a respectable citizen in Wigan, and died feared, and long remembered I should think by all her relatives and connections. The humble but vehement and unusual story was set down by her, year in year out, in vigorous diaries, and in letters which she copied and embodied very carefully in the diaries. These were neglected and ignored by her people after her death, but by chance in the '30s of this century fell into the sympathetic hands of Mr Edward Hall and, edited by him, were published by the Oxford University Press in two volumes, in 1936 and 1939. They run from 1807 to 1825, and give a close, realistic picture of small-town life in England at that time—while building up with amazing strokes of humour, coarseness, truth, self-acclamation, pride and intelligence, a full-size portrait of a very remarkable female—one who in an easier walk of life, or with even an ounce or two more of education or of luck, might have done remarkable things, or given a lot of trouble, or somehow made herself remembered. Space forbids me to linger with Miss Weeton—I can only commend her in passing to those who like originals, and do not mind being bludgeoned—at a remove of more than a hundred years.

HENRY CRABB ROBINSON, 1775-1867
Drawing after a miniature by Masquerier

In the great world at this period, far from the Lakes and from Upholland—in Fanny Burney's world—a great many journals were piling up, in secret or in semi-secret. The first half of the nineteenth century saw well to its own documentation. Creevey, Greville, Croker: Joseph Farington, Benjamin Haydon ; Lady Blessington, Lady Holland ; Moore, Byron, Rogers, Telford, Scott—these and many others consumed a great deal of ink in their day, assembling what were to be their 'papers'—memoirs, reminiscences, letters—not always diaries. Thomas Creevey, for instance, who moved in Prince Regent and Holland House circles, was believed by Greville and others to have kept 'copious diaries,' as to the destiny of which there was some anxiety at his death in 1838. But when his 'papers' were published there was found to be almost no diary—only an occasional passage in that form wedged in among his letters to his wife and to his

214

stepdaughter. These letters are, however, so lively and malicious that one cannot but regret the diaries of which he was suspected, but which perhaps he never wrote.

Charles Greville, who held the post of Clerk to the Council and was intimate with statesmen of all parties, and particularly with the Duke of Wellington and with Palmerston, kept journals from 1818 to 1860, had a wonderful *flair* for the right kind of backstairs news, and has provided posterity with some excellent entertainment. Joseph Farington R.A., an inconsiderable painter, but a man of authority and shrewdness who devoted himself zestfully to Academy affairs, kept a diary from 1793 to the last day of his life, December 30th, 1821. Everyone who is anyone appears in it, and therefore it is a useful reference book for historians or biographers of the period ; but in manner and tone it is dull, and does nothing to attract us to its writer.

A very different kind of man, Benjamin Haydon—resembling Farington only in being a bad painter—also kept a journal, from 1821 to his death, by suicide, in 1846. Haydon was energetic, pugnacious, intelligent, most naïvely conceited and never out of trouble—and his diary reflects him vividly, and is alternately maddening and very entertaining. He has a good narrative manner and plenty of humour, except about himself, a subject on which he could not look unemotionally. He makes good observations on painters : 'Tintoretto has not the solidity of Rubens or Titian ; Titian was full of sensation.' And he reports parties well—the terrible christening party for Hazlitt's child, and an evening when Mrs Siddons read *Macbeth* to a number of gentlemen who were eating toast and drinking tea, they in an agony lest they clatter or crunch. 'Curious to see Lawrence in that predicament, to hear him bite by degrees and then stop for fear of making too much crackle.' Haydon was a friend and correspondent of Keats, of whom he says with absurd complacency: 'Poor, dear Keats. Had Nature but given you firmness as well as fineness of nerve . . .' Yet, years after Keats' death, he writes touchingly : 'I dreamt last night of dear Keats. I thought he appeared to me and said : 'Haydon you promised to make a drawing of my head, . . .' Haydon died in sudden despair, after years blustering for solvency and fame—and he is remembered now not as a painter, not even as the man who fought the Academy in the cause of the Elgin Marbles, but merely as a friend of Keats, and perhaps also because Hazlitt said he was the best talker he ever knew.

But the period of all these journals, indeed the first sixty years of the nineteenth century, have been recorded quite superbly—from the point of view of historians, biographers and gossip-hunters—by a prince of extrovert diarists, Henry Crabb Robinson. What we have in published form of this indefatigable man—reminiscences, letters and diaries—and a very great deal has not been printed—makes an invaluable body of information and eye-witness comment. To try to catalogue Crabb Robinson's famous friends, or his interests, or his travels, or his social activities would be absurd. He had, since he must have been abnormally sociable, a wonderful life. He was of respectable, modest origin, the son of a tanner in Bury St. Edmunds. He spent his youth as an attorney's clerk; then, inheriting an income of £100 a year, he went to Germany when he was twenty-five, and remained there five years, studying at Jena and Frankfurt, and later meeting in Weimar all the greatest Germans of the century—Goethe, Schiller, Wieland, Herder, Schlegel. Also he met the ubiquitous Madame de Stael, and 'mon Benjamin,' Benjamin Constant. In England, to which he returned in 1805, his earliest friends—but he never seemed to lose a friend or to slacken in the upkeep of friendship—were Hazlitt, the Lambs, Mrs Barbauld, Coleridge, the Wordsworths, the Flaxmans, Blake, Miss Mitford—but eventually every interesting, intelligent or especially gifted person in England was on his list, never to be removed from it. He joined the staff of *The Times* and was its correspondent in Sweden and in Spain in 1807-1808. From 1813 to 1838 he practised at the Bar and having made enough money with which to be solvent and generous for the rest of his days he retired, to give himself up to a variety of good works and pleasant pursuits.

He was not a brilliant man; but he had a sound understanding, was industrious, loyal and balanced, and he must have had a genius for friendship. His diaries are innocent of malice, but they are not at all fatuous. His sturdy devotion to Coleridge through thick and thin, his unflurried interest in Blake, and his wise, calm passion—if passion *can* be thus qualified—for Goethe prove capacity of mind and an appetite for the difficult. And the value for us of his devotion to genius is the simplicity, unaffected and pure of sycophancy, with which he writes down his impressions. When he notes some of Blake's difficult aphorisms: 'I regret that I have been unable to do more than put down these few things,' he says. 'The tone and manner are incommunicable. There are a natural sweetness and gentility about Blake which are delightful.'

The modest diarist might have been surprised to learn that *his* readers in their turn would find, all through his laborious contributions to posterity another kind of 'natural sweetness and gentility . . . which are delightful.'

Crabb Robinson does not appear to have known Caroline Fox, although many of his friends were also hers, and he would have sympathised with her intellectual interests and with her spiritual idiom. She kept a diary, from 1835, when she was sixteen, to her death in 1871. She was born and always made her home in Cornwall. Her father was Robert Were Fox, Quaker, distinguished geologist and F.R.S. Caroline, who never married, was herself a devout Quaker, and of intellectual and austere tastes—though warm and humorous too, very quick and appreciative with life and people. Chief among her famous friends were John Stuart Mill, John Sterling and the Carlyles. She regularly paid long visits to London,

and went abroad with her father on his travels and, towards the end of her life, in search of health. Her *Journal*, though in fact a touch too impersonal for all its air of ease and intimacy, is a very intelligent record of the observations and moods of many great and distinguished people; there are attractive notes on the diarist's own reading, and there is a sense of sweetness and natural holiness throughout. Good anecdotes too: Jane Welsh Carlyle reporting of Geraldine Jewsbury that she 'declares herself born without any sense of decency; the publishers beg that she will be decent, and she has not the slightest objection to be so, but she does not know what it is.' Sir Henry de la Beche and Warington Smyth being unnerved at a dinner party by the young Florence Nightingale, who led them *via* geology 'into regions of Latin and Greek' and Egyptian inscriptions. 'But when she began quoting Lepidus . . . "A capital young lady that, if she hadn't so floored me with her Latin and Greek!"' Tennyson, in 1860: '. . . but when he heard the name of Hallam, how his great grey eyes opened, and gave one a momentary glimpse of the depths in which *In Memoriam* learnt its infinite wail.'

In 1938, '39, '40 there appeared for the first time in print—published by Jonathan Cape—three volumes entitled *Kilvert's Diary*. Mr William Plomer was their editor. He had found a prize indeed—and the prize fell luckily into discreet and sympathetic hands. Anything might have happened to Francis Kilvert when being dressed for presentation to the reading public of the past twenty years, for he lays his soul right open to the mockery, the cleverness or the portentous psycho-analytical wisdom of our time. Mr Plomer, however, was content to read and enjoy him, assemble all available facts and associations, and present the diarist to us with only the necessary amount of just and friendly comment.

Francis Kilvert was born in a Somerset rectory in 1840. He went to Oxford and took Holy Orders. After a period assisting his father, who was then rector of Langley Burrell in Wiltshire, he went as curate to Clyro in Breconshire, where he worked for seven years. Afterwards he had a living at St. Harmon's in Radnorshire, and finally that of Bredwardine in Herefordshire. He married when he was thirty-eight, and five weeks after his marriage he died very suddenly of peritonitis. His published diary runs, with breaks, from 1870 to the spring of the year in which he died, 1879.

Its most obvious merit is the clear and detailed picture it gives us of life in the English countryside seventy years ago. Kilvert gets it all in, and makes it much more vivid and worth reading about than do the eighteenth century parsons, because he has enthusiasm for living, takes pains, has an unusually eager, bright eye, and—being very sentimental—gets all external things related to himself. He gives us, like a painter, not the flat actuality but his own composition of it. He gives us all the 'properties' of his kind of life indeed, all the things we know that are almost 'stock' now, and that we have encountered over and over again in period novels and family albums, but he gives them *as he feels them*, and as partaking of his vitality: walks, sermons, frosty mornings, visits to parishioners; toothache, confirmation caps, talk of the Franco-Prussian War, 'a letter from my mother'; girls and kisses and 'mischievous, saucy glances from beautiful grey eyes'—a very great deal about girls and glances; croquet parties, chubby babies, news from India, the funeral of an eccentric aunt (this last being quite superbly done); archery, dances, kisses—'ten miles for a kiss'; prayers by the bedsides of dying children; a great deal of scenery; visits to Oxford; pious reflections, and sudden 'romps' (undefined)—'a screaming romp with Lucretia who in rolling about upon the bed upset the candle on the coverlet and burst into peals of inextinguishable laughter . . .'; talks with Mr Barton, 'a clever, well-read man,' about the Holy Grail; 'sun on the lawn . . . claret cup iced . . . after dinner we had archery.' It might be dull, it might grow tiresome—even though on plain, objective merits many passages are lovely—crystal clear and complete. 'Chippenham bells pealing and firing all day for the Queen's birthday. Perch fished while I lay on the sloping bank and read *The Spanish Student*. The river was very low and the roach and dace have not yet come up. The air was full of "green drake" or mayfly just come up and all swarming over the river, and the little bleak leaping at them every moment.' Or this—a different statement, quite as clear and complete : 'Just as I heard the breakfast bell ring across the Common from the Rectory and turned in at the black gate a man crossed the stile carrying a basket. He said his name was Summerflower, that he had fasted since yesterday morning and that he could buy no breakfast before he had got watercresses to sell.' Yet such things, though they need not be any better done, would not in themselves bestow its curious originality and freshness on this diary. Nor would it be truthful to say that Kilvert always describes as well as in these passages. 'Considered simply as a writer of prose he shows a decided talent,' says Mr Plomer. Agreed ; but it is talent only—that is, talent undeveloped, unconsidered by its owner, and therefore too frequently unbridled. I am willing to be indulgent, with his editor, to his 'copious flow of adjectives'—but not for their own sakes, and not for the prose they give us when they are let loose, but because they are an unavoidable part of Francis Kilvert, they express him, for better or worse, in terms of his period and of himself—and so must be accepted with the rest of this remarkable self-portrait. But I do not think that he was more than a potential writer of good prose—for it always seems to have been hit or miss ; an atmosphere, a memory, a mood could control him and make him write as it dictated ; but *he* could not control those masters—which only means that he never *learnt* to write, but simply wrote ; in the most alarming, rich gushes, if that was how he felt—*vide* the entry 'From My Bedroom Window' for July 11th, 1870—or gently, objectively or humourously, when such states ruled him. I do not believe that he considered his writing at all, save with the pleasure of a boy in doing something which everyone could not do. And in the period in which he lived, with its influences of eloquence, colour, tears and tenderness, that was not a safe way to be a prose writer. Not that there is any safety—artistic or emotional—in Francis Kilvert ; I think indeed that he got through so decently, as man and as writer, simply by the grace of God and the luck of the innocent.

Sometimes, taking his prose at its wildest, he reminds one of all our great-aunts, and of the poems and letters which they used to write when an infant died in the family, or had a birthday. 'Then the girls would have me go into the next room to see Janet in bed. So we went in and found her pretty and rosy with tumbled curly hair lying in her little soft white nest contentedly sucking chocolates. I sat down upon her bed and the rest gathered and so Queen Janet held her court as pleased as possible . . . soon had her round plump limbs out from under the sheets with the innocent simplicity of childhood and her pretty little feet in my lap . . .

rosy and curly and still contentedly sucking her chocolate. Dear Ruthie stood by her little sister, kind, sweet and motherly. They share their little bed together, "two dumplings" as Ruthie said . . . Then the father dressed for dinner came in to see his children and to wish them Good-night. It was a lovely family group, a beautiful picture.' Or read' him as he muses over a silk bookmarker with 'Forget-Me-Not' embroidered on it—'the short, simple prayer.' 'It was a gift from a child sweetheart. But from which ? I gazed at the words conscience-stricken. Forget-me-not. And I had forgotten . . . The whole scene rose before me, the old cottage fireside at evening and the fair head and pure eyes of a child bent earnestly over her work, and the little hands eager about her labour' of love . . . "Forget Me Not. I will send it to-morrow and he will not forget." And I have forgotten. The vision faded. Oh, the fickleness and forgetfulness of man and the faithfulness of woman. Alas, it is the old story . . .' It is a shame to have to chop up such a passage, but Kilvert is not economical when he dreams. And I do not quote it so much *pour rire* as to show that he wrote without judgment, though in a sense with an abundance of talent.

It is the unevenness, the eccentricity and the sheer naturalness of the writer which distinguish this diary. Kilvert puts down everything and anything, a landscape, a joke, a prayer, or a rhapsody about yet another girl ; and, whatever it is, he lights it up ; by some curious trick of his vitality and his innocence, he makes everything *live* that he touches.

Except perhaps girls. Because girls render him helpless. Any girl, from two years old to twenty-five, in her perambulator or at the churn or in Sunday school or being a bridesmaid or playing croquet or castrating a lamb or lying on her deathbed—any girl sets him off ; about her sweet blue eyes and bright sweet morning face and rounded arms as creamy as the milk and her tossing curls and teasing glance and half-veiled charms. Girls, from their cradles to their wedding beds, moved him so much that he quite simply was unable to see them for emotion, and can be said to have been girl-blind. For it is impossible that Wiltshire, Radnorshire and Breconshire could have contained such an extraordinary number of shattering, innocent, merry beauties in that one decade seventy years ago. It is just that they were girls. 'O my child if you did but know ! ' and 'Ah Gipsy ! ' and 'Angels ever bright and fair' and 'Farewell, farewell ! ' and 'I thought—was it so ?—that there were tears in those blue eyes when we parted.' No reader could keep track of the journey of this clergyman's heart—for apart from official wooings, of 'sweet Daisy Thomas,' of 'Kathleen Mavourneen' or of 'bewitching Etty Brown,' he records very, very many other strongly protested loves. 'Lovely Florence Hill' and the 'Gipsy Child' and his 'mountain maid,' and the girls he 'romped' with, and the girls he longed to know better, and the little girls at Sunday school, and the girls he visited in sickness, and the girls he buried.

'THE NUTTING IN SEAGRY WOODS'
Verses and drawings by Francis Kilvert

Parallel with this ever-rushing emotionalism runs a good rough stream of coarseness, of plain sensuality in thought, and of shameless enjoyment of the beating of children. Yet he was kind—and good. He was limited indeed by his own *naïveté* and his acceptance of outward forms, and by the characteristics, some of the worst characteristics, of his age. But he was loved in his parishes; he knew his people well, frequented them, helped them, grieved with them and 'romped' with them. He preached the Christianity of his time, and clearly he did his best to live as a Christian. He worked tirelessly and without self-pity, and in little things he was kind. If he met an old woman carrying buckets of water he carried them for her; he carried his musical box up a considerable mountain climb 'for the blind child'; in his way he understood children and made good jokes about them, and noted what they said with an unusually selective ear. And he really loved the beautiful country about him, its ancientry and simplicity, and its seasonal changes and occupations. He seems to have been a happy man on the whole in spite of his sensitivity; he had an outgoing, generous temperament, and great consideration (despite the flogging complex) for the feelings of others; he was tolerant, and touchingly easy to please. 'The morning was perfectly glorious, a brilliant cloudless blue sky . . . and the gossamers shone and twinkled into green and gold in the grass which in the shade of the wood was still hoary with the night's frost . . . After luncheon I played croquet with the girls.'

And now we will leave all this Victorianism with a salute to its Queen, who also was a diarist. Many people have read the excerpts of her diaries which are published with her letters, and many more, of the older generations, are familiar with the once very popular *Leaves From The Journal Of Our Life In The Highlands.* By reason of her place and greatness any writings of Queen Victoria must have interest, and some have found much to admire, or even to charm them, in the closer revelation of her personality which the diaries give. Some, on the other hand, have not, and remain unattracted by the dauntless, arrogant, obstinate little old lady. But certainly the Highland Diary is good fun, for us who can view those perpetual, freezing expeditions and picnics in the rain at our very safe remove. And Francis Kilvert, at least, would have admired the Queen's extraordinary prose, and shared her enthusiasm for scenery—and even perhaps for lunching 'on a cairn of stones, in a piercing cold wind.' For he was polite and adaptable in a way we have forgotten, and certainly he was a most loyal subject of Her Majesty.

So far the twentieth century, pre-war, war and post-war periods has shown no sign of dropping the well-established diary habit. And now war again—we assuredly have plenty to record for those who come after. It is as well, I suppose, that the diarists should persevere. But out of the stream already published, from Sir Algernon West and Wilfrid Scawen Blunt, by way of Colonel Repington, Sir Henry Wilson and Arnold Bennett down to Ego 1, 2, 3, 4 and 5, I choose here to make reminder of only three diaries—and those reminders shall be brief. All three were written under exceptional stress and ordeal, and bear little spiritual relation to traditional English diaries—therefore they seem particularly representative of our time.

The last diary of Captain Scott is good to read now, for morale's sake, as a reminder of the power of courage, and of the dignity of men. Everyone knows the magnificent story of his last journey to the South Pole, and whoever knows the story knows the diary, which was found in the tent on the Barrier with the three dead men. The entries of the last two months are immortal. 'Wednesday January 17.—The Pole. Yes, but under very different circumstances. We have had a horrible day . . . Now for the run home and a desperate struggle. I wonder if we can do it.' 'Jan. 24th. . . . I don't like the easy way Oates and Evans get frost-bitten.' 'Feb. 8th. A lot could be written on the delight of setting foot on rock after 14 weeks of snow and ice . . . It is like going ashore after a sea voyage.' 'Feb. 24th. It is great luck having the horsemeat to add to our ration . . .' 'Feb. 29th. Every day we have been ready to start for our depot 11 miles away but outside the door of the tent it remains a scene of whirling drift . . . we are getting weaker, of course, and the end cannot be far. It seems a pity, but I do not think I can write more. R. Scott. For God's sake look after our people.'

That was the end of one of the greatest of all stories, which can be read at any time with benefit ; and now is a good time for such a cold, astringent tonic.

The Journal Of A Disappointed Man was first published in March 1919, and on its last desperate page carried the italicised announcement that Barbellion, its remarkable author, had died on December 31, 1917— about two months after making the diary's last entry, which is the solitary word : 'Self-disgust.' Later it was found that this announcement was untrue, a curiously ill-advised piece of 'effectiveness' ; Barbellion was alive when his *Journal* appeared, and died on June 3rd, 1919. This was— from the detached point of view of readers of the *Journal*—a discouraging discovery, and could not but chill sympathy ; but the fact that he *did* live eighteen months longer than he, we must suppose, expected to—in pain, weakness and discomfort which it is torture to read about—was of ultimate great value, to him and to us ; for it gave him time to write *A Last Diary*, which is not nearly so well-known as the *Journal*, but which supplements and supports it—explaining, resolving much of the confused, knotted misery of the first book, and showing the disastrously unlucky man with his burden of wasted gifts and passionate regrets outgrowing, much more than the uneven courage of the *Journal* had shown him to, his terrible personal misery—and growing sweeter, lighter, truer and wittier in obser-vation, gentler and more calm in habit of thought, as his body pressed home its violent defeat of him, and the real hour of his departure from it came in sight.

The two journals, read together, make a fine record—for they assemble *all* the essential truth about a personal tragedy which can be described as total. They take the unusually bright schoolboy—whose real name, by the way, was not Wilhelm Nero Pilate Barbellion but Bruce Frederick Cummings—with his spontaneous passion and genius for natural history from his poor and often happy days at home to the first chances, the successful examination, the post in the Natural History Museum, the stirrings of ambition, and then of love—to the premonitory encroachments of ill-health, and the beginning of a tragic, useless struggle. They give us truth about a love and a marriage, and show the goodness and necessity of that love as well as the doubts and second thoughts, not merely from the point of view of the diarist but, very justly and penetratingly, from the probable point of view of the girl who became his wife and bore him a child. They show all the theatre, all the self-pity, disgust and bewildered loneliness of a young, egoistical and brilliant man caught in a terrible trap ; but also they give flashes and passages of peace, that increase and grow truer as sorrow deepens, spreading at last to an almost constant witty sweetness, a near-gaiety, in *A Last Diary*. And because of this completion, because of the clear thinking, the control, the loving-kindness and the *fun* of the end, which justify and greatly ennoble him, we can surely rejoice a little in the hard extension by eighteen months of a life which—since by endowment he could have made it so fine—Barbellion had so often and so bitterly desired at an end.

He was very intelligent, in many directions. So his diaries, which exist to explain his personality and his fate to the world, as he intended them to, are not solely about himself, in the direct sense. They contain a great deal of objective observation of things and people, lively snatches of conversation, quick character-sketches and vigorous comment on books. And some of the best of these are in *A Last Diary*. His disrespectful admiration of Emily Brontë is amusingly expressed, for instance. 'One might almost write her down as Mrs Nietsche . . . no fit companion for the young ladies of a seminary. . . "No coward soul is mine" she tells us, with her fist held to our wincing nose.' In December 1918 he was writing : 'James Joyce is my man. Here is a writer who tells the truth about himself. It is almost impossible to tell the truth.' 'What I have always feared is coming to pass,' he says, with death well in sight, 'love for my little daughter. Only another communicating string with life to be cut.' 'I take my life in homeopathic doses now,' he says gently. Somewhere he says : 'Sir Thomas Browne was my father and Marie Bashkirtseff my mother.' It is an amusingly good shot. 'I am the scientific investigator of myself,' he says. He was greatly gifted ; and reading some of his character-impressions, and especially his conversations with his nurse towards the end, one feels that among the many things he might have done excellently the writing of novels was one.

It is curious that the last two diaries we shall speak of here, Barbellion's and Katherine Mansfield's, should be those of sick people, people doomed to die young and frustrated, and that, with Captain Scott's, their personal notes should stand for our century so far. But I cannot help the too-obvious symbolism ; it has worked out that way—and need not be taken too pessimistically. For all three were brave, exceptionally brave, and all were ultimate masters of their own tragedies, though we may proportion those tragedies as we choose in relation to universal things. Katherine

Mansfield's story needs no re-telling. She has left it to us in her work, in her letters, and in what she left undestroyed of her 'huge, complaining diaries.' That residue, published under the title of *Journal*, covers her life from 1914 to her death at Fontainebleau in October 1923. It is very personal, moody, self-pitying and brave. It contains notes for work, much discussion of work, sudden memories of childhood, outbursts of love, of gaiety and of desolation, and amusing, bitter, accomplished sketches of people encountered—and as it advances towards the darkness courage and ambitious desires rise up in greater waves, harder to meet, but which are met in fact by wisdom which has enlarged itself too, imperceptibly purified by detachment and humour—and by gentleness. The last pages of the *Journal* are clean of the occasional whimsicalities and false ironies that disfigure the earlier part; and there is a workmanlike, non-invalidish quality in the passages of rough notes, mere reminders for the professional —like the colour notes a painter makes. There is courage and goodness in this hard passion for work, and in the sick woman's lonely debates on the personal question of her illness and her love. And at the end she writes, thinking of another and of how to help him : 'And when I say "I fear" don't let it disturb you, dearest heart. We all fear when we are in waiting rooms. Yet we must pass beyond them, and if the other can keep calm, it is all the help we can give each other.'

Recollecting that I began this book by saying that the best English diaries have been written by bores, I can now only hope ruefully that I have not too much justified that sweeping statement. Yet I adhere to it—as I meant it; *i.e.*, that the best and most typical English diarists would probably have been bores if they had not kept diaries—for they possessed that first attribute of the bore, the need to mention everything. And now, after much reading of diaries, and while allowing for all kinds of exceptions, the feeling I am left with is that the traditional, the generic English diary, from Pepys and Evelyn through the parsons and the political gossips to Crabb Robinson and Queen Victoria, is the escape, the safety-valve of the otherwise bore, the bright reverse of natural dullness. Facts, actions, lists of things and people, details of movement, exact information, plain observation—all valuable and some enchanting, as it happens, after fifty or a hundred years—but *accidentally* so; not designed expression, not making the exciting claims of works of art, but set down in routine, because of somebody's neat habit. Lucky for us. How much luckier we are, after all, to know Crabb Robinson in his diaries, as a whole, with all his illustrious friends massed about him on parade, than to have been mere acquaintances in his time of the busy, ubiquitous, unremarkable man with the absurdedly crowded engagement-book!

The women diarists are in a special case however. They are not as a genus bores *manquées*, because they very likely would not have been diarists if they could have been something more directly self-expressive. They are diarists *faute de mieux*, whether they knew it or not. Dorothy Wordsworth kept journals and did no more creative writing only because, consciously or unconsciously, she had decided that devotion to William was her clearest and most necessary duty; Fanny Burney wrote diaries because she should have been training herself to be a great novelist and had not enough decisiveness for that, so escaped, with ease and brilliance; Miss Weeton wrote them because she was obscure and lost, half-mad with a sense of frustration, and the need to say something, somehow; Caroline Fox was a natural intellectual who played second fiddle modestly to all her brilliant male friends. And the Queen? The Queen is above common rules, and in any case Victoria sweeps them away, as she should, by being perhaps at once a diarist *and* a bore.

ENGLISH NOVELISTS

ELIZABETH BOWEN

THE English novel, from its beginning on, has been the subject of so much critical writing that one may feel there remains little to add. Its characteristics have been defined; its development has been noted; influences upon it have been traced. In so far as all this may enlarge our pleasure in reading, we owe thanks to the critic. I do, however, see one danger—that too much information about great novels may make us less spontaneous in our approach to them—though they offer entrancing subjects for study, they were in the first place written to be enjoyed. It would be sad to regard as lecture-room subjects books that were meant to be part of life. As things are, are our classical English novels not often left to the honour of our high-up shelves, where they receive little other attention than the periodic dusting of their tops, while that place for which their lively authors designed them, the place on the book-table by the arm-chair, is taken by modern writers whose chief attraction is that we have not yet been required to find them "good" ?

We lose much if we ignore, or honour in name only, so living a part of the English heritage. And now, when the English spirit stands at its full height, to do so would be a double loss. England's past in art, as well as in history, has helped to build up her heroic To-day. It is natural to want our writers beside us as we face this new phase of human experience. And painters and writers, however long dead, however far back their place in actual time, remain, in their living art, our contemporaries. Their domain is always the domain of living men; it is to us, the living, that they are speaking now. This is as true of the novelists as it is of the painters or poets—as true, but not so easily recognised. Why? Because while in painter or poet we expect the sublime (or timeless), in the novelist we expect the familiar, the day-to-day. The novel, we feel, should keep close to life. Whatever seems unlikely is fatal to it. The novelist must be a man of his own day—and, as that day of his gives place to another, and as that other gives place to our own, may we not feel that he depicts only what was, so that his judgments seem to lose their point ? How, the would-be reader may ask, can I find the familiar, the convincing, the likely, in a novel written two hundred years ago ?

The answer, of course, is that while novelists must belong to their own day, the great novelist is not confined by that. Poor novels do pass away with their time ; they pass because they concerned themselves only with the ephemeral parts of human experience, not with its lasting essentials. But in the great novel, we recognise those essentials that run through all experience, independent of time. We may, in fact, see for the first time what those essentials are. We see, too, why fundamentally men and women have changed so little. In a novel that has been great enough to survive the years, we shall find very little that is unfamiliar or queer. Any feeling of queerness evaporates in the course of the first pages. Differences of speech, costume, habits, manners do not affect us as we had thought they would : instead, we are made aware of the underlying likeness of life then to life as it is to-day.

The English novel, the novel proper, began in the Age of Reason—in fact, at a time when people thought for themselves—and reason has continued to be its godmother. But the genius that gave the novel its truth and life is, at the same time, something beyond the scope of reason ; a sort of romantic miracle. In the course of the English novel, since its beginning, the English have continued to show and to see themselves—islanders, haughty, puzzled, at once saved and graced by a comicality to which they are not blind. The novel has been an overflow of a number of English people's feeling for their own life—and, also, it voices a criticism. It is as givers of one particular sort of pleasure, and inspirers of a particular sort of interest, that I shall discuss the English novelists. While I shall hope to be fair, I cannot avoid the influence of my own taste. I read for pleasure, and it must be remembered that I write as a pleasure-seeker and not a judge.

O F the English novel, before the eighteenth century, there were several curious false dawns. These attempts at the novel have a sort of interest for their own sakes. In the England of Queen Elizabeth the demand for entertainment was general, and the arts made a noble response to it. English drama then came, as we know, to its greatest height—and, as the mass of the people could still not read, drama continued to be the popular art. Writers who wrote anything other than plays addressed themselves to a literate, elegant upper class, and Elizabethans who did experiment in the novel either shared or flattered the Court's taste. The way was prepared for story-tellers by an existing vogue for Italian tales—this not the first nor the last of invasions of foreign fancy

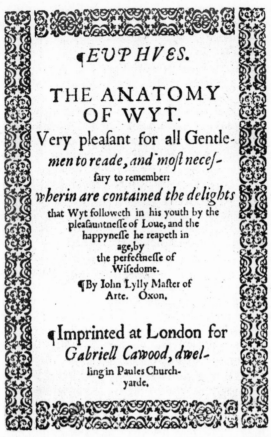

TITLE PAGE OF JOHN LYLY'S *EUPHUES OR THE ANATOMY OF WIT*
First Edition, 1579

that have reached the English shore. First by late Renaissance Italy then by France, the English have been at once englamoured and shocked. By the time John Lyly, a Kentish man born in 1553, brought out his *Euphues*, translations from the Italian had set up a pretty high standard in artifice. Of this Lyly was so careful not to fall short that he decidedly over-reached himself ; also, he gave his first story a foreign scene. In *Euphues, the Anatomy of Wit*, published in 1579 and followed a year later by *Euphues and his England*, all late Renaissance influences appear. There are great flights of discourse ; everything is kept at the highest possible level above the everyday. The hero Euphues, his romantic friend Philautus and the lady who proves false to them both, leave few subjects of gallant or

229

philosophic interest untouched. In the second half of the story the high-minded Euphues visits England, and comments on much that he finds there. *Euphues* had an immediate, hectic success in circles for which it was designed. But the success was brief—against Lyly's wrought-up style, with its hollow elegances, strained ingenuities, and overload of classical references there came a revulsion that was severe. Common sense began to assert itself, and enthusiasts felt that they had been fooled. Ridicule swept away *Euphues*—which is now chiefly remembered as having added a word to the English vocabulary. . . . The *Arcadia* of Sir Philip Sidney (born at Penshurst, 1554) fared a good deal better, as it deserved. The *Arcadia* is a sort of sustained dream, and also it has the consistency of a book written to please oneself—for Sir Philip, by himself for some time at his sister's house in the country, undertook the *Arcadia* for this reason alone. Courtier-soldier, traveller, lover, poet and man of the world, Sir Philip brought to his narrative prose-poem unusual feeling and innate stylishness. In the *Arcadia*, pairs of lovers wander in the seclusion of a pastoral world—though on this is imposed a complex plot. When, in 1590, four years after its author's death in battle, the *Arcadia* appeared (against his wishes, for he had asked that it should be burned), it went straight to the hearts of the *beau monde*, to whom, in the heated pressure of Court life, pastoral distances seemed idyllic—in fact, the theme of Arden was here. Though Sidney's lovers show less spirit than Shakespeare's, the breeze from *Arcadia* continued to blow sweet ; and, not in itself deeply original, for pastorals had already been done abroad, the book was to be in its turn followed by a number of imitations in this genre.

John Greene (born in Norwich about 1560) belongs with the rakes and the realists. When he left Cambridge for London it was not to come to Court but to pick up a living by pamphleteering and the writing of plays. His trade was tough, his companions low. In this milieu, a gust of contempt for the unreal made him discard the *Euphues* influence under which his own first story, *Mamillia*, had been penned at Cambridge in 1583. So his succeeding stories, though still romantic, have that progressive strength that comes from a truer view. But more important were his pamphlets, that, in story-interest and length, began to approach short novels ; in these he broke away from the courtly idea and wrote of the stinking, stewing London he knew—whether fine nostrils liked it or not. In this break with flattery and illusion, Greene came to be followed by "ingenuous, ingenious, fluent, facetious Thomas Nash" (born at Lowestoft, 1567), who also developed the satiric attacking style.

So the Elizabethan period closes with two very opposite tendencies in the air. And a place for the narrative that was to become the novel had been at least made—though now that place was to stay empty for some time. With the end of Elizabeth's reign some creative urge subsided, and experiments came to a standstill.

ROBINSON CRUSOE
An illustration to Daniel Defoe's *Robinson Crusoe*
Engraving by Clark and Pinese for the first edition, 1719

I N the seventeenth century, in which so much happened, little worth
speaking of happened to the novel. John Bunyan was, it is true, to
give, with his *Pilgrim's Progress* (1678), one of our grandest examples of
story-telling. But first, the theatre kept its hold over the people—though
drama was in a state of noisy decline ; then, battles and metaphysics came
with the Civil War. In 1642 the Puritan parliament closed the theatres,
and, to escape from an oversevere world, pleasure-loving society turned to
reading, and sought again—this time as an anodyne—the seductions of the
imported romance. France now supplied the demand. Long-winded
reconstructions of chivalry helped the ladies and gentlemen of the defeated
faction through the Commonwealth gloom, and when the Restoration
brought out the sun again the French romances could more freely circulate.
For the English, the Frenchmen could hardly write fast enough—and quite

231

soon English imitators sprang up. One cannot praise, and need not discuss, the results. However, with regard to the novel, the century had not a quite barren close : in 1692 one exquisite tale, *Incognita*, came from Congreve the dramatist. But the theatre was entirely to claim Congreve—it was having another tremendous boom. Literature, apart from dramatic art, was to be the domain of a few exquisite but rather detached minds. Vigorous invention and curiosity went, rather, to scientific research.

Story-telling, however, had one more likely recruit in the person of Mrs. Aphra Behn. Though there were unkind judgments of this lady, she had one great merit : she wrote from experience. She had lived abroad, and she had lived to the full. Though subject to flights and foolishness, she had energy—more energy, some people considered, than was becoming in her sex. There was a tendency, due to last a long time, to regard professional novel-writing as an immodest, too dashing occupation for women ; in fact, well on into the nineteenth century gentlewomen whose novels found publication remained anonymous, or used pen-names. When, in 1698, Mrs. Behn's two best-known novels, *Oroonoko* and *The Fair Jilt*, appeared, she had already been dead some years. *Oroonoko*, with its negro hero, put out that idea of the noble savage that Rousseau was to make popular with a romantic age. Aphra Behn is at least a landmark : the rest of the sub-heroic nonsense of her period vanished, leaving behind for the novel only a bad name.

The seventeenth century, all the same, produced the England that was to produce the novel. Out of the Civil War a new kind of English self-consciousness had been born. Social thought was already upon its way. The new interest in science had made people objective, curious, analytical. The complexity of the spirit of man was recognised—and, with this, his tie to the natural world. Most important, a new class had come into conscious power—the middle class, self-reliant, anti-feudal and sturdy. This class was to ask from art something new. The courtly idea had gone for ever, to be succeeded by the democratic idea.

DISABUSED, critical, liking fact and inclined to rate fancy low, why should the eighteenth century have given birth to the novel ? For some time, indeed, the brilliant essayists reigned. But it was two of these, Steele and Addison, who by their sketches in the *Tatler* (1709-1711) and the *Spectator* (1711-1712) made a step forward towards the novel by creating interest in character—or, should one say, heightening interest that had begun to exist? The members of Mr. Bickerstaff's Club (in the *Tatler*) and Sir Roger de Coverley and his friends (in the *Spectator*) stepped from print into life with an utter convincingness. These were individual people ; no longer the dreary "types" who had dominated the English story and play. Only continuous narrative of their actions was

JOSEPH ANDREWS AND MR. ADAMS WITH FANNY AT THE WAYSIDE INN
An illustration to *Joseph Andrews* by Henry Fielding
Water colour by Thomas Hearne
By courtesy of Walker's Galleries, London

MR. BURCHELL RESCUING OLIVIA PRIMROSE
An illustration to the *Vicar of Wakefield* by Oliver Goldsmith
Water colour by Thomas Hearne
By courtesy of Walker's Galleries, London

needed to make Sir Roger and the others into characters in a novel—but this their creators did not choose to supply.

Daniel Defoe (a butcher's son born in London in 1660) perceived character, though he put action first : though what straighter approach to character could there be than the story of a man alone with himself ?— and *Robinson Crusoe*, Defoe's first great work of fiction, was published in 1719. Defoe started late in fiction but not in writing : pamphlets, verses, satires, treatises had for years poured from his ready pen. Disgrace, a stand in the pillory and the loss of his business (he had started a brick kiln at Tilbury) had, by following on his double-edged pamphlet, *The Shortest Way with the Dissenters* (1702), already shown him his pen's danger—and power. He paid high for a laugh that no one else had enjoyed. When Defoe returned to his craft it was in a desperate spirit ; starvation faced him and his family. By this time, however, he had the public taped ; he resolved to make profit out of its gullibility, and the possibilities of fiction, to this end, at once presented themselves to him. He wrote up the case of a Mrs. Veal who after her death appeared to a friend in Canterbury, and he did not fail to put Mrs. Veal across. Defoe developed two great assets : plausibility and a superb style, at once matter-of-fact and evocative. His English has, to my mind, never been bettered : it is the ideal narrator's prose. After *Robinson Crusoe* came, in 1721, *Moll Flanders*—a great fascinating acute short book on no account to be missed by anybody. The bad beauty who names it is immortal : never was a life lived with more style. *Colonel Jack* came in 1722, and *Roxana* in 1724.

Everything that Defoe wrote reads as true. (He carried this so far as to be able to fake memory in his *Journal of the Plague Year*.) He sets up for us the important rule that a story-teller must be believed. It is true that he tested his plausibility on no subject so fantastic as that of the *Gulliver's Travels* (to give the book its short name) of Dean Swift—published in 1729. Swift's vast satiric imagination did not disdain, in *Gulliver's Travels*, the minutest details that would convince. Though the head may say to the reader, You know, this could not have happened, the imagination answers, It surely did. We see—and so we believe. In fact, to Defoe and Swift the English novel owes its powerful start. We have come to the end of the false dawns. The novel could only come into power when it took account of the forces of common sense.

Two elements of the novel were, thus, waiting—likely and living character, likely and living plot. But a third was needed, to merge these two. What was this ?—interest in human relationships. The tract in which men and men, or men and women, affect, act on and conflict with each other was still waiting to be explored. It had been accepted that it is from a man's character that his actions spring. One had now to see the effect that one man or woman, by acting in character, had on the action or character of another. It had, too, to be seen that human behaviour seldom follows a set course (or course planned in the head), being often deflected by accidents. The nature and cause of the accidents that deflect behaviour might be called the stuff of the novel. Most often, these are psychological : conflicting desires between two people are more important than a tempest or a coach being overturned. One can see why the novel must have love interest—though in as wide a sense as you like.

And the novelist had to accept a fact known to his readers—that behaviour, however wide its zigzags, very seldom goes over certain set bounds. What sets these bounds ? Society, what one might call the world of the everyone-else, that world in which each man or woman, by being born, takes up his or her inherited place. The relation of a man to society is an integral part of the concept of any novel. In the eighteenth century, the idea of society crystallised : the novel, in fact, was the product of a great social age. A man's relationship to society was seen as his first important and human one—he might fly from or defy society by becoming a hermit or vagabond, but he could not ignore it, for its existence gave him his meaning and shape. It was seen, I think rightly, that the fact that human beings do not live for themselves only, in vacuo, makes them more rather than less interesting.

This new contemplative interest in human beings was not on the level of poetry : sublimity played little part in it. The medium for its expression was prose narrative—but this would have to contain much. England being now ripe for the novel, the novel came. The public sprang to meet *Pamela*, published in 1740.

SAMUEL RICHARDSON, the middle-aged London printer who became the author of *Pamela*, was a pursy, not interesting little man. Born in 1689, son of a joiner in Derbyshire, he had received a limited education, had come to London as an apprentice, done well and married his master's daughter. His experience of the world was limited—as some absurdities in *Pamela* show.

His life was troubled more by domestic griefs—there were many deaths in his family—than by emotional storms. His personal tameness makes all the odder his faculty—one is entitled to call it genius—for the analysis of the human heart. He is said, as a prim cold-blooded little boy of thirteen, to have been the confidant of a group of young ladies for whom he indited love-letters ; and this precocious knowledge of love, at an age before one feels love, may account for much. Certainly, given the masculine temperament of the eighteenth century, Richardson's knowledge of women is extraordinary. His detractors might say that he spied on women rather than felt for them—certainly Richardson's heroines arouse (as he intended) solicitude rather than desire. (Fielding's heroines, on the other hand, are desirable before everything.) In *Pamela*, marred, as I say, by absurdities

SAMUEL RICHARDSON 1689-1761
Oil painting by Joseph Highmore

and more than a little shocking in its success philosophy, Richardson no more than foreshadows his coming powers. The *réclame* that *Pamela* gained him, the many new doors that opened to the successful author, he was artist enough to put to a good use. Also he learned a lesson from the experience of having *Pamela* ridiculed—of Fielding's ruthlessness I have yet to speak. In the eight years between *Pamela* and *Clarissa*, Richardson came out of his chrysalis. *Pamela* is a slight story brilliantly told. Of *Clarissa*, at the end of two hundred years, we may say : this remains one of the finest novels we have.

But *Pamela* is more than an innovation. To what can we trace the charm of this shocking book ? Partly to the unerringness with which the sense of predicament is sustained. Partly to the vivacity of the dialogue. Partly to the intimacy of the manner—the book is written in letters, but it is more than that. Richardson not only adored detail but had an unfailing sense of its place in art.

235

Those who do not like him find his atmosphere too indoor—claustrophobic, in fact. It is true that his characters are constricted by their emotions into a tiny, oppressive world. . . . Pamela Andrews, little waiting-maid of fifteen, adorably pretty, a chaste minx, is left, by the death of her mistress and patroness, exposed to the evil designs of that lady's son, Mr. B. From the slender defences she clings to at his Bedfordshire country house, Mr. B. whisks Pamela off to his still more lonely estate in Lincolnshire.

"About eight o'clock at night" (Pamela writes to her parents, for whose peace of mind she seems to have no regard) "we entered the courtyard of this handsome, large, old and lonely mansion, that looks made for solitude and mischief, as I thought by its appearance, with all its brown nodding horrors of lofty elms and pines about it. Here, I said to myself, I fear is to be the scene of my ruin. . . ."

Crude is hardly the word for Mr. B's goings-on. And he is not even high-spirited. There comes the crucial occasion when Pamela's virtue is only saved by her collapse into alarming fits. Mr. B., unnerved, thinks again : he ends by proposing marriage. Whereupon, Pamela, idealist in behaviour, accepts the husband she has up to now considered a mean, inestimable young man. The book's morality founders on this rock, and Pamela's bridal prosperity, though described with spirit, leaves one cold. The book, with unconscious cynicism, is sub-titled *Virtue Rewarded*.

One stands dumb, all the same, before the accomplishment of this first English novel. So did the world of its day. But the moral flaw in the book was perceived, without mercy, by at least one mind. It was on *Pamela's* weakness that Fielding pounced. Henry Fielding, Richardson's junior by nine years, had been born to many advantages that the printer, through no fault of his own, lacked. Fielding was a gentleman, a wit, a rake and a scholar. Born at his grandfather's country house near Glastonbury in 1707, educated at Eton, he had found himself with remarkably little money and had been by turns journalist, playwright, barrister. By the time he read *Pamela* he was tough, poised, satiric—but something more. The full possibilities of this new form, the novel, may or may not at first have appeared to him. We know that he set out on his *Joseph Andrews* in a spirit of pure burlesque.

In *Joseph Andrews*, published 1742, Fielding gives Richardson's Pamela Andrews a brother Joseph, virtuous as herself and exposed to equal difficulties. The handsome young footman too well pleases his widowed employer's eye. His employer is Lady Booby, the aunt by marriage of Richardson's sinister Mr. B. Mr. B.—it could not have been more annoying—is thus made to enter Fielding's pages as young Mr. Booby, with Pamela as his exceedingly snobbish bride. Richardson called *Joseph Andrews* "a lewd and ungenerous engrafture"—and probably did not stop at that. But neither did Fielding stop at his burlesque—the novel ran far away from it, to our eternal gain. Joseph may be the hero, but he is soon eclipsed

HENRY FIELDING 1707-1754
Engraving after William Hogarth

by the outsize figure of Parson Adams—Joseph's friend and patron, with
his big heart, big family and big fist, his erudition and innocence, his
Christian humility and his hot temper, his astounding get-up, optimism
and constantly mislaid and forgotten horse. When Joseph flies from Lady
Booby's in London, he meets Parson Adams, who is looking for him.
Fanny, Joseph's young village love, has also left home to seek him—so
these three range the country together on a much-interrupted journey
home. And what country they travel, and in how roaring a spirit! If
solicitude is the note of Richardson's novels, zest is the note of Fielding's.
Strongly under the influence of Cervantes, he loved movement, the fantastic, the outdoor. In this first book we feel the author getting into his
stride. Fielding had more to carry than Richardson, and so the content of
every one of his novels is always a little more than their form will hold.
But his very prodigality is superb. He is the masculine writer par

excellence ; in no other Englishman who has written has the masculine quality been so pure. Among the other sex one might say that only Jane Austen has been his counterpart—she wrought her own femininity into an art as tempered and as dispassionate.

On Richardson, the umbrage occasioned by *Joseph Andrews* had been having a far from bad effect, for in 1748 he published *Clarissa*—which one might call the corrective to *Pamela*. Here is the same situation, but with another approach—and from it breathes the real horror *Pamela* lacks. In her bitter struggle with Lovelace, Clarissa Harlowe has—unlike Pamela in her struggle with Mr. B.—nothing to gain. She is a young beauty, born to her own position, till lately adored by her proud family, and asking no more than to go on being tranquilly happy in her country home, Harlowe Place. In fact, she asks no more than to keep herself—but this is what Lovelace hates her to do. Threatened at home by an odious marriage, Clarissa is tricked into flight with Lovelace, who has continued to offer her a protection that should be completely disinterested. No sooner is she upon the road with him than he justifies her instinctive mistrust, and by a series of outrages breaks down—here is the core of the tragedy—the love for him she had been so ready to feel. In his hatred of what he calls her pride—though this hatred is knit up with a desperate love—he makes her suffer every abuse of the power from which she is unable to free herself. Clarissa, in the end, dies, but dies with her colours flying : though Lovelace, having drugged her, has once stolen her body, they both know that her spirit remains intact. Steadily, she has refused the marriage he offers: she cannot marry without love, cannot love without honour, and cannot honour the man who, by every action, has ruined his (not her own) honour in her eyes. One may say that, in this stand she took up, Clarissa was not only high above Pamela but very much in advance of her own time—in which (with a cynicism that was to last) marriage was supposed "to make everything all right." Clarissa may well have been found exacting. Was she, perhaps, proud ? Her sense of her own pathos does a little alienate us from her—"A young creature like I am," she often says.

The story is (like *Pamela*) told in letters : Clarissa and Lovelace each have confidants of their own sex. But the letters read more like journals : there are pages and pages of brilliant dialogue. Also, a circle of other characters is made to surround the hating lovers—most notable is the figure of Anna Howe, Clarissa's high-spirited, gallant girl friend, who has Mr. Hickman for quiet *fiancé*. But the outstanding figure of the book is not Clarissa ; it is Lovelace himself—the brilliant neurotic rake. The pathological complexities of Lovelace, the extravagance of his reactions are, I say firmly, absolutely convincing; I say this firmly because, by some critics, Lovelace has been denounced as "impossible."

Clarissa has a compactness (in spite of its great length) and a saturation in its own moral atmosphere to which few novels have so completely

TOBIAS SMOLLETT 1721-1771
Oil painting by an unknown Italian artist

attained. It has a convincingness nothing can break through. . . . In 1753
Richardson followed up with *Sir Charles Grandison*, the tale of a model
baronet and his ladies, but after *Clarissa* this lacks emotional power and
seems diffuse, artificial and slow. France as well as England wept over
Clarissa—but France was shocked by Fielding's ultra-English *Tom Jones*.
It is interesting to compare Fielding's masterpiece—published in 1749,
one year after *Clarissa*—with Richardson's. Fielding's conscience—or
call it morality—was a thing tempered out of his own furious living;
Richardson's conscience remained a theory—though a theory brought to
a fine point. The predicament of the conscience is the real preoccupation
of *Tom Jones*, in spite of the novel's lordly, spacious, picaresque overlay
and its rough-house scenes. Tom Jones, the handsome foundling, is a
bad lad who constantly disappoints the squire who brought him up and

deviates from his ideal love for Sophia. Circumstances combine to treat Tom hardly, and he hardily does what he can with them. Turned out by the squire, he rides the country with his self-seeking Sancho, Partridge, and, coming to London to seek Sophia, is more than half embroiled by all the wiles of the town. In Sophia Western, who "with all the gentleness which a woman can have, had all the spirit which she ought to have," Fielding creates the first of the English novel's adorable heroines. The book is, again, pre-eminent in its comedy characters : to have sat through *Hamlet* with Partridge, as Tom did, can have been only second in pleasure to sitting through *Hamlet* with Miss Bates. And there is Squire Western, baited in argument by his sister, that blue-stocking and snob, till "Damn Milton !" roars the suffering Squire. Squire Western remains the prototype of one very marked kind of landed English commoner. "I hate all lords," he says simply, "they are a parcel of courtiers and Hanoverians, and I will have nothing to do with them." That is that. The other type— more thoughtful but as feudal—is represented by Squire Allworthy. "Love," says Squire Allworthy, to the (apparently) erring Jenny Jones, "however much we may corrupt and pervert its meaning . . . remains a rational passion."

This idea—or ideal—of the rational passion is strong in Fielding, as it is in his race, as it was in his century. It had even been, in a sense, to this ideal that Richardson's bewildered Clarissa clung. And the idea of love on this plane has continued to rule the English novel—one may say that, to an extent, it has limited it. The French and the Russians have been left to explore love's inherent principles of disorder and pain.

Fielding's *Amelia* followed *Tom Jones* in 1751. While Fielding wrote this last novel he had been at once an ailing and, as a Westminster magistrate, a very busy man, and though the book shows no descent in feeling, it does show a certain decline in force. Amelia, the heroine, is a married woman, constantly tried but never disillusioned by the weaknesses of her husband, Captain Billy Bond. Her patience, with its triumphant saneness, on the whole suffers less than poor Billy's conscience—sporadic though that conscience may be.

I have given to Fielding and Richardson what may seem by the end of this book to be too much space. But surely they are important ? Not only are they our two innovators, but it seems to me that, in their different work, all later English novels are present in embryo. These two represent two opposed, but equally real, aspects of the English temperament—in a sense, all succeeding English novelists descend from one or other of them. Also, these two men, by the time that their work was finished, had sent out like a challenge their sense of the novel's power, and had shown, without attempting to limit, what was likely to be the English novel's

A GIPSY TELLING THE FORTUNES OF PAMELA AND MRS. JEWKES

An illustration to *Pamela* by Samuel Richardson

Oil painting attributed to J. F. Nollekens after the engraving by H. F. Gravelot

YORIK, THE MONK AND MADAME L— IN THE INN COURTYARD AT CALAIS
Water colour by Adam Buck
An illustration to *A Sentimental Journey* by Laurence Sterne

scope. I am sorry that, because of my use of space, I shall not be able to do anything like justice to Tobias Smollet, the Scotsman who, born in 1721, published his *Roderick Random* in 1748—the same year as *Clarissa*.

Of Smollet, it may be said briefly that he perfected the picaresque romance—he had all the stuff for this, for, disappointed in his early hopes as a dramatist, he had, a navy doctor, gone to sea. After five years of adventure he returned to London, where he set up as a surgeon in Downing Street. *Roderick Random*, with its attractive hero and quick-moving scenes, obtained a success that justified him in trusting his fortune to his pen. Smollet was—as far as I know—the first novelist to attempt to define the novel. "A novel," he says in one of his dedications, "is a large diffused picture, comprehending the characters of life, disposed in different groups and exhibited in various attitudes, for the purposes of a uniform plan. . . This plan," he adds, "cannot be executed with propriety, probability, or success, without a principal personage to attract the attention, unite the incidents, unwind the clue of the labyrinth, and at last close the scene, by virtue of his own importance." One criticism of Smollet is that his heroes fail to unite the incidents in the novels that they so often name—the incidents being too various for any one character to unite. He has, again, been accused of coarseness. In reality, the touchy, difficult Scotsman (few people knew him well) had a more delicate stomach than his contemporaries : the brutality that was the dark side of our Age of Reason inspired a sort of nausea in him—his reactions were the reactions of nausea. He excelled, perhaps overreached himself, in burleque. . . . His *Peregrine Pickle* came in 1751, *Ferdinand, Count Fathom* in 1753, and his last and best novel, *Humphry Clinker*, with its postillion hero, in 1771. He admitted he owed much to foreign influences, to Cervantes and to Lesage's *Gil Blas*. His great lack, as an artist, was equanimity. And he bred, through no fault of his own, a most regrettable host of imitators, who threatened again to bring the name of the novel down.

The subtlety lacking in Smollet was brought to a fine point in Laurence Sterne. Born in 1713, at Clonmel in Ireland, son of a poor lieutenant, Sterne, upon leaving Cambridge, took holy orders. During his twenty years cure of a Yorkshire parish his cloth did not debar him from the enjoyment of privileged eccentricity : he fiddled, shot, had a circle of wild friends, wrote sermons, and all the time revolved a number of matters in the white heat of his curious intellect. The result was to be *Tristram Shandy* —written in Yorkshire, published in London 1759. Contemporary London, dazzled, hardly knew what to think, and we hardly know how to speak now, of this unique book. *Tristram Shandy* bears no intellectual date. It is dementedly natural in its course, surrealist in its association of images. One does not attempt to "follow" *Tristram Shandy* ; one consigns oneself, dizzily, to it. This seems all the odder, because the plot

—in so far as there is any plot—is static. The characters—Mr. and Mrs. Shandy, Uncle Toby, Corporal Tim, Yorick the parson, the dapper doctor —stand still, but soar and enlarge from their roots like trees. Young Tristram spends much of his time as an embryo : by the end of the book he is about five years old. The Widow Wadman's appearance is brief and fatal. One may say that, in the pages of *Tristram Shandy*, one finds the whole of English fantasy charted—and what a fantasy! This is a book that inspires volumes : one cannot do much with it in a paragraph. Some people hate Sterne : they say he is maddening and indecent. He is indecent : whether he is maddening depends on you. . . . In 1768 he published the *Sentimental Journey*—a fluid, delicious, capricious and on the whole "easier" book.

Dr. Johnson's *Rasselas*, not exactly a novel, left its impressive mark on the century. It was Johnson who, through an act of kind interference, brought to light the distracted Goldsmith's *Vicar of Wakefield*. Oliver Goldsmith, born in Ireland 1728, and educated at Trinity College, Dublin, had come grimly poor to London, after a series of Continental adventures, only to find a grimmer poverty there. The manuscript of *The Vicar of Wakefield* had moved about with his person, in and out of debtors' prisons, for some years : when the book did come to be published, in 1766, the author still maintained in his preface, "There are an hundred faults in this thing." He can but have felt, however, how his book's spirit transcends possible faults. With *The Vicar of Wakefield*, the eighteenth century's first note of intimate tenderness has been struck. Here is true virtue— humble and tried. The Primrose family, with their innocence, their hopes and fears, their lyrical domesticity, exist in an element that seems hardly literature, so unlike is this to the air of another book. Here are the beauty and pathos of youthfulness—the Vicar himself seems hardly old. And when poor lovely Olivia stoops to folly, never did such true sadness surround a fall. As to writing—Goldsmith is the most delicate narrative stylist the eighteenth century put out. He adds to Defoe's directness a poetic lucidity of his own. His comic sense has something rueful about it—all the same, he adds, with the figure of Mrs. Primrose, to the English gallery of great silly women. Mrs. Shandy was there before her ; Mrs. Bennet is to join her soon. With this gem, *The Vicar of Wakefield*, the first great age of the English novel closed.

But the age has a footnote, or epilogue, that one must not miss. Miss Fanny Burney, though only born, at King's Lynn, Norfolk, in 1752, by which year Fielding and Richardson had already finished their best work, comes in time to contribute the woman's view of the Age of Reason and its society. In view of the prejudice against lady writers, Miss Burney not only published anonymously but wrote in secrecy and with some sense of guilt. However, Dr. Johnson's approval was later to justify her career. She was sheltered and nicely bred—the daughter of a doctor of music,

FRONTISPIECE TO FANNY BURNEY'S *EVELINA*
Engraving by Mortimer from the edition of 1791

whose move with his family up to London added interest to without ever
disturbing the tenor of his domestic life—and when she wrote her two
most successful novels she still knew little directly of the world. She,
however, contemplates scenes of callousness that amount to brutality with
just that equanimity Smollet lacked.

Fanny Burney lived to be Queen Charlotte's attendant at the secluded
Court, to be chased round Kew Gardens by poor King George III in one
of his fits of maniac playfulness, to record all this in a lively journal, and
to marry and share the misfortunes of a French emigré, M. D'Arblay.
Perhaps real life a little diminished her, for her early work is her best—

as having the freshness of someone who still expects much from experience. This freshness endears to us her young heroines. She is not a great novelist—her men are flat figures, though expertly cut out, and her women lack what she lacked : intellect, passion, irony—but she is an engaging, ingenious, often convincing one. *Evelina*, her first novel, published 1778, is the story of *A Young Lady's Entrance into the World*, with the vicissitudes —largely aggressions by vulgar people—that attended it. Fanny Burney's heroines, unlike Jane Austen's, seldom rise above those social miseries that it is their creator's special joy to describe. Could Evelina, for instance, had she found herself in Clarissa Harlowe's position, have suffered more than she does in being seen about with the awful Branghtons ? One doubts it. A subtle falseness of values impairs Fanny Burney's novels, for all their charm. In *Cecilia*, following *Evelina*, this weakness more plainly appears. Burney women, though they protest and blush, are made up of tacit acceptances. A *roué* could have seen Woman in these feminine novels and felt few stirrings of self-reproach ; he could ask, "Can one fundamentally wrong Woman, when she is not able to feel fundamental wrong?" The ardent spirit in woman had been already saluted by Fielding and Richardson : Jane Austen and the Brontës were later to make its voice heard.

W E must take it that now, for a few decades, the first great English impulse towards the novel, the social impulse, seemed to come to a pause. Already a revolt against Reason, and against its controlling effects, seemed to be on its way. The escape from society, this time, was not to be to the green glades of Arcadia but to the haunted castle and beetling crag. Fancy, so long kept down, now violently reasserted itself. Horace Walpole's *The Castle of Otranto* (1764) was followed by a whole spate of horrific-fantastic tales, featuring demon lovers, shrieks, vaults. This gothic sub-literature is a specialist's subject : I have only room here to name two of its practitioners, Monk Lewis and Mrs. Radcliffe—who closed the century with her *Mysteries of Udolpho* (1794). This crude opening of a romantic revival is, however, important, and must be noted : in it appears that shadowy, deep underneath of the English nature—a nature of which, in the great eighteenth-century novels, we have so far seen only the daylit, orderly top. (Though the dark has already come up through Richardson, with his "brown nodding horrors of elms and pines.") We shall observe how the nineteenth-century novelists attempted to keep in balance the English darkness and day. Apart from its gothic movement, the novel now tended to lapse and fall into disrepute. In quality it grew vapid ; in quantity it was overproduced. Extravagant sensibility gave it its strongest colour ; it was felt to threaten the not strong fortress of reason in a generation of Lydia Languishes.

JANE AUSTEN 1775-1817
Engraving after the water-colour drawing by her sister Cassandra Austen

JANE AUSTEN seems to belong to no century. Her "modernity" has been commented on—which is, I suppose, an agreeable way of saying that she is still some distance ahead of us. I have, earlier, coupled her name with Fielding's : she is like him in her feeling for comedy, her highness of spirit, and, most of all, in so completely not being a muff. She was born in 1775, in Hampshire, at Steventon, of which her father was rector, and her earlier novels were written, though not published, within the bounds of the eighteenth century. Publication dates—*Sense and Sensibility*, 1811 ; *Pride and Prejudice*, 1813 ; *Mansfield Park*, 1814 ; *Emma*, 1816 ; *Persuasion* with *Northanger Abbey*, 1818 (after her death)—do not represent her novel's actual order in her working life. *Persuasion* was, in fact, her last novel, but *Northanger Abbey*—which owes its initial satiric idea to Mrs. Radcliffe, as *Joseph Andrews* owed its to Richardson—had been written as far back as 1798, and *Pride and Prejudice*, under another title, was the first of her published novels to be written—in 1797, when she was twenty-two.

245

Herself a delighted reader of novels, Jane Austen saw no reason, and was to show no reason, why the novel should lapse from that place of honour that Fielding and Richardson gained for it. Her own and, I think, only explicit defence of the novel is to be come on early in *Northanger Abbey*, and here the spirit matches the irony. "Yes, novels," she says, ". . . performances which have only genius, wit and taste to recommend them." She took up her own pen, however, in no dogmatic spirit. She wrote, at her edge of the family parlour table, with just that zest for the scene and joy in discrimination with which she chose new ribbons, flirted and danced. But her genius was imperative. She surrounded each subject she took up with every feeling and faculty that she had. There has been a tendency to accept Jane Austen as no more than a faultless practitioner of the minute : her own remark (to a too fervent clergyman) about the two inches of ivory has been held against her. It is true that she made no effort to pass, through art, outside the range of her own, a gentlewoman's, experience : her novels depict the lives of leisured young men and women in country houses or on visits to Bath or London. Men (and women) in action were her subject, and with her vivid precision she placed action where, by the chance of her birth, she most often saw it—in drawing-rooms and ballrooms, on lawns, in shopping streets. But what she at once depicted and penetrated was not just *a* world, it was *the* world. She arrived at, and was able to fix for us, the denominators of desire, self-delusion and passion that are common to every kind of human experience. Her view of life, in fact, if confined to, was not confined by, drawing-rooms and lawns. She applies big truths to little scenes—so no scene stays "little" under her hand. The constraints of polite behaviour serve only to store up her characters' energies ; she dispels, except for the very stupid, the fallacy that life with the lid off—in thieves' kitchens, prisons, taverns and brothels—is necessarily more interesting than life with the lid on. It is true she has drawn no rebels : her people expect, and derive, pleasure from the straight-forward living of life. But they plan ; they seek, with degrees of determination, ideal circumstances, ideal relationships inside that world they already know. They locate, and never far from themselves, possible darkness, chaos ; they feel the constant threat of the wrong—be this only a mean act, a callous or a designing remark, a subtly deceiving proposition, a lie. The world Jane Austen creates remains an absolute world because of its trueness to its own scale.

Not only the charm but the strength of Jane Austen's novels resides in their being so innately grown-up. In enjoying the youthfulness of her women—most youthful of all in their mistakes—we are at the same time conscious of something in them that remains ageless and poised. So high is this norm of maturity that infantilism, in one form or another, appears as the root of all faults and absurdities : it is imperfect grown-upness that makes people brag, fuss, prattle, play-act or flatter themselves. Among the heroines, poise appears most in her first, Elizabeth Bennet, and in her last, Anne Elliot. But also, Emma Woodhouse retains a lovable balance throughout her headstrong career, and deluded, naïve little Catherine Morland keeps not only Henry Tilney's but the reader's respect. Fanny Price and Elinor Dashwood remain just a shade too sober for many tastes. But one must see that Fanny's sobriety gives much to the structure of *Mansfield Park*, while Elinor acts as the counterpoise to unstable, brilliant Marianne. . . . Jane Austen has also been criticised for an imperfect evaluation of love : it is said that her leisurely, civilised young creatures deny to the passion its true place. She was a great supporter of the rational passion, and the young men allowed to inspire this in her brilliant and her fastidious women are not—with the major exceptions of Mr. Darcy and volatile Henry Tilney—men whom one feels would inspire much. Her tempting alternatives to reason—Willoughby, Frank Churchill, Henry Crawford—are always better done. But, as against this, with what gallant sparkling composure, almost Shakespearean, her heroines' flirtations are conducted, and with what fineness the early shades of attraction are recognised ! Silence always falls on couples of plighted lovers—as though feeling paused outside a door. And, *Persuasion*—could there be a deeper picture of a woman loving too late, apparently without hope ?

Technically—that is, as to matters of form, plot, characterisation, dialogue, setting—Jane Austen remains the most nearly flawless of English novelists. She could not have been other than English—yet she stands a little apart from other writers we have in an artistry that no sentiment blurred, no theory narrowed and no rancour or prejudice side-tracked.

BORN, north of the Border, four years before Jane Austen—in fact, in 1771—Sir Walter Scott was to release England's imagination. Desire for exaltation, love of strangeness, had so far given birth only to gothic tales : Jane Austen had ridiculed mystery. Scott's majestic narrative poems—*The Lay of the Last Minstrel*, 1805 ; *Marmion*, 1808 ; *The Lady of the Lake*, 1810—had first made England look North, and look North with awe. One was met by a landscape dark with clouds and feeling, charged with the past, lost battles, old memories and relentless dreams, a landscape against which the human figure could only stand out in heroic acts. England, who long ago with the Stuarts had accepted a line of Scottish kings, now began to drink in the Scottish tradition—a tradition that returned Fate to its place. (Eighteenth-century England, in common with most of rational Europe, had up to now stressed will rather than fate.) Scott, when he turned to the novel, showed the first great impulse that owed nothing to the sense of society—though it owed everything to the sense of race. What Scott did for his own country in giving voice to its nature is Scotland's and not England's affair : what is certain is that he rushed in on England to fill an emotional vacuum. For the mannered, dry-witted age of the Regency, Jane Austen perfected the novel of manners but this same age received, as though it were parched, Scott's novels that rolled down on it like rain-clouds. And about the man himself there was something warm and commanding that seemed to mellow the air.

The first of his novels, *Waverley*, appeared in 1814—same year as *Mansfield Park*. *Guy Mannering* followed in 1815 ; *The Antiquary* shared 1816 with *Emma*. From then on, the Scott novels are too numerous and regular to enumerate ; outstanding names and dates are : *The Heart of Midlothian* (1818), *The Bride of Lammermoor* (1819), *Ivanhoe* (1820), *Kenilworth* (1821), *Peveril of the Peak* (1822), *Quentin Durward* (1823), *Redgauntlet* (1824), *Woodstock* (1826), *The Fair Maid of Perth* (1828). *Count Robert of Paris* and *Castle Dangerous*, his last two short novels, appeared in 1832—the year of his death.

The idea of the historical novel was in itself, to the England of that day, new. Novelty, linked with its own outstanding power, secured for *Waverley* immediate success. The past, with its accumulation of feeling, was presented with the likeliness of the present day. And when Scott dealt with his own day, as in *Guy Mannering* and *The Antiquary*, past-like emotion gave depth to the scene. He was less happy when, as a *tour de force*, he adventured—as in *Ivanhoe*, *The Talisman*, *Kenilworth*—into English history : reconstruction here is too obvious ; the scenes seem to be cardboard, the people thin. He cut his art off, in fact, from its natural source when he detached himself from his own native mystery. He was truly creative only in regard to his own land. His people are epic figures or nothing, and he could see the epic only in people he instinctively knew. So his novels have their own psychic atmosphere.

Most of the plots contain some major heroic passion. The characters range from great to lowly—many are simple, wanderers, naïve narrative talkers, the trustful, the half-crazed. Scott's treatment of sexual love is stilted—less dishonest than shy. Love with him is always involved with some other aspect of fate. His style depends on emotion for force and lift; so that, when at times the emotion behind it lapses, one feels let down, and resents the verbosity. But such a style, with its poetic richness, was bound, coming when it did, to fecundate English prose. I am less concerned to claim Scott's Scottish novels for England than to show their effect on the English novelists.

The effect was, on the whole, a loosening one. As such, it was strongly resisted by William Makepeace Thackeray, who, son of a British official in India, had been born near Calcutta in 1811. Thackeray vowed himself to the anti-heroic. Consciously unfortunate Victorian, he was preyed upon by nostalgia for the eighteenth century—seldom does a nostalgia set in so soon. With him it was a case of "Of thee I dream. . . ." Not only did he regret his own place in time, but he is said to have felt that he could

'GEORGY MAKES ACQUAINTANCE WITH A WATERLOO MAN'
An illustration to Thackeray's *Vanity Fair*
Engraving by Thackeray for the first edition, 1849

have written better had he not been English : this seems strikingly true.
Also, much happened to damp down in Thackeray anything like a spontaneous love of life—having received a gentleman's education, and formed
along with that a gentleman's ample tastes, he lost his money and was
condemned for some time to a seedy existence abroad : when he married,
his wife became insane after four years. He lacked the resilience of Fielding,
whom he so much admired ; and in his attempts at realism he was infected,
more than he may have realised, by the insincerities of his period.

Need to repair his fortunes in the first place drove Thackeray to the
pen. He had been writing for papers for some years, under varying pseud-
onyms and with increasing success, when *Vanity Fair*, with his own name
on the covers, began to appear in monthly parts in the year 1847-8—all
but a hundred years after *Tom Jones*. This first and great novel of Thackeray's creates for itself an epoch. It was an ambitious book that had not
failed. Prodigal in incident, character, sense of period, saturated in
humour, spontaneous in its criticism of life, it is in form, at the same time,
absolutely controlled. Possibly Thackeray's natural bent was to write
about wicked people rather than good. The *Vanity Fair* characters, stamped
with life for ever, are headed by that great bad girl Becky Sharp, whose

249

career across other lives her creator follows with a submerged laugh and, I think, some submerged love. The good—through their imperfect virtue —are fooled : Thackeray sees the vice in a sentiment. The length and variety of the book—there is everything in it from a good-bye to a girl's school to drama before the battle of Waterloo—are part of its merit : it suited Thackeray's powers to take a panoramic view of experience. He here uses perfectly his astringent style. The sub-title is *A Novel without a Hero*—and, in fact, there is no one central character, and nobody that one is enjoined to admire ; he gave the book a moral rather than human plan. But this does not make it either abstract or cold. *Vanity Fair* is entrancing, engaging from first to last.

What happened to Thackeray after this ? His powers, after *Vanity Fair*, seem to me to have horribly misdirected themselves. His conceptions remain spacious, his style sometimes masterly and always efficient. But I think he made a mistake in abandoning the complete moral detachment of *Vanity Fair*. In attempting to put across "good" people, in attempting to make disillusionments a matter of tragedy rather than comedy, he commits himself to a sentimentality that is at once laboured and insincere. His anti-heroicism involves every character in the same tepid atmosphere. His *Esmond* (1852) is important as being the first *English* historical novel : the period of the story is Queen Anne. Thackeray, steeped in the Augustine Age, could now give his nostalgias rein : Steele, Swift, Addison walk and talk through the pages—but they seem to creak. In fact, throughout *Esmond* one gets the feeling that damp has got into the works. The triangular situation between Esmond, Lady Castlewood and her daughter Beatrix is boldly conceived but timidly handled—Thackeray may have had this in mind when he implied that he would have liked to be French.

Pendennis (1848) had preceded *Esmond* ; *The Newcomes* (1853-5) followed it. These two novels are interesting as documents of Thackeray's own class—the upper-middle—and age—the early Victorian. They contain some portraits of detestable women, fatally well drawn. *Pendennis*, *The Newcomes* are shells of great novels—or should one say great shells of novels ? But life—and surely they once had life ? seems to have evaporated from them. Over good Colonel Newcome does anybody survive who could shed a tear ? . . . No, the loose rich romantic fullness of Scott certainly did nothing to Thackeray.

As an acknowledged influence on Dickens, I do not remember having heard Scott named—but there must have been something propitious to Dickens's temperament in the atmosphere Scott had left behind. Dickens's subjects are as superficially prosaic as Scott's are evidently poetic, but romantic energy is common to both. Charles Dickens was born at Portsmouth in 1812—a year after Thackeray. His father was a dockyard clerk whose character was to be idealised into Mr. Micawber ; his mother is said to have inspired Mrs. Nickleby. Such an alliance was not likely to

'I AM HOSPITABLY RECEIVED BY MR. PEGGOTTY'
An illustration to Dickens's *David Copperfield*
Engraving by H. K. Browne ("Phiz")

make for domestic stability : the family tottered along and now and then crossed the line that divides fecklessness from declared ruin. After a move to London there came a crash, and little Charles, as a debtor's visiting son, became familiar with the Marshalsea debtors' prison.   To support himself, the boy of twelve worked in a blacking factory, filling and labelling pots. His father's release from prison set him free to attend a seedy school ; he picked up enough learning to make himself into a solicitor's clerk. Later he taught himself shorthand, and, as reporter for several papers, sat in the gallery of the House of Commons. This was to be only one phase of his career as a journalist. He knocked about England, saw and tackled life, drew conclusions, collected fantastic facts. All his youth he had been an omnivorous reader ; his feeling for "story" had been developed young. So he wrung the most out of every experience : nothing that happened to Dickens went to waste. The class from which Dickens sprang—the English shabby-genteel, holding tight to the fringe of respectability—had been up to now ignored by art and society. It was the pathetic product of an age ruled by commercial ideas of success, in which human values were crude and on the whole mean. England was still unwilling to cope with the bad conditions industrialism created. Can one wonder at Dickens's exaltation—call it sentimental—of the good heart ? Can one wonder at his tenderness for the devices of fancy by which underdog people manage to live ? The sociological aspect of Dickens I have not got room to discuss here. But remember that he had first been thrust into, and had later explored by his own will, abysses of injustice and human waste. Though success met him early—in fact, with the publication of the *Pickwick Papers*, in monthly parts, in 1836—he never ceased to feel what he had seen. The buoyancy of his spirits did not make him a less implacable moralist. He brought up his picturesque, persuasive, sometimes extravagant art against the well-fed callousness that comes largely from lack of imagination—and he did live to see some reforms. He chose to appeal to feeling rather than thought—he *was* violently sentimental : leave it at that. But defiantly, perhaps involuntarily, what an artist he was! There is something superbly childish—I mean, unspoilt—about his imagination. He gives a child's value—a poor child's—to the enjoyment of sheer physical bliss—warm lit rooms, trustworthy faces, the roar of a fire, the succulence of a chop. At the same time, he keeps a child's apprehensiveness of the weird, the unknown, the unsubstantially threatening. He gives loneliness, sense of loss or sense of betrayal all the frightful force they have for a child. Though he draws unconvincing or sugary pictures of "straight" love, he is first-rate at depicting the sinister attachment—such as Rosa Dartle's to Steerforth—also, in the depiction of hero-worship. In fact, into all the love affairs in his books a queer adolescent strain of hero-worship, or idealisation, enters on one or the other side. His linked senses of threat and of friendliness make him second to no other writer in penetrating the atmospheres of landscapes, houses and streets. And he is frightening in his sense of the power of all kinds of obsession and fantasy.

He was too much embroiled with his subject to be detached in his style. But his emotional vision sometimes produces the most mobile kind of English romantic prose. Read, for instance, the passage beginning "The waters are out in Lincolnshire . . ." in Chapter II. of *Bleak House*. *Bleak House* (1852-3) seems to me the most impressive, *David Copperfield* (1849-50) the most august and tender, and *Great Expectations* (1860-1) the most original of Dickens's novels. But no name of a novel of his is unknown, and few of his novels, I think, remain unread. In him the English genius finds a wide course : he is as comprehensive as any writer we have. His zest and humour have been likened to Fielding's. But he has in common with Richardson his perception of the nervous, or dusky, side of the human make-up.

When Dickens died, he left unfinished a mystery story, *Edwin Drood*. His growing preoccupation with mystery was due to his friendship with Wilkie Collins, who, born in 1824, was to do brilliantly in this genre. Wilkie Collins, in fact, may be called the grandfather of the English detective story. He had not only a great sense of human drama but a

A LITERARY GATHERING IN 1844
Charles Dickens reading *The Chimes* to his friends in Forster's chambers
Pencil drawing by Daniel Maclise

command, to be envied, of "atmospheric" style—see the description of the tree-muffled Hampshire mansion at midnight, and of the dead lake, in *The Woman in White*. He also created—as in Count Fosco—superbly sinister figures, and drew some unforgettable scenes. His two greatest stories are *The Woman in White* (1860) and *The Moonstone* (1868).

Anthony Trollope, another friend of Dickens, has only lately come into his own again. Less intellectual and fastidious but also less arid than Thackeray, more stolid and less fantastic than Dickens, he seems to me the most sheerly able of the English Victorian novelists. He was honest enough about his own age to be able to give an objective picture of it ; he was less affected by pruderies than prepared to make discreet allowance for them. One cannot deny that, with the nineteenth century, a sort of fog did begin, in the English novel, to obscure some vital aspects of life. It became more difficult to write greatly because it became less possible to write truly. There was facetiousness on the subject of class, squeamishness on the subject of sex. One could no longer travel straight across country, as the eighteenth-century novelists had done. Evasions made for sentimentality. Anthony Trollope probably recognised that, for the Victorian novelist, absolute integrity was impossible ; but he made towards an integrity of his own. . . . Born in 1815, three years after Dickens, he had an unhappy childhood (see his *Autobiography*) : he seemed to himself to be born at a disadvantage—which makes one all the more admire the

253

CHARLOTTE BRONTË 1816-1855
Chalk drawing by George Richmond

saneness with which he reconciled himself with life. First as a clerk, then as a civil servant (travelling in the pay of the Post Office), he had had usefully varied experience : he got to know all grades of society and to enjoy the stretch of the English scene. The geniality that he arrived at breathes, never speciously, through his novels—whose increasing success made him able to leave the Post Office and give to his new profession his full time. He wrote hard, and under prosaic conditions.

Trollope is most remembered for his clergymen : in the famous Barsetshire novels he seals up for ever the atmosphere and the personalities of an English cathedral town. He immortalised also English squires, peers, professional people and politicians. Also, I know few writers better than Trollope at conveying the charm of a charming scene. Many of his comedy characters—for instance, the incorrigible Bertie of *Barchester Towers*—are first rate. He can—as in *The Warden*—at once honour and analyse the English conscience at its most austere. He has the merit of being a very masculine writer. If he fought shy of passion, he created

MRS. GASKELL 1810-1865
Chalk drawing by George Richmond

women who could inspire it : he puts the English heroine back on the map again ; his young women are lovely, ardent, intelligent, capable, true. In some of them—especially Mary Thorne—the gallant spirit once more appears. After several early tries at the novel, Trollope arrived with *The Warden* (1855). The rest of the Barsetshire novels followed. He embarked with *Phineas Finn* (1869) on a political series—less well known now because less well done : Disraeli was far better in this genre. In *Can You Forgive Her?* (1864) he tackled the subject of erring womanhood. Before he died he had written sixty novels in all.

THE Brontë genius remains a phenomenon of all, not only of English, literature. Haworth vicarage, exposed on the wilds of Yorkshire, was the home of this family : pilgrims now gaze around the vicarage as though the force of the Brontë living must have left its mark on these darkish walls. The Rev. Patrick Brontë had come from the North of

Ireland : of his marriage, in 1812, there were six children—two daughters who died at a boarding-school for the daughters of clergymen, then Charlotte (1816), Patrick Branwell, Emily (1818), Anne (1820). By 1822 the family were motherless : poverty, isolation, very delicate health made up the medium of their existences. As children they roamed the moors. Charlotte went for some time to the school—the Lowood of *Jane Eyre*—that had killed her sisters. Branwell—a character so sinister that he started a darker part of the Brontë legend—took drugs, wasted money and kept the family feeling at burning point. The sisters went out as governesses : Charlotte and Emily, in order to learn languages, attached themselves for a time to the Pensionnat Heger, in Brussels. In 1846 the three sisters together published *Poems by Currer, Ellis and Acton Bell*. Charlotte's first novel, *The Professor*, failed to find a publisher, but in 1847 *Jane Eyre*, "by Currer Bell," appeared. And in that same year came *Wuthering Heights* by the "Ellis Bell" who was Emily. Anne Brontë published two gentler novels, *Agnes Grey* and *The Tenant of Wildfell Hall*. By the close of 1849 Branwell, Emily and Anne were dead—it was a wonder that they had lived so long. Charlotte, in that year, published *Shirley ; Villette*, a reconstruction of *The Professor*, appeared in 1853. A year later she married her father's curate, but she was to die in 1855. *The Professor* was published after her death. Old Mr. Brontë was left alone at Haworth : none of his children had reached the age of forty.

But it is an ageless fire that burns in the novels the Brontës left. The sisters were young chiefly in having lost none of their vehemence ; they were involved with little outside themselves—only Charlotte at all came to terms with life. Emily, having consumed her own lonely experience, translated experience to an unearthly plane. *Wuthering Heights* is a book of fire and ice : no book has ever been better named. It is raged through, as by a wind, by a damned soul—the fated, fatal Heathcliff. The love in it is relentless, as pure of hope as it is of flesh. The house is solitary, exposed . . . . here is the real English dark tower of passion above all rationality. All the same, the material setting is circumstantial; the story is full of pictures stored in Emily's living eye—the feathers plucked from the pillow, the two children in the tree in the wind. The Thrushcross firelight, with its domestic promise, by contrast darkens the darkness that is the lovers' home. And the love of Heathcliff and Catherine gains in poetic intensity by being set back inside a complex prosaic form—much of the narrative is in the idiom of "ordinary" people ; the consternation of limited people frames the unlimited tragedy.

Wuthering Heights bears no definite feminine stamp—though perhaps only a woman could have liberated her spirit so completely. Charlotte Brontë's *Jane Eyre*, on the other hand, gains force by being woman from beginning to end. Made in this voice, the plain, proud, unhesitating assertion of woman's feeling for man—Jane's for Rochester—shocked the

SIR WALTER SCOTT 1771-1832
Oil painting by Sir Thomas Lawrence

WILLIAM MAKEPEACE THACKERAY 1811-1863
Oil painting by John Gilbert

'OUR SOCIETY'
An illustration by Hugh Thomson to Mrs. Gaskell's *Cranford*

England of 1847. It had been the accepted idea that, while woman might, by very judicious degrees, respond to declared love, she did not initiate love on her own account—to do so was more than doubtful, it was "unwomanly." So *Jane Eyre*, in spite of its actually faultless morals, took on an odour of impropriety—which is not to say that it was not read. If Jane, the plain little sprite of a governess, does not court her employer Rochester, she challenges him in Cleopatra's voice : their scene in the July dusk of the garden is unforgettable. Jane wants much more than love ; she wants human fullness of life—the book voiced, for the first time, woman's demand for this. Read the scene where, alone on the roof of the country house, Jane looks out over the country and cries for movement, achievement, adventure—feeling the masculine part of her spirit stir. Might this be called the first feminist novel ? The nature of her struggle with Rochester, who, when his existing marriage has been discovered, wants her to be his mistress, shows the hundred years' difference between Jane and Clarissa. But Jane, like Clarissa Harlowe, still identifies virtue with the power to keep her fate in her own hands. . . . *Jane Eyre*, set nearer to every-day life than *Wuthering Heights*, has a few social improbabilities in which the Brontë lack of worldly experience shows. Temperamental black-whiskered Rochester may fall a prey to our laughter ; the black-souled Heathcliff never does. Charlotte Brontë, naïve, starved of beauty and luxury, rather over-describes gilded scenes—the drawing-room lit for a party, the harpy charmer's veneer. But there is something endearing about this weakness of hers. In *Shirley* she also portrays glamour—the glamour of Shirley's dashing temperament. After *Jane Eyre, Villette*—with its foreign atmosphere of waxed floors and cold windows, the romantic rigidity of the boarding school—is her best book. . . . At a time when male approval, coupled with money, gave woman the only status she had, it is remarkable that the only giant novels should have been written by spinster daughters of an obscure indigent clergyman.

After the Brontës, George Eliot—really Mary Ann Evans—may seem opaque and pedestrian. Not for nothing did she assume a masculine name. Her intellect must be honoured—it is more constructive than brilliant—her emotion is gravely coloured by it. She was at grips with the problems of her day. If not an attractive, she was a great, woman : as an artist she is never to be despised. Born in 1819, daughter of a land-agent, she, in helping her father with his business, early took a hand in practical life. Courageous in her emotions, she lived for years in free union with George Henry Lewes—not the least of a group of advanced thinkers to whom her propensities had attracted her. Experience had made her know many people ; imagination made her penetrate them. Provincial-Midland-England is the scene of her best books—and, above all, she knew the yeoman class. She had her own sense of beauty—best seen in *Middlemarch* (1871), *Scenes from Clerical Life* (1858), and *The Mill on the Floss* (1860). She had humour, but is greatest in tragedy, which with her is found more in character (with its misuse or vain sacrifices of will) than in fate. *Felix Holt the Radical* was, in 1866, the rather stark intellectual high-point of her career. For the emotional interest one expects from a novel she is best in *Adam Bede* (1859) and *Silas Marner* (1861). She can write with a faultless convincingness, and with a noble sweep of imagination—apart from this, her books, with their palpable truth to life, are important as documents of their day.

All the same, in my heart I prefer Mrs. Gaskell—as sincere a person, a less major artist and a more feminine soul. Born in 1810, she had been a beautiful Chelsea girl, reared on a succession of country visits. She married a Unitarian minister and lived, worked and felt with him in Manchester, among "the dark satanic mills." Her reaction to the injustices she found in industrial England of that day was of the heart, but was ruled by her steady head : unlike Dickens, she never overpainted ; truth seemed to her good, and bad, enough. She never lost her love—and perhaps her nostalgia—for the sweet, the comely, the orderly, the agreeable, though these, to warrant her love, must be founded on moral right. Happy in her own life as a woman, she was keenly aware of injustices done to her sex in the name of morality—she wrote her bold *Ruth* in 1853. Before this had come *Mary Barton, a Tale of Manchester Life* (1848), which is a document of the Chartist year. Called the first "labour" novel, it prays for improved understanding between masters and men. *North and South* is much in the same vein. *Cranford*, that delicious idyll of gentility, appeared the

'GEORGE ELIOT' 1819-1880
Chalk drawing by Sir Frederick W. Burton

same year as *Ruth*—to which it is a counterpoise. It is *Cranford*, with its immortal old ladies, that keeps Mrs. Gaskell's name so widely known and loved in the world. Reading *Cranford* after Jane Austen's *Emma*—that other picture of an enclosed society—one is conscious of the change there had been in England in the forty years between those two books. Emma Woodhouse's Highbury is unthreatened ; Miss Matty's Cranford is not— behind its orderly, small-town silence one feels vibrations from "Drumble" —the not distant out-spreading Manchester. . . . In the *Wives and Daughters* she did not live to finish (she died in 1865) Mrs. Gaskell returns to the Southern scene. With these four Victorian women writers we seem to come to the close of a period : we pass from the Mid-Victorian to the Late. The change is, rather, in attitude : the actual dates of authors overlap.

Several of George Meredith's novels, for instance, were contemporaries of George Eliot's, and his first, *The Shaving of Shagpat*, appeared only nine years after *Wuthering Heights*. He was born in 1828—and was to live on into our century. He was of Welsh extraction, and went to a Moravian school in Wales : his grandfather had been a successful tailor—a fact that was to be dug up by those enemies who accused him of snobbery (there was something less arid than snobbery in Meredith's love of the truly grand). On his return from school to London he became a solicitor's clerk, but published his first *Poems* (containing *Love in a Valley*) in 1851. These drew the attention, and later the friendship, of Rossetti and Swinburne to the brilliant young man. In fact, he was able to develop his talents in an atmosphere that was most propitious to them. He became the first English novelist with a conscious aesthetic—this may account for the *hauteur* of his style—and, more, he had a philosophy, as opposed to a general theory of right and wrong.

His poetry provides the key to his novels. Able to leave the solicitor's office for journalism, Meredith, from his room in Rossetti's house, wrote only for papers whose reputation did nothing to damage his promising name. Grub Street never really impinged on him. His first marriage failed : in 1864, one year after his second, he went to live at Flint Cottage, Box Hill, Surrey, which remained his home for the rest of his long life.

As a novelist Meredith has been found obscure, besides being a little too unaware of the banal side of human experience. The complex content of his prose does sometimes choke it—his poetry, on the other hand, continues to burn with intellectual vision. It has been argued that he should have kept to poetry. But his poems—culminating in *Modern Love* and *The Woods of Westermain*—are essentially those of a novelist. And without his novels, his smashing intellectual humour, his capricious descriptions would have been lost. Perhaps as a novelist he suffers from having lived too much in an eclectic world—unlike Thackeray, Dickens, Trollope, he can seldom have been mortified or bored. He tends to precipitate his characters—who are themselves, from their start in his brain, dynamic—into rather too special an atmosphere. His novels are, in a sense, too like operas.

All the same, it was Meredith who produced that almost faultless novel *The Egoist* (1879), in which the best of the English comedy spirit flowers—at once satirical and rotund. The plot ?—a high-minded baronet is more truly, less kindly seen by a young lady than was Sir Charles Grandison. Here, too, Meredith perfects, in the best tradition, a purely English scene. One might say that his scenes are more likely, on the whole, than his characters—these, though vivid, being at times out of drawing. His sense of heroic promise in people is shadowed by his sense of their weaknesses : "We are betrayed by what is false within." He adored love, and shows it as adorable—all the same, he sees it as an ordeal—his early *The Ordeal of Richard Feverel* (1859) even takes its title from this idea. His stories about the youngness of young men deal with evolution rather than with adventure. Sometimes he applies his vision to politics, to national aspiration, to the

GEORGE MEREDITH 1828-1909
Chalk drawing by William Strang

international scene : some of his novels range far abroad. His heroines move through Olympian air : one charge against them has been that they talk too much. In his famous *Diana of the Crossways* (1885) he undertakes the defence of a noble creature. *Evan Harrington* (1861), *Rhoda Fleming* (1865), *Vittoria* (1867), *Beauchamp's Career* (1876), *The Amazing Marriage* (1895) also stand high with Meredith readers. He may be attacked, but he cannot be overlooked : I feel certain that he will stand the test of time.

Samuel Butler belongs in this period from having been born in 1835. His reputation, however, has been cumulative, and his importance continues to grow to-day. Grandson of the great bishop of that same name, he, on leaving Cambridge, renounced the intention of taking holy orders and went out to New Zealand, to sheep-farm. Successful in this, he also began to write. Returning to London he took up painting, and exhibited at the Royal Academy. It was in 1872 that he published his satire *Erewhon*— which has been likened to *Gulliver's Travels*. Butler might, indeed, be called the nineteenth-century Swift—comprehensive, at once enraged and precise. Grievance—his whole bent was to science, but he held himself to be boycotted by a group of accredited scientists—at once warped him and steeled his curious power. He has many aspects, but comes into the scope of this book because of his one novel, *The Way of All Flesh*. He began this in 1872 ; he laid it aside in 1885—and it was not published till 1903. It is at once a hate-charged and scientific analysis of English middle-class family life (as embodied in the Pontifex family), especially of the relationship between parents and children, and its effects. It was well for the English eighteen-seventies and 'eighties, with their placid system of family reverence, that *The Way of All Flesh*, though in their time being written, was held up and did not explode on them. 1903 was quite soon enough. *The Way of All Flesh*, coming just when it did, has inspired a whole school of iconoclast novels.

Thomas Hardy was born, near the Dorchester he was to rechristen Casterbridge, in 1840, twelve years after Meredith. These two Late-Victorian novelists have in common that they were both poets. But while Meredith might be called a magnificent by-product of the English genius, Hardy is a figure in its direct line. In fact, his is a figure in which many tendencies culminate. The strangeness of his novels—a strangeness as great, at times, as that of *Wuthering Heights*—is counterpoised by their pervasive physical naturalness. He was England's first regional novelist—setting his stories in a tract he called Wessex, that centres on his own county of Dorsetshire. But whereas other regional novelists simply use, Hardy created, local colour : he confers a sort of super-existence on the region he wrote about. It would be true to say that Hardy did for his part of England what Scott had done for the Border. But a whole extension of complex human experience lies between the two. Scott's country people are walking traditions ; Hardy's are sharply individualised : there is not one "type" in the whole of his gallery. Scott revived the dignity of the past ; Hardy, although the past works in him, is moved by a philosophic consciousness of the future.

Of the hero of *The Return of the Native* (1878) he says, for instance : "In Clym Yeobright's face could dimly be seen the typical countenance of the future. Should there be a classic period to art hereafter, its Phidias may reproduce such faces. The view of life as a thing to be put up with, replacing that zest for existence which was so intense in early civilisations, must ultimately enter so thoroughly into the constitution of the advanced races that its facial expression will be accepted as a new artistic departure. People already feel that a man who lives without disturbing a curve of feature, or setting a mark of mental concern upon himself, is too far from modern perceptiveness to be a modern type. . . . The observer's eye was arrested, not by his face as a picture, but by his face as a page ; not by what it was but what it recorded. His features were attractive in the light of symbols. . . ." "The view of life as a thing to be put up with"—what a long way the human spirit had travelled by the time Hardy wrote that. There is, throughout his feeling for nature, the same sublime awareness of an endurance. Egdon Heath, in the timeless November dusk, as yet crossed by no figure, occupies the first chapter of *The Return of the Native*. "It was at present a place perfectly accordant with man's nature—neither ghastly, hateful nor ugly : neither commonplace, unmeaning or tame ; but, like man, slighted and enduring, and withal singularly colossal and mysterious in its swarthy monotony."

But meekness is no note of Hardy's characters. His young men and women, each one singularly alone, each raise a kind of cry for perfection—through intellectual or moral achievement, through love. Each one is made dynamic either by a desire or an idea. The most alive of the men are creatures of intellect ; the most alive of the women are creatures of passion. But he has also created the character that is stable and philosophic—born, one might say, already half reconciled. Very often such people are very simple : old lore, inherited wisdom speak through them.

The Return of the Native (1878), *Tess of the D'Urbevilles* (1891), and *Jude the Obscure* (1896), all three of them tragedies, have been recognised as the greatest of Hardy's novels. All have their superhumanly human scenes—Eustacia tending her solitary beacon fire, Tess waking from her bridal sleep to the fatal sunrise of Stonehenge, Jude's love Sue raising her sick husband to see the sunset reflected in a bedroom mirror. Hardy's art is, above all, diverse. His comedy spirit is, therefore, august and mellow. Merry-making, weddings and village dancing, the comic charm of bravado, naïve, racy talk, the emanation of magic from a beautiful woman, the delicious negligent poise of a pretty one, the fine day and the fine fellow, the strong sweep of hope and the long sweep of open country come equally into his range. His style, sublime at its greatest, does sometimes lapse into bathos ; his dialogue, at its best idiomatic, alive with natural rhythm, has reaches of stilted unlivingness. But the architecture of his novels cannot be criticised : it is beyond praise. Hardy, after a meagre education, did in fact qualify and for years practice as an architect—so from one art to another he carried sound rules. And, his conception of life being elemental the poet in him fused with the novelist. His outstanding novels, other than those I have mentioned, are : *Under the Greenwood Tree* (1872), *Far from the Madding Crowd* (1874), *The Mayor of Casterbridge* (1886), *The Woodlanders* (1887).

ENGLAND cannot really claim Henry James, though he claimed England by coming to live here and becoming in 1916 a naturalised Englishman. An American, born in New York State in 1843, he became, while still a young man, familiar with what was civilised in both hemispheres. In their high, wise kind of sophistication, his novels are cosmopolitan. At the same time, he keeps, in his observations, the alert austerity of the pioneer. He writes at once with the detachment of a spectator and the close-upness of someone under a spell. He might be called the analyst of civilisation—and from this point of view England, with its enigmas, its inconsistencies, its puzzling, superb survivals, fascinated him. And, as a novelist, he was fascinated by the phenomenon of the English conscience. His affinities, as an artist in writing, were to artists abroad—Flaubert, Turgeniev—but he was to crown England, at the close of one century and the start of another, with a series of novels that penetrated to the essential Englishness of her scene. One might say that she had not been so completely perceived before.

One may say that James's perceptions only worked in the particular area of his social tastes. He had an aesthetic love of the *beau monde*—whether it be of artists or aristocrats. As in Meredith's case, desire attracted him to the people and settings of which he wrote. Any character in a Henry James story or novel, however low his or her stated class in life, is promoted—by being made articulate or susceptible—to his or her place in James's *beau monde*. And he makes the same promotions in age as he does in class : even his children are, in their fineness, mature. In a sense, his adults are child-like, in having crystalline natures. The fact was, that James could only use the *fine* nature—whether evil or good—for his very special treatment of the predicament. And predicament was his subject, at every time. His sense of beauty is matched by his sense of evil : his villains do worse than oppress or threaten—they subtly and immeasurably corrupt. His innocent characters move through danger zones ; the spirit is in peril, seldom the flesh. Evil only operates quite directly in a few of the James stories—the great example is *The Turn of the Screw*. Elsewhere, its action is indirect ; it may work through the most apparently natural affections, desires and loyalties . . . see, for instance, *The Spoils of Poynton* (1896). In *The Golden Bowl*, with its London scene of poised and controlled cosmopolitan people, he shows the implicit rather than the conventional ugliness of an adultery. Under Henry James's adroitness, behind his complex constructions, is the simple pattern of the morality play. In the end, he sees nothing as beautiful that has not been proved good. He subjected to moral examination the grace, the privilege, the mystery, the tradition of the age-polished England he loved so well.

Henry James's great novels and stories are astoundingly many. His style became more and more involuted ; his later novels are not found easy to read. His first long novel was *Roderick Hudson* (1876). Landmarks in his work have been : *The American* (1877), *Daisy Miller* (1878), *The Portrait of a Lady* (1881), *The Princess Casamassima* (1886), *The Spoils of Poynton* (1896), *What Maisie Knew* (1897), *The Two Magics* (which contains *The Turn of the Screw*) (1898), *The Awkward Age* (1899), *The Wings of the Dove* (1902), *The Ambassadors* (1903), *The Golden Bowl* (1904). Though

THE VISIT TO THE MAD WOMAN AFTER THE INTERRUPTED MARRIAGE

Illustration to *Jane Eyre* by Charlotte Brontë

Water-colour by Frederick Walker

THOMAS HARDY 1840-1928
Oil painting by Augustus John

he did not die (in England) till 1916, his great fiction period had closed years before that.

So Henry James has carried us over from the nineteenth century to our own. The same transition was made by a number of novelists whom, alas, I have no room to name here. In fact, the great Late-Victorians I have discussed were in reality far from isolated : to let them seem so gives an incomplete picture of their day. It has taken years for them to stand out from among their more popular contemporaries. I am now conscious of two very bad lacunæ in not having mentioned either George Gissing or George Moore—the first a "straight" realist, the second an æsthete-realist, Irish, much touched by French influence, whose work has an outstanding quality. And a still graver omission is Robert Louis Stevenson, the second great Scot to influence England. In his power to raise the story of action to a heroic, sometimes poetic, level, Stevenson was to be approached by Joseph Conrad—the Polish sea captain who added to English writing a sort of fervour and glory—a temperament. I can name, in the space that is left to me, only four novelists who carry forward into, or at least touch, our own time.

There is Rudyard Kipling, for instance. The artist in him has been quite wrongly obscured, in some views, by the Imperialist. Actually, he was realistic, quite disabused, about English life abroad as well as at home. The dramatic side of the Empire did appeal to him—but he knew its plain working side well, as a journalist. He likes energy, courage, action in any form : if he salutes these in the English one cannot blame him. His best work is in the field of the short story—setting and incident interest him more than character, though his touch on character can be devastatingly sure. His long novel, *The Light that Failed*, is, though moving, on the sentimental side. No English writer has been more mobile and vivid in his depiction of action. Also, he makes one see, smell, touch what he describes : his descriptions are charged with reality. For a number of untravelled English people he has, for instance, "created" India for ever. He has, and quite often likes to use, a real English-gothic command of the horrific. In *Plain Tales from the Hills*, and other collections, he has written some ruthless love-stories : love does not appear to Kipling to be a rational passion. Anglo-Indian life, boy life and the British Army are, in general, taken to be his province. In his children's stories he shows pure imagination in his treatment of the past and of animals. He was born in Bombay in 1865, and the publication dates of his books extend from 1881 to 1930. He has left us some classic tales of the last war.

H. G. Wells, born 1866, has, like Samuel Butler, the scientific approach to life. He applies science to the novel. Like Hardy, he has a constant sense of the future—but, whereas Hardy apprehended the future only as the extreme of a psychic state, Wells commits himself to exact material prophecies. Science has justified his predictions by already coming abreast of several of them—but the stories have their independent place in art as being magnificent fantasies. *The Time Machine*, for instance, came in 1895, *The War of Worlds* in 1898, *The Food of the Gods* in 1904, *Men Like Gods* in 1923. It may be said that Wells's rationalised Utopias offer no place for the human soul—which, one takes it, will no longer exist. If so, in the future there will be no more great novels. . . . The Utopian novels have made great impacts : fearless, iconoclastic, impertinent from the point of view of tradition, they do always stimulate thought. But it is in consciousness of his own age, of the maladies and the aspirations of men as they are to-day—in fact, as a straightforward novelist—that Wells seems to me to excel. He has a truly Dickensian eye for the comic. *Kipps* (1905) and *The History of Mr. Polly* (1910) are novels that could not be better. *Ann Veronica* (1909), *Marriage* (1912), *Joan and Peter* (1918) are milestones in the analysis of his age. Wells is at once engaged and fascinated by the impossibility of rationalising love : sex seems to hold up progress, the way things are. Others of the novels—outstandingly, *Mr. Britling Sees It Through* (1916)—fall into the document group : they crystallise the feeling and the conditions of a particular period. From the first, Wells has been liked or disliked for a particular boldness—*Tono Bungay* (1909) and *The New Machiavelli* (1911) made revolutions in their day. And the present day has not yet caught up with his thoughts : for our own generation he flies a tremendous flag.

In his move from the social novel, with its acceptances, to the sociological novel, with its attacks, Wells was accompanied by Arnold Bennett (1867-1931). But in the Bennett novels—which at their finest, for instance, *The Old Wives' Tale* (1908), stand up to anything Europe has put out—the artist towers over the man of ideas. In fact, general conditions chiefly interested Bennett in so far as they serve to explain particular lives. Like Hardy, he re-created a region—the Five Towns, in the northern Midlands, dark with the smoke of the potteries. In him appears, at its most lively, the English satiric sense—and as success closed in on his own life, how freely he satirised success ! He became accomplished enough as a writer to explore every genre—the thriller, the domestic comedy. After the *Old Wives' Tale*, among his serious work comes the *Clayhanger* trilogy (1910-15), and *Riceyman's Steps* (1923). He lived years in France, loved her and learned from her the uncompromising regard that is due to art. The French æsthetic ideal—detachment—was always uppermost in his mind : to this we owe his objective view of England—as valuable in an Englishman as it is rare.

John Galsworthy's novels have not worn so well. His dates are 1867-1933. The *Forsyte Saga* novels (1906-28) have their first interest—and are much read abroad—as documents of the English upper middle class. They have the merits of all his other writing—intellectual scrupulousness, sense of beauty, a rather hopeless passion for social justice, and, with regard to

RUDYARD KIPLING 1865-1936
Oil painting by Sir Philip Burne-Jones

women, a serious but exotic sentimentality. His pictures of men of property, men created by their sense of their own position, are more searching than Thackeray's, more fastidious than Trollope's—yet somehow the different Forsytes fail to be major figures. Possibly Galsworthy was not ruthless enough ; perhaps he failed (while he did boldly attempt) to objectify the tradition in which he had been brought up. He attacks privilege, but in a privileged way. His disinterested ambitions deserve praise : one would not be so much aware of his limitations had he not attempted to do so much. As a dramatist—and he was called the English Ibsen—he learned how to give the fullest force to a scene—so it is the scenes in his novels that are remembered ; one tends to lose sight of their continuity. In his sense of place he excels ; he has immortalised London ; he has a sensuous feeling for countrysides. His characters, with their ascetic wills, dread beauty because of its dangerous power : in fact, you could not have a fairer example than Galsworthy of one kind of English romanticism. His novels most to be recommended are : *The Man of Property* (1906), *The Patrician* (1911), *The Dark Flower* (1913), *In Chancery* (1920), *To Let* (1921).

These four writers—Kipling, Wells, Bennett and Galsworthy—have been in their time, and each in his own way, more revolutionary than any younger men. We now take for granted a great deal that they achieved. The novelist of to-day has less to react against. So we feel some break in temperament between these four last Late-Victorians and the novelists who are at their maturity to-day—for instance, Aldous Huxley, Somerset Maugham. Has there come, too, a break in the English novel tradition ? Looking back, we may say that the English novelists have, from the eighteenth century up to some years ago, excelled in the creation of character, and, secondarily, in the drawing of scenes, rather than in the analysis of ideas and passions. They have left us a gallery of immortal English creatures—eccentrics, haphazard fine young men, fantasists, optimists, blackguards, silly women, dashing bad women, lovely spirited girls ; they have left us English landscapes as various as ever came from the sweep of an English brush. Hardy and Meredith, poet-novelists, were the first to indicate any change.

There is, I think, a change now, though not a break. D. H. Lawrence has come and gone : his explosive novels have had the effect of a sort of depth-charge, bringing much to the surface. Lawrence was, it would seem, at once behind and in advance of his own time : his puritanical antipuritanism was paradoxical. In writing of worlds he knew, he commanded an admirable realism, tinged with poetry, and a simplicity that has not been praised enough; these having been obscured, for the general reader, by his "prophetic" quality, and by his (apparent) doctrine of purification by fire—*i.e.*, sexual passion. At any rate, D. H. Lawrence played a major part in shifting the stress from character—in which, ever since, our contemporary novelists show an interest that is much less exclusive. They continue to turn, instead, to just those ideas and passions in which individual destinies count for less, in which people take less colour from their surroundings because those surroundings change from day to day ? One great war has already left, another is in the act of placing, its mark on English habit, feeling and thought. I do not think English essentials will ever change—but events make us sharply conscious of what these are. The novelist to-day must think for himself : this is no time to add random comments to life. So the English novel gains in self-consciousness—it may have lost some of the old spontaneity.

I cannot see my contemporaries as I see the earlier novelists : that is, I cannot see them down the perspective of time. They are many, and vitally on the move. To attempt to judge them would be to attempt to immobilise them. I may have been arbitrary about the dead ; I will not be misleading about the living. With every day, values go up and down. So I shall close with a reference only to two modern novelists whose work

ARNOLD BENNETT 1867-1931
Caricature by David Low

seems to me to have attained a position clear of the daily critical flux. One,
Virginia Woolf, is recently dead ; the other, E. M. Forster, has not published a novel since 1924. These two seem to me both to epitomise English
tradition and to have moved forward along lines of their own.

E. M. Forster's novels are more straightforward, more (at least apparently) in the familiar manner than those of Virginia Woolf : they have
developed plots, they give place (though not the first place) to character ;
they have a high ironic level of comedy, and their dialogue comes abreast
with Jane Austen's. What is new in them is their particular mental
climate ; also, the nature of other people's predicaments. Contrast does
much to give these novels structure and meaning—contrast between one
country, with its inherent spirit, and another (suburban England and hill-
town Italy in *Where Angels Fear to Tread*, between England and India in
A Passage to India), between convention and passion (in *A Room with
a View*), between illusion and truth (in *The Longest Journey* and *Howard's*

269

End). In each, the central character is kept at the high tension of a continuous decision. Through experience the character seems to make a journey—an often lonely destination is reached. The controlled, level style of the narration can be penetratingly beautiful.

In Virginia Woolf's novels the characters are less mobile ; they seem to stand still, amazed, while experience ripples past. The men and women have an intense inner existence ; each generates his or her own world. Imagination of this pure power has not been brought to narrative style before : Virginia Woolf has been likened to Sterne—but her imagination is less contused than his. I have not heard her compared with Emily Brontë—but Emily Brontë has been the only other woman capable of this upward sweep. While the *Wuthering Heights* setting is in itself extraordinary, Virginia Woolf's choice of settings has been the reverse, and her characters are, in their outward aspects, made almost deliberately tame. She chooses, in fact, unlikely matter to kindle—but, once kindled, how high she makes it burn ! She has put behind her, having no need of, devices that make all other stories work. The towering inner strangeness of her people appears not at all in their outward actions (which appear conventional and compliant), but in the manner in which they see and feel. Only in the earliest of her novels, *The Voyage Out*, do the characters actually make a journey : they go to South America. Otherwise, they are confined to the experiences of London, the English countryside and seashore. But never before has England appeared as it appears under this burning-glass of her art. Once, in *Orlando*, she turns the glass on the English past. Otherwise, all her titles—*Night and Day, Jacob's Room, Mrs. Dalloway, To the Lighthouse, The Waves, The Years, Between the Acts*—suggest the familiar "now"—the familiar scene, in cycles of light and darkness, in hearing of the rhythm of tides. Time, not passion, spins any plot that there is —and yet Virginia Woolf has been supreme in her power to place the life art touches beyond the power of time.

I have tried, as I promised at the start of this book, to make felt the wideness of the To-day of art, and return past novelists to their place in its light. So it is fitting to close with Virginia Woolf's name : she lived as well as wrote in the presence of that To-day.

BRITISH PHILOSOPHERS

KENNETH MATTHEWS

I

TWO major influences have shaped the philosophy of modern Europe: the British and the German. It is true that Descartes, who is generally regarded as the founder of modern European philosophy, was a Frenchman and Spinoza, the saintly, Ghandi-like refugee who polished lenses and discoursed with princes, was a Spanish Jew. No science can be confined behind national frontiers. But just as in Ancient Greece an extraordinary coruscation of intellectual curiosity took place in a brief period and within the limits of a single language, so in Britain a tradition of philosophy arose and flourished, having its special native characteristics; and so in Germany a rival succession of philosophers flourished in their turn, following different gods.

The native characteristics of British philosophy are these: common sense, dislike of complication, a strong preference for the concrete over the abstract and a certain awkward honesty of method in which an occasional pearl of poetry is embedded. It is as easy to perceive a common parentage in the philosophies of John Locke and Bertrand Russell as in the seamanship of Francis Drake and Horatio Nelson. We might vainly enquire whether climate or language or some original hereditary strain or a combination of all three produces the distinguishing marks of national character, but their existence cannot be denied. The British philosophers, at least the most typical of them, stand with both feet on the ground. They are, compared with the great German system builders, Kant, Hegel, Leibniz and the others, earthbound and pedestrian figures. But then, they would say, a sound philosophy is a utility product, which must be capable of taking hard knocks.

A crucial incident in the history of European philosophy was the discovery of David Hume by Immanuel Kant. The German philosopher tells us in a memorable phrase that he was suddenly "awakened from his dogmatic slumbers." We do not know which of Hume's books provoked this event, nor exactly when it happened. It was probably one of the passages in the *Treatise of Human Nature,* one of those destructive analyses of the idea of causation, which struck Kant as somehow darkly anarchic and led him to create the elaborate philosophic structure of the *Critique of Pure Reason.* It would be too much to attribute all the ambitious philosophic systems which were evolved by German philosophers after Kant to the seed sown in Kant's mind by the Scottish philosopher. There are fashions in philosophy, as in everything else; and in the Romantic Period, people were ready for philosophies in the romantic spirit and on a romantic scale. The fellow-countrymen of Wagner supplied them. They had their influence in the world; and they had their imitators in Britain. But when a philosophy erected like Kant's or Hegel's, tier upon tier of abstract superstructure upon a pinpoint of experience, falls out of fashion, it falls like Lucifer, never to rise again. The philosophy which touches the ground at many points has a much greater survival value.

Moreover, common sense is not a dull quality. Rather the contrary. Nothing is more calculated to shock people than common sense applied to long established but unexamined beliefs. This was the indiscretion which long ago put a cup of hemlock in front of Socrates.

The British philosophers provoked the same reactions, but on the whole did not go to the same lengths of contumacy Sir Thomas More was the only one to lose his life and that for annoying the King rather than writing *Utopia.* Thomas Hobbes, the truculent author of *Leviathan,* went more often to church when a Bill denouncing his famous work as blasphemous literature was introduced in Parliament. Locke went into exile, as Socrates might have done; his *Letter of Toleration* was published in Holland. Hume, than whom no man lived a more blameless life, ensconced in his Edinburgh house, with his sister, maid and cat, was regarded with such distrust that hostile demonstrations were expected at his funeral; and on the advice of his friends, he kept the *Dialogues Concerning Natural Religion* unpublished during his lifetime. Undoubtedly a certain mellowing in the public attitude towards philosophic speculation was taking place even at that time; philosophers, like heretics and witches, had succeeded in somewhat modifying their professional status. But it was still possible for Jeremy Bentham to horrify the Romantic Age by the classical simplicity of the Utilitarian doctrine: the greatest happiness of the greatest number. John Stuart Mill tells us how he read Bentham in his teens with an effect of revelation; and no doubt (though this is not recorded) there were murmurings in conservative households that Mr. Bentham must have picked up these immoral ideas during his travels in Russia.

Bentham journeyed to Russia and wrote one of his books in the form of letters from Russia. We have noted the practical spirit of British philosophy ; and it should not surprise us to find that the philosophers themselves were practical men. Men of affairs would be an even juster description. Two of them, Francis Bacon and Thomas More, occupied the office of Lord Chancellor ; hence Harvey's celebrated taunt, that Bacon wrote philosophy like a Lord Chancellor. Locke was offered the post of Ambassador at Vienna or Berlin ; and actually filled the offices of Secretary to the Board of Trade, Commissioner of Appeals and Commissioner of Trade and Plantations. Berkeley spent ten years of his life on a plan for a college in the Bermudas, whose purpose would be "the reformation of manners among the English in our Western plantations and the propagation of the Gospel among the American savages" ; and if the project never matured, it must be recorded that a grant of money was made by the almost unanimous vote of the House of Commons. Bentham was one of the pioneers of British prison reform. J. S. Mill was for twenty years in charge of the East India Company's relations with the Indian native states. Those philosophers who, like Hume, had none but literary ambitions, regarded philosophy not as an end in itself, but as a foundation of other researches ; they concerned themselves with history, social problems, economics and theories of government. We may conclude either that the common sense which we have mentioned as a characteristic of British philosophers derives from this catholic experience, or that both philosophy and experience derive from an innate realism of mind.

What is Philosophy ? The old Greek word meant simply "love of wisdom." In the popular sense, philosophy means any deeply reflective study of abstract subjects, like God or Beauty. In this sense the poets are philosophers ; and Browning and Wordsworth are more philosophic than Herrick or Keats. This opinion seems to me to be true as far as it goes.

But in a narrow sense philosophy means what Aristotle first called metaphysics. By metaphysics we understand the science which supplies the answer to the question : what is the nature of the universe ; or to break up the subject into its component terms, what is space, what is time, what is the mind of man made of, what is the difference between mind and matter, what do we mean when we say that a thing exists, and so on. Closely associated with metaphysics, we have ethics, which purports to answer the question : what is the Good and how ought man to behave ; and logic, which is the formal analysis of our methods of reasoning. It is clear that no exact dividing line exists enclosing philosophy on one side and non-philosophy on the other. There is rather a progress from questions which are felt to be absolutely fundamental and secondary questions which arise therefrom. Like most living things, philosophy does not easily submit to academic definitions. But it will probably be most useful if we think of philosophy mainly in the narrow metaphysical sense but without altogether excluding the more generous interpretations.

II

SOME of the most remarkable relics in England are the churches and monasteries surviving among the Northumbrian shipyards from the days of the Venerable Bede. We shall not claim Bede as a philosopher, although he died like one, surrounded by weeping disciples and dictating the last words of his English translation of the Gospel of St. John.

Small, isolated communities like Bede's kept a candle burning in Britain during the early Middle Ages. But the centres of learning were on the Continent of Europe : the Frankish Courts, the Vatican, the University of Paris. Charlemagne wanted to see the intellectual life of Europe revolving round his own person ; while he exchanged gifts with the Caliph of the Arabian world, he called scholars from south, north, east and west, including Alcuin from Britain. We shall not call Alcuin a philosopher ; nor yet Erigena, who travelled from Ireland to the Court of Charles the Bald. Both were theologians, for whom philosophy was one of God's handmaids, subject both to divine discipline and original sin. All through the Middle Ages you were allowed to philosophise only if your conclusions served to buttress the current dogmas of the Church ; Aristotle, read in Latin translations, was the "set book." The story of British philosophy is the story of how this ghostly tyranny was broken, how independent thought on fundamental questions was achieved and what it accomplished.

We might do worse than begin with the Franciscan mission which landed at Dover on September 10th, 1224, not for the mission's own sake but because of its connection with Britain's first full-size philosopher, Roger Bacon. What strange invasions the coast of Kent has seen—the legions of Julius Caesar, the war-craft of the Anglo-Saxons, St. Augustine's little Christian band, and, on this old September Tuesday, the nine friars sent by St. Francis, three of them Englishmen, who journeyed to Lincoln, London and Oxford to set up new standards of scholarship in England. The Franciscan School in Oxford was of especial importance ; there an infant university was arising which was soon to rival Paris, and the Franciscans played a great part in its development. We are told how the friars used to walk barefoot through the cold and wind to attend the Oxford theology classes. They quickly produced philosophers pre-eminent in their generation : Thomas of York, whose *Metaphysics* was preserved in Italian libraries in Florence and the Vatican ; Friar Robert of Cornwall "whom fools thought wise and wise men crazy" in Roger Bacon's biting phrase (he was rash enough to differ from Bacon on a point of logic !) ; and Stephen the Englishman who lectured on philosophy in Genoa and Rome and who, when dying, besought his friend to have masses said for his soul "because he used to go too often to a certain religious matron, to console her."

'THE PHILOSOPHERS ON THE SUMMIT OF MOUNT ATHOS TAKING OBSERVATIONS OF THE STARS
AND WRITING WORDS IN THE DUST'
Illumination from the Travels of Sir John Mandeville. 15th century

Roger Bacon (Friar Bacon) joined the Franciscan Order in Paris; between Paris and Oxford he divided his life. A prodigious figure! He has survived in legend as the inventor of gunpowder. Popular opinion is at least right in judging him to be the sort of person who might have made this discovery. Popular opinion has also dressed him in a long black necromancer's cloak and pictured him concocting nefarious substances in mortars and retorts, rather like that friar whom we have all seen on the stage concocting a death-brew for Romeo. But if we strip off the fancy dress and try to reach an understanding of the man as he really was, we find only a shrewd, tough, tirelessly inquisitive and irrepressibly argumentative character who lived to a ripe old age and spent a great part of it deliberately shocking people: a figure rather like that of Thomas Hobbes, though Hobbes seems to have known a little better when to stop.

He was born about 1214 and took Holy Orders before he was twenty. The cast of his mind is shown when he first of all refuses to read Aristotle in the accepted Latin translations, learns to read the original Greek and then declares that if he had his way, every translation of Aristotle would be burned.

From Aristotle in Greek he proceeds to the Arabian scientists who, in the mediaeval world, were the natural successors of the Greeks. He turns to "speculative alchemy," which he presently declares to be one of the three foundations of true science. Here already we have the foundations of the Baconian legend, although Bacon's "alchemy" was practised in as dispassionate a spirit as modern chemistry. He was known, even among his contemporaries, as the Marvellous Doctor (Doctor Admirabilis). But as he pursued his researches, it is clear that a vision dawned upon him which lifted him clean out of the surrounding world: the vision of man's future power over nature. He writes of boats which shall be driven without oars, bridges which will stand without supporting piers, self-propelled carriages and other possible mechanical inventions. At the same time, his contempt for orthodox thought, as practised in the schools of Oxford and Paris, gathers head. He takes, not only his science from the Arabians, but also his invective. He criticises a learned rival in these terms: "His works have four faults. The first is boundless, puerile vanity; the second is ineffable falsity; the third is superfluity of bulk ... and the fourth is ignorance of the most useful and most beautiful parts of philosophy." The style, which would have delighted the taste of Haroun-Al-Rachid, fell less gratefully upon the ears of the reverend scholastics of Paris. They shut him up for ten years in 1257; he wrote his *Opus Majus* in prison. Scarcely had he been released when he offended again. His *Summary of Philosophical Study*, written about 1271, probably caused the second scandal. At the age of sixty-four, he was summoned before the Chapter of his Order and condemned for "making innovations"; this time it was fourteen years' imprisonment. The aged philosopher emerged

ROGER BACON d. 1294
Illumination from a fifteenth century Ms.

from prison, wrote a book upon theology and died : worthy, if any man
ever was, of a philosopher's grave on British soil.

What was the system of philosophy which emerged from this stormy
life ? It had two sides, negative and positive. The negative side was the
rejection of contemporary methods of reasoning. Mediaeval or "scholastic"
philosophy reposed, like modern law, upon precedent ; the truth had been
revealed and one had only to refine upon it. Bacon dismissed this philosophy as a compound of four errors : of obsequiousness to authority,
ingrained habits of thought, deference to the unlettered crowd and the
empty ostentation of knowledge. The positive side of Bacon's work represents his greatest contribution to philosophy. "There are two modes in
which we acquire knowledge, argument and experiment. If any man who
had never seen fire were to hear proved by satisfactory argument that fire
burns and destroys things, his mind would not rest satisfied, nor would
he avoid fire ; until by putting his hand or some combustible thing into
it, he proved by actual experiment what the argument laid down ; but
after the experiment has been made, his mind receives certainty and
rests in the possession of truth." A thirteeth-century philosopher who
proposed to divert his learned colleagues from their transcendental hair-

splitting to the practical untidy work of the laboratory, was as if a physician in the years of the Great Plague should have told his profession to cease their incantations and look for the germs.

We can better appreciate the quality of Roger Bacon by comparing him with another British Franciscan : John Duns Scotus. Duns is a Scottish village lying about halfway between Berwick and Edinburgh, almost on the English border ; here Duns Scotus is said to have been born about the year 1265. He, like Roger Bacon, studied both in Oxford and in Paris but in all probability missed the influence of the older man. He had spent four years at Paris and at least ten years in Oxford before he began the Oxford lectures on theology in 1300 which constitute one of his surviving works. Later, he lectured in Paris ; and as Bacon was termed the Marvellous Doctor, so he earned the name of the Subtle Doctor (Doctor Subtilis), a happy example of popular discernment. He was an infinitely more conventional figure, a true "scholastic," who took part in the current scholastic controversies. He argued about such matters as "the hylomorphic composition of angels." The word "dunce" (from Duns) indicates the contempt which a later age felt for the whole scholastic tradition. But even Duns Scotus disturbed men's minds in his time ; it is said that his books were publicly burned in Oxford by his philosophical opponents.

In the year of Bacon's death (1294), when Duns Scotus was at the height of his career, we read that the number of foreign students at Oxford was so great that they could not be accommodated in the city. The prestige of English scholarship was already rising fast. Two hundred years later it is no longer surprising when one of the greatest continental scholars, Erasmus, visits Cambridge. It was at Cambridge that Erasmus first met the author of *Utopia*—Sir Thomas More.

More is perhaps not strictly a philosopher. He is *anima naturaliter philosophica*. His *Utopia* which is a description of an ideal society or commonwealth, must be taken as a profound fable rather than an enquiry into the principles of knowledge. But it shows the new renaissance temper abroad in England, the switch of interest from Aristotle to Plato. And a liberal, even radical spirit of criticism. The citizens of Utopia enjoyed complete religious toleration ; they had "priests of exceeding holiness and therefore very few." They had a law that those who would marry must approve each other's naked body before the ceremony was performed. They considered war "as a thing very beastly" ; yet their women accompanied their husbands into battle. *Utopia* was published in 1516, when More was thirty-eight years old ; and with its old-fashioned Latin dress and new-fangled ideas, it stands as a bridge between Mediaevalism and the Elizabethan Age of Enterprise.

"As water ascends no higher than the level of the first spring, so knowledge derived from Aristotle will at most rise no higher than the

FRANCIS BACON 1561-1626
Oil painting. Studio of Paul Van Somer

knowledge of Aristotle." This forthright pronouncement occurs in the first philosophical work written in the English language. It demolished in one sentence the whole laboured edifice which had been raised in the Middle Ages. The author was a second Bacon, Francis, later Baron Verulam ; and the work, the *Advancement of Learning.*

The *Advancement of Learning* was published in 1605, two years after Queen Elizabeth's death. It ante-dated by 32 years the publication by

Descartes of the *Discours sur la Methode*, which is conventionally regarded as the fountain-head of modern philosophy. Descartes' revolutionary method consisted in building up knowledge from the beginning by rejecting every belief which could possibly be doubted ; but Francis Bacon before him had declared : "Our one hope is to begin the whole labour of the mind again." The *Advancement of Learning* stands as a landmark, not only in British, but in European philosophical history.

Francis Bacon, even more than his namesake, presents us with a personal enigma. He, too, trails his clouds of legend. One of the wildest fables which has grown up round his name is that which credits him with the writing of Shakepeare's plays. This may at least be taken as a tribute to Bacon's vast intellectual powers. He has said many things worthy of Shakespeare. The magnificent boast : "I have taken all knowledge to be my province" might well have come from the same pen as wrote of the Roman Triumvir : "Why man he doth bestride the narrow world like a Colossus." Yet, although there is grandeur enough in Bacon, there is little lyricism and less humour. Bacon is at bottom practical. Some of his most memorable sayings are the stuff of politics. Consider this, upon war resources : "The sinews of war are not money ; if the sinews of men's arms be wanting, they are a soft and effeminate nation." Or this, upon seapower : "The being master of the sea leaves a nation at great liberty to act and to take as much or as little of the war as it pleases, whilst those who are superior in land forces have yet numerous difficulties to struggle with." How often these words are quoted without regard to the author of them !

The enigma of Francis Bacon resides in his personal character. His public career was stained continually by treachery and self-seeking. He betrayed his friend and patron, the Earl of Essex. Under King James I we see him putting neither his own integrity nor the public good before personal advancement. He schemes for the extension of the King's Prerogative and the hoodwinking of Parliament at a time when the authority of Parliament was the supreme condition for the further advancement of British liberties. Presented in a certain light, his elaborate machinations to protect the Duke of Buckingham's monopolies appear more odious than royal tyranny. He achieved his aim of becoming Lord Chancellor but was brought down by his accumulating enemies within three years. He was convicted of taking bribes in the discharge of his judicial duties. The legitimate receipts of his office were about £2,790 ; his actual income was about £16,000.

Bacon's philosophy was that of a man of the world. He says roundly of his system : "The matter in hand is no mere philosophy of speculation, but the real business and fortunes of the human race." Here, certainly, we have the note, never long absent from our island philosophy, struck with surpassing vigour and boldness. Knowledge for its own sake means

NORTH VIEW OF FRIAR BACON'S STUDY AT OXFORD

Coloured aquatint by T. Rowlandson, 1756-1827

Johannes Duns Scotus, Doctor Subtilis

By courtesy of the Bodleian Library, Oxford

DUNS SCOTUS
17th Century oil painting

nothing to Francis Bacon. Knowledge must be justified by works ; true knowledge means power over nature. It is easy to see how a man who held these views would not readily accept the status of an academic philosopher. He even says in one place, that those who spend their whole lives in writing books do so because they do not realise that there are other easier roads to fame.

It is a fantastic coincidence that Francis Bacon should have shared with a thirteenth-century predecessor not only a name but also a great part of his "new method." Francis, like Roger Bacon, discovered precisely four causes of human error. He describes Four Idols which delude the human mind : Idols of the Tribe, Idols of the Cave, Idols of the Marketplace and Idols of the Theatre. The word "idols" sounds picturesque ; it is a direct translation from Plato. The Idols of the Tribe are those fallacies which arise from the very structure of men's minds ; for example when we jump to a general conclusion on the basis of one example. The Idols of the Cave are the errors peculiar to the individual ; for example, when a man thinks a subject is specially important because he himself has studied it. The Idols of the Market are the errors caused by the misleading use of words. Nothing, as we shall see, is more up-to-date in Francis Bacon than his analysis of the fallibility of words. He says in one place : "In Physics, where nature is to be caught by works and not the adversary by argument, truth in this way slips through our fingers, because the subtlety of the operations of nature far exceeds the subtlety of words." The Idols of the Theatre are the narrow systems of philosophy which have hitherto gained currency in the world. Bacon says that time is like a river ; it brings the refuse down to us and leaves the solid stuff behind !

Then, too, Francis Bacon, like Roger, bases the new method entirely upon *experiment*. Philosophers, he says, must become like little children, examining the elements of nature. But—and this is the startling suggestion —nothing else will suffice than the assemblage of all existing instances of the object studied and no generalisation will be valid unless it is based on all the instances. Bacon realises, of course, that a literal interpretation of this method would make all generalisation impossible. He allows a sort of tentative generalisation which he calls, picturesquely, the First Vintage. In this Bacon shows remarkable anticipations of modern thought. The final generalisation, which can be made after the active researches described have been completed, Bacon calls the Form. When we have understood the form of anything, we shall be able to exploit our knowledge and achieve supremacy over nature. Such is the Baconian method or Baconian Induction as it is sometimes called.

What Bacon planned was a sequence of six mighty works; he catalogues them for us in the preface to the *Advancement of Learning*. 1. A Survey and Extension of the Sciences. This was the *Advancement of Learning*, published by Bacon, as we have seen, in 1605. 2. *Novum Organum*. This work was published in 1620. 3. *Phenomena of the Universe*. This was to be the vast natural and experimental history on which the new philosophy was to be founded. This was never written. Many writers have declared that the collection which Bacon proposed was too comprehensive to be possible. 4, 5 and 6, *Ladder of the Understanding, Precursors of the Second Philosophy* and the *Second Philosophy*, were likewise unwritten. In them Bacon imagined the development of the philosophy or science which would put all nature at man's disposal and create undreamed of sources of power. Once again, we detect the faint spark which was to light the Industrial Revolution.

In the *Novum Organum* Bacon attempts to show the new method in operation. He applies it to the notion of heat. First he collects all the known instances of heat. It is an astonishing list, ranging from the rays of the sun, ignited meteors and volcanic flames, to "all shaggy substances," "fresh horse-dung" and even old nasturtium applied to the palate. He then collects instances where we might expect heat and find none : as from the light of the stars, from phosphorescence, and so on. Finally, he examines the variation of heat in a number of instances. As the collection of instances is acknowledged to be incomplete, he can only proceed to a tentative generalisation : the First Vintage of the Form of Heat. This Bacon defines as follows : "Heat is an expansive motion restrained, and striving to exert itself in the smaller particles." John Stuart Mill says that Bacon's mistake was in assuming that *one* cause produced all instances of heat ; in the real world there is always a multiplicity of causes.

On Easter Sunday, April 9th, 1626, Francis Bacon died, poor, disgraced, but still experimenting. He had been riding out to Highgate, and got down from the coach to stuff a newly-killed fowl with snow ; he was investigating "the conservation and induration of bodies." He was taken ill and had to seek shelter in the house of Lord Arundel, to whom he dictated a letter of apology. "My Very Good Lord, I was likely to have had the fortune of Caius Plinius the elder, who lost his life by trying an experiment about the burning of the mountain Vesuvius." So passed Francis of Verulam, perhaps to be called first of a long line of modern European philosophers, whom Pope, in a cruel epigram, styled "the wisest, brightest, meanest of mankind."

A more generous epitaph, and one better fitted to our purpose, has been left by Charles Darwin who, more than two hundred years later, wrote that he had "worked on true Baconian principles and, without any theory, collected facts on a wholesale scale." Nothing would have more gratified the originator of the Baconian philosophy, who had wished his work to be translated into Latin for the benefit of posterity, than that his influence should have reached down the centuries and touched, among all others, the author of the *Origin of Species*.

THOMAS HOBBES 1588-1679
Engraving after Casper by Wenceslaus Hollar

III

AFTER Francis Bacon, we enter upon the Great Age of British philosophy. It was also the age which saw the mortal struggle between King and Parliament, the Puritan dictatorship of Oliver Cromwell, the Restoration and the English Revolution and the early stages of the imperial struggle with France.

The outstanding names are those of Hobbes, Locke, Berkeley and Hume. Greatness is not an easily measurable quality ; and if we are to attempt to distribute it among four such competitors, we might fall into the error of Paris, who should have excused himself from passing judgment. Let us say that these four men were collectively great and ask what they collectively achieved. They broke down any intellectual basis that may have remained for controlling the free exercise of human thought. Hobbes assailed the temporal power of the Church. He was not the first nor the last to denounce ecclesiastical vested interests but he was certainly one of the most effective. Locke's work on religious and political toleration chastened the powers of civil government. He, like Milton, hated censors, the miserable creatures who imposed a tax of 6/8d. per volume upon a set of Cicero imported from Holland. From the sailing of the Mayflower in 1620 to Hume's *Dialogues upon Natural Religion* it is as if a new intellectual climate has descended upon the land. Instead of the harsh recurring frosts, there is a reign of scarcely interrupted sunshine. Such a liberation based, not on accident, but upon that fundamental effort of thought which we call philosophy, was necessary to the century of science which immediately followed and which the philosopher-pioneers foresaw.

To begin, then, with Hobbes. Hobbes as a young man used to walk with Francis Bacon in his garden. It was the pupil's task to imprison upon paper the ideas which flowed from the master's conversation; and we hear that his lordship "better liked Mr. Hobbes taking his thoughts than any of the others because he understood what he wrote." But Hobbes was not the man to remain a taker-down of other people's thoughts for long. He was what is called in the vernacular a "character." His inordinate vanity, his eye darting like a "live bright coal," his endless disputatiousness, combined with a rare capacity for friendship, caused people to take sides for and against him even though they had never read his works. He laid down the law on all subjects indifferently. He hated bishops and all persons of unnatural unction. He was a confirmed bachelor, though he is said to have had an illegitimate daughter whom he referred to as his *delictum juventutis*. He was still publishing his latest philosophic discoveries at the age of ninety. He lived to be ninety-one. He was the George Bernard Shaw of his day.

Hobbes was by no means born into philosophy. He was lucky to get any education at all. His father was a disreputable country parson. One Sunday, after playing cards all night, he startled his congregation by waking from a snooze in the pulpit and shouting : "Spades are trumps !" Presently, after a brawl at the church door, he disappeared, deserting his family. An uncle sent the young Hobbes to Oxford, where he distinguished himself in Latin and Greek. Then, after leaving Oxford, he secured a tutorship which shaped his whole life—in the family of Lord Cavendish, later first Earl of Devonshire. He never broke his friendship with the Cavendish family; he lived and died in their ancestral homes of Chatsworth and Hardwicke; through them he met the Kings of Europe and, more important, the great scholars, Descartes, Galileo. He was over forty before that critical incident occurred which has, perhaps, been somewhat overdramatised. "By God !" says he, looking at a proposition of Euclid

TITLE PAGE OF HOBBES' *LEVIATHAN*, 1651

in a friend's book, "this is impossible!" But following the proof from proposition to proposition, he becomes convinced and begins to dream of establishing a philosophical system as logical and remorseless as Euclid's geometry. This philosophy took on a political bias because, says Hobbes, the country was "boiling hot with political questions, the forerunners of an approaching war." The philosophy he wanted to write would have been in three parts : the first dealing with matter, the second with human nature and the third with society. Actually he carried out something like this plan ; only in the stress of the Civil War, he wrote the last part first. This was *Leviathan :* Hobbes' masterpiece and one of the great monuments of the English language. The first part of the system, the analysis of matter, was developed in a later book *De Corpore*, written in Latin ; and much of what Hobbes had to say about human nature was telescoped into *Leviathan* and an earlier work upon the social organisation of man *De Cive*. Hobbes was, in the strict philosophical sense, a materialist. He believed that nothing existed except matter—matter in motion. Just as he ascribed the phenomena of Nature to the ceaseless motion of its elements, so he thought he could reduce all human affairs to "the internal motions of men" ; he was an exponent of that oldest Greek philosophy which dismissed all reality in the words πάντα ρεῖ —everything flows. Something in the primeval iconoclasm of this doctrine appealed to Hobbes' temperament.

Hobbes wrote to hurt and counted nothing well said which did not strike a telling blow against someone or something. Consider some of his typical pronouncements. That the first passion which inclines men to peace is fear of death. That the essence of commonwealth is rule by terror. That the only difference between monarchy and tyranny or between democracy and anarchy resides in the outlook of the governed. That liberty consists in submission to the monarch. That the prosperity of a people depends, not on their form of government, but on their obedience, and that those who preach disobedience and revolution as a means to reform are like the daughters of Peleus who, desiring to renew the youth of their decrepit father, cut him in pieces and boiled him but made not of him a new man. That a man may deny the true God at the command of his sovereign, because profession with the tongue is but an external thing. That a king must either rule or be ruled by the Pope because the distinction of temporal and spiritual power is but words. And so on.

These are some of the findings of *Leviathan*, in which the essence of Hobbes' thought is concentrated. Leviathan is the name given by Hobbes to the "mortal power" exercised by governments. The political theory of the book can be summarised quite simply: it is that the natural man, swayed only by selfish passions, must be for ever at war with his fellows unless he *contracts* to submit to Leviathan, that is, to a *sovereign*, conceived as an absolute and external power. The contract is cemented by *fear*. The reduction of all human activities to selfish elements is so ruthlessly urged and argued, with such savage excursions against certain social groups, like the clergy and the universities, that parts of *Leviathan* read like a forerunner of Freud's analytical psychology, and parts like a Shaw preface. The book was published in 1651 to greet the first years of Cromwell's dictatorship. It was not unacceptable to the rulers of the Restoration. But of the opinion of the mass of the people we can perhaps best judge by the fact that, after the Great Plague of 1665 when God's displeasure became a matter of public enquiry and concern, *Leviathan* narrowly escaped suppression by Act of Parliament.

Hobbes' unorthodoxy flashed like a meteor through the sky dazzling the beholder ; Locke put a new star among the constellations which has never ceased to light men's way. Locke was nineteen years old when *Leviathan* was published. His *Two Treatises of Government* were directed, not against Hobbes, but against a lesser disciple of Hobbes, Sir Robert Filmer ; yet ever and again, by a turn of phrase or a pointed allusion, Locke shows himself conscious of the older master-spirit. I take the innermost essence of Locke's political philosophy to be contained in this proposition : "He who attempts to get another man into his absolute power does thereby put himself into a state of war with him." This superb declaration may be found in the seventeenth paragraph of the second *Treatise*. From this follows Locke's view of monarchy, that where-ever the King may be found exercising absolute power over his subjects, whether he be called the Czar or the Grand Signior, such a society is the most primitive possible. From this follows the memorable dictum which justifies war and in extreme cases revolution : "May the commands, then, of a prince be opposed ? To this I answer, that force is to be opposed to nothing but to unjust and to unlawful forces." Locke held the very moderate view that government was a responsibility delegated by the com-munity for the purpose of protecting each member's life and property. Its function was to safeguard, not to restrict, the liberty of the individual. The *Epistle on Toleration* (*Epistola de Tolerantia*, one of the last English philosophical works to be published in Latin) carried the same theme ; and if, as is sometimes pointed out, he himself failed to tolerate Papists and Atheists, he surely hastened the day of their toleration.

Locke, too, had a sounder initiation into government than Hobbes, the tutor of earls and princes. He was born in a cottage. He was by turns doctor, university professor, diplomat, civil servant ; and he was turned out of a university post by one of the arbitrary acts of King James II. When the revolution broke out, Locke had been seven years in exile in Holland. He returned in the same ship which carried the Princess Mary and was invited to become William of Orange's Ambassador to one of the German capitals, Berlin and Vienna. Nothing is more revealing of Locke's personal character than the letter in which he declined this employment.

What is most serious in the letter is too long to be quoted ; but like Ambassador Dodd of the United States, apprehensive of the summons to adapt himself to the habits of the Nazi leaders, Locke takes alarm at the German reputation for hard drinking. "It is no small matter in such stations to be acceptable to the people one has to do with, in being able to accommodate oneself to their fashions. I should think it more for the King's interest to send a man of equal parts that could drink his share than the soberest man in the kingdom."

Modest, efficient, scholarly, democratic (his father fought in the Civil War on the Parliament side)—these qualities would have inevitably ranged him against Hobbes, would have gone far to account for his essays on political matters and the kindred work *Some Thoughts Concerning Education* in which he makes many practical and modern-sounding suggestions for forming the minds of children. They would never explain that towering intellectual achievement, the first full study of the nature and limits of philosophic knowledge in modern times, the *Essay on Human Understanding*. Locke came to this by a sort of revelation. The scene was such a one as Plato often describes and Locke's description of it is strikingly similar. Five or six of his friends were talking in his room about morality and religion. "It came into my thoughts that we took a wrong course, and that before we set ourselves upon enquiries of that nature, it was necessary to examine our abilities and see what objects our understandings were, or were not, fitted to deal with." Locke parted from his friends that night with the promise that he would write down his thoughts upon these first principles. The task took him nearly twenty years.

What Locke did was to map the human mind. Like the old geographers who charted Africa, he coasted patiently from bay to bay, measuring distances, dropping his plummet into every firth and inlet and, on occasion, making exploratory forays into the interior. The immense and original labour which Locke performed opened up a new philosophical continent. None of his successors but was constrained at some time or another to say : "John Locke travelled this way before me"; they acknowledged his achievement by the glee with which they corrected a detail here and there in his plan.* Locke made certain large assumptions. He called all the objects of the human understanding *ideas* and treated them neutrally. That is to say, *seeing a tree* and *thinking about God* were both *ideas*, according to Locke ; and it was wildly exhilarating in the seventeenth century that anyone should hold the balance so evenly before dropping two such traditionally uneven ideas upon the scales. Next, he regarded the mind as a blank upon which the ideas were imposed, like pictures on a screen. There were no such things as innate ideas ; all ideas entered the mind from outside, although some of them, the compound and abstract ones, had been worked up by the mind, as raw material is worked up into a

*Locke's map is not inaccurately drawn even by to-day standards.

288

JOHN LOCKE

Oil painting by Sir Godfrey Kneller, 1646 - 1723

EDINBURGH FROM THE WEST, IN THE TIME OF DAVID HUME

Coloured engraving by Paul Sandby, 1725 - 1809

complex finished product. Perhaps his most characteristic assumption was that the ideas sit somewhere midway between the mind and the external world. This is the very battleground of philosophy, the question what is the relation between the mind and its ideas and between ideas and external things. Locke said that the ideas were "in the mind" and that some ideas "resembled" external things ; that was as far as he went into the matter. But one cannot in the same voyage circumnavigate a continent and trace all its rivers to the source.

He takes his ideas, then, and examines them from various angles, holds them up to the light, so to speak. First, he classifies them according to their origins. Ideas originate from *sensation* or *reflection* or both. The ideas of sensation are, of course, the shapes, colours, tastes and smells which come to us from the outside world. For example, we look at the sun. We have various ideas of roundness, whiteness, and heat : all simple ideas of sensation. The roundness is a *primary quality, resembling* something in the sun ; because although it may not be the real size and shape of the sun, yet the sun has *some* size and shape. The whiteness and heat are *secondary qualities*, because these are wholly begotten upon the mind by the senses and neither they nor anything like them exist in the sun. The distinction which Locke made between primary and secondary qualities stirred up a philosophic controversy which has lasted to this day. The ideas of reflection appear when our mental faculties of memory, will-power, discernment, knowledge and so on begin to work upon the raw material of sensation. When we remember the sun and when we deliberately think of the sun, we have simple ideas of reflection. When we bask in the sun, we have an idea of pleasure ; when we are blistered by the sun, we have an idea of pain : and these are also simple ideas, but of sensation and reflection mixed.

We come next to the complex ideas. The sun is, of course, itself a complex idea ; it is an idea of something which is at once round and white and hot. The mind constantly builds collections of qualities like these into ideas of *substance*, from which is finally built our idea of the world of nature. It compares one idea with another to produce ideas of *relations* ; for example, we say "Queen Elizabeth lived 69 years," an idea which we get by comparing the duration of one substance (Queen Elizabeth) with 69 annual revolutions of another substance (the sun). The mind also has the power of abstraction, that is to say, it can combine ideas regardless of their relations with things. The ancients produced their idea of a Sun God by combining the ideas of the sun and of a very powerful man. Locke rightly saw that language itself is an act of abstraction and that to call every leaf on every tree in the world by a particular name would be the very negation of language, because no man would understand what another was saying. There is a very modern spirit in the way Locke bases much of his reasoning on the behaviour of animals and young children. He reminds us in one passage how children invent their own words to represent their real ideas of things, reversing the habit of parsons and schoolmasters who repeat other men's gibberish with the utmost persuasiveness in spite of the fact that it represents nothing really existing in nature.

After assembling the contents of the mind (and no brief summary could so much as suggest the vigour and richness of the detail), Locke asks : "What is knowledge and how much can we be said to know ?" To the first question : "What is knowledge ?" he answers that knowledge consists in the agreement which we perceive between our ideas, or the agreement which we perceive between our ideas and reality. We know that two plus two equals four because this idea agrees with all other ideas and never comes up against an idea that two plus two equals five or fifty. We know that the sun exists because our idea of the sun agrees with something real in the outside world. Locke held that knowledge of substances, that is to say, the outside world, was very incomplete. We knew substances only through sensation ; and to find out that the sun hardened mud but melted wax required patient observation and experiment. Beyond the region of our certain knowledge, said Locke, stretched a twilight region in which the judgment operated. We could judge of many things which we did not know, but only on probability. Of the pitfalls which beset the fallible judgment of man, Locke tells a story which he must have heard with delight during his residence in Holland. The Dutch Ambassador to the Court of Siam was trying to explain to the Siamese King how the northern rivers froze in winter time ; the ice was so thick, he said, that an elephant could stand on it. But the King of Siam, applying his own system of probabilities, was merely confirmed in his previous belief that the Dutch Ambassador was a liar.

Locke put the problem of knowledge upon a psychological basis. Indeed the *Essay* may be read as the first great study in analytical psychology. It has, as we have already indicated, a truly superb completeness. It is not hard to lose one's way in the *Essay ;* but it is extremely hard to find any point which Locke has entirely neglected. Many of the criticisms of Locke fail before the simple fact that Locke himself answered them, but in a different place. This applies not only to the criticisms of the egregious Bishop of Worcester, to whom Locke made three public rejoinders, but even to Berkeley and Hume who owed to Locke the main body of their theses. The *Essay* must, in fact, be one of the world's hardest books to index properly. Locke is not over logical. He will never force a fact to fit his theory. Locke's habit of walking round his subject and commenting on it from various directions makes for occasional inconsistencies, which are the professional critic's delight. The whole is dominated by the intense conviction that philosophy is for use, not for empty debate. If knowledge be a sun, let us work in sunlight ; if a candle, by candlelight : but let us work !

GEORGE BERKELEY 1685-1753
Oil painting by Vanderbank

The Bishop of Worcester's fears were not unjustified. The young took up the New Philosophy with enthusiasm, even the future bishops. A twenty-year old theological student of Trinity College, Dublin, organised a study-circle to discuss the *Essay on Human Understanding*. It was George Berkeley, later Bishop of Cloyne. This engaging young Irishman—for that he was engaging we have more tangible evidence than his charm of style—believed that he could resolve the difficulties and uncertainties of the famous *Essay* by a single stroke of intuition. In 1710, when he was only twenty-five, he published the *Principles of Human Knowledge*. His three best-known philosophical works, the *Theory of Vision*, the *Principles* and the *Dialogues Between Hylas and Philonous* were all written before he

291

was thirty. After that, his interests in philosophy slackened as his ecclesiastical career matured. His later books, which mix Christian apologetics and Platonic mysticism, are of interest only to the specialist.

What was the young man's inspiration which was to make all Locke plain sailing ? Berkeley assailed the New Philosophy at its weakest point, the junction between the *idea*, which Locke said was in the mind, and the *thing* which the idea represented and which was assumed to exist in a world outside the mind. Why, asked Berkeley, if all that the mind knows is its own ideas, do we assume that an outside world exists at all ? "Some truths there are so near and obvious to the mind that a man need only open his eyes to see them. Such I take this important one to be, that all the choir of heaven and furniture of the earth, in a word, all those bodies which compose the mighty frame of the world, have not any subsistence without a mind, that their *being* is *to be perceived*, that, consequently, so long as they are not actually perceived by me or do not exist in my mind or that of any other created spirit, they must either have no existence at all or else subsist in the mind of some external spirit."

Two amusing comments on Berkeley's theory may be recalled. One of them is the immortal anecdote about Doctor Johnson. "After we came out of church," says Boswell, "we stood for some time talking of Bishop Berkeley's ingenious sophistry to prove the non-existence of matter, and that everything in the universe is merely ideal. I observed that, though we are satisfied his doctrine is not true, it is impossible to refute it. I shall never forget the alacrity with which Johnson answered, striking his foot with mighty force against a large stone, till he rebounded from it : "I refute it thus !' " It may be pointed out in Johnson's defence that Bertrand Russell borrows the essential part of his argument when, after observing that Berkeley is "very hard to refute," he adds that his commonsense revolts against the consequences.

Less reasonable but more witty is the limerick attributed to an Oxford professor :

"There was a young man who said 'God
Must find it exceedingly odd
That this sycamore tree
Just ceases to be
When there's no-one about in the Quad'."

This limerick, like the equally celebrated one about Einstein's Theory of Relativity, is unfair. Berkeley never maintained that the sycamore tree simply ceased to exist when there was no-one looking at it. What he said was that the "matter" or "substance" or whatever was supposed to cause the greenness of the leaves and the jagged shape of the branches and to persist when there was no image of a sycamore in any mind *did not exist at all or at any time*. But the whole sensible world of Nature did exist, not only during the transient perceptions of men, but also permanently, in the ideas of God. Nature was a manifestation of God's ideas; and there are passages in Berkeley which approximate to the extreme Spinozan view, that Nature *is* God.

Berkeley is important in the history of philosophy because he produced a very pure form of a theory which constantly recurs in philosophic literature under the general title of *Idealism.* This theory represents the Universe as of mental stuff and is opposed to *Materialism*, which represents the Universe as basically material and derives all mental phenomena from the motions and properties of matter. Hobbes was an out-and-out Materialist; Berkeley an equally thoroughgoing Idealist. The key work is the *Principles* from which we have already quoted the key-passage. Second ranks *Hylas and Philonous*, in which the three main ingredients of his life-work are all attractively deployed : the Idealist theory, which was his own ; the arguments, which were broadly Locke's ; and the manner which was Plato's.

Philonous : Can any doctrine be true that necessarily leads a man into an absurdity ?

Hylas : Without doubt it cannot.

Philonous : Is it not an absurdity to think that the same thing should be at the same time both cold and warm ?

Hylas : It is.

Philonous : Suppose now one of your hands hot and the other cold, and that they are both at once put into the same vessel of tepid water, will not the water seem cold to one hand and warm to the other ?

Hylas : It will.

Philonous : Ought we not therefore by your principles to conclude it is really both cold and warm at the same time, that is, according to your own concession, to believe an absurdity ?

Berkeley makes a brilliant splash upon the pages of British philosophy but with a talent which shines, perhaps, a little too smooth and easy against Locke's rugged genius.

Hume rounded off the Great Age. The *Treatise of Human Nature*, which was to jerk all European philosophy into a new groove, ripened as young as Berkeley's masterpiece. It was begun in 1734 when Hume was twenty-three and finished three years later. If he had not written it then, the world would almost certainly have lost it altogether, for Hume craved for popular fame and when he discovered that philosophy did not bring it, he turned to other subjects. In later years he was so ashamed of the neglect into which the *Treatise* had fallen that he set himself to rewrite it in a more popular style. Such are the aberrations to which even the most powerful mind is liable.

Hume was of a simple, generous, gentle nature—sharper in his writings than in his dealings with mankind. His friend Adam Smith, the author of *The Wealth of Nations*, declared after Hume's death that he was an example

of the wise and good man.   Yet there was a ruling vanity in Hume which,
if less assertive and angular than that of Hobbes, at least suffices to make
his virtues interesting.   It may be seen in the brief autobiographical sketch
he left behind him, *My Own Life;* and his letters from Paris, describing
the compliments which the Dauphin and Madame de Pompadour showered
upon him, are models of eighteenth-century complacency.   Poor Hume,
who wrote to Hippolyte, Comtesse de Boufflers : "Commonsense requires that I should keep at a distance from all attachments that can imply
passion !" Not Gibbon himself spurned a lover with more self-consciousness or less charm.

My Own Life is what we should call nowadays a literary success-story.
Hume spent his mature powers upon three massive English Histories and
fitted in, so to speak, his occasional digressions into Philosophy and Religion.
Twice he held public appointments.   From 1746 to 1748 he was aide-de-
camp to General St. Clair.   He took part in a "Commando" raid against
L'Orient on the coast of Brittany.   He also accompanied a British Military
Mission to the Courts of Vienna and Turin ; he has left in his letters a
fascinating account of the Court of Maria Theresa, the goitre in the Ba-
varian valleys, the lovely Slovene countryside and his homage at Virgil's
birthplace.   Then from 1763 to 1765 he was Secretary to the Embassy in
Paris, for a few months actually Chargé d'Affaires.   He presents these two
episodes of public service as interruptions in a scholar's life ; and he
comments here and there upon royalties and copyright payments in the
modern manner.   He is very conscious of his "public."   At first they
reject him ; generally they are violently agitated by him ; but all goes
right in the end.   The *Treatise of Human Nature* "fell dead-born from the
press" ; but in the final years "the copy-money given me by the book-
sellers much exceeded anything formerly known in England."

The great *Treatise* has the marks of youth upon it.   It begins weakly.
There is a sort of insolence in places—much talk of "profound reasoning,"
a gulf like a caste-system fixed between "philosophic" and "vulgar" minds,
no acknowledgment of the debt to Locke, of which the most casual reader
must be instantly conscious.   For Hume takes over entire that part of
Locke's system which atomises the mind into *ideas*, except that he calls
Locke's ideas of sensation *impressions*.   He even attempts a superficial
catalogue of his *ideas* and *impressions* in the Lockian manner.   But these
are preliminary hesitations : we are soon to launch once more into un-
charted seas.   We are going to apply Locke's psychological method with
a subtlety and accuracy for which Locke had no time and from the consequences of which he would have certainly shrunk.   *Ideas*, such as the
abstract one of "humanity," differ from *impressions*, such as "seeing the
sun," only because the idea is faint and the impression vivid and strong.
The fact that I believe that the sun exists, while I do not believe that
"humanity" in the abstract exists, is, for Hume, simply a sign of the

DAVID HUME 1711-1776
Oil painting by Allan Ramsay

vividness of the impression as against the idea—certainly not a proof of
the existence of a physical sun. If any impression or idea strikes in on
our minds with particular force, we are said to believe it ; this, according
to Hume, is all that knowledge means. And further : we believe what we
believe out of habit. For example, when we believe that the sun will rise
to-morrow, our belief is simply a strong idea, based upon the habit of
observing the sun rise upon innumerable morrows in the past. Thus, for
all natural laws, based on the operation of cause and effect, Hume substitutes
simply a *feeling* of belief, based on habit. It was this destructive criticism
of the idea of cause which set Kant's mind working. For if one could not
be, but only *feel*, certain that the sun would rise next day, it would seem
that all science was illusory and indeed impossible.

We have no space here to follow the *Treatise* along all its ramifications. But to take a specimen of Hume's method : his treatment of the problem of the external world. Locke had, as we have seen, assumed that there was an external world, corresponding in some respects to our ideas of it. Berkeley had declared that there was no need to assume an external world at all—at least, not in the usual sense of the term. Hume said : since philosophers agree that all we can know is our own ideas and since we are not in direct contact with the external world at any point, how do we come by this extraordinary notion ? Note the form of the question—not how can the notion be justified, but how do we come by it. Well, the philosopher looks at his desk and papers ; here they are, here they were yesterday and the day before. He looks at the fire ; it certainly has sunk since he last looked at it, but by natural degrees, so that it is visibly "the same fire." From these observations, Hume concludes that when certain impressions return to us, either unchanged (like the desk) or with expected and coherent changes (like the fire), our imagination (like a boat which continues in movement when the oars are lifted) insists on filling in the spaces between the interrupted impressions and making one identical object out of them. Hume then refines upon this analysis. Where do we get this idea of "one identical object ?" The only identical object of which we have experience is an uninterrupted perception. (Hume now uses Berkeley's word "perception" instead of his own "impression"). If, now, we have a succession of interrupted but similar perceptions (as when we "see the sun" on several occasions) and if imagination fills in the gaps between them, we still only have one identical *perception*, not an external object. But a human mind, according to Hume, is simply a bundle or chain of perceptions (how close we are to modern forms of mental theory at this point) ; so there is no difficulty in supposing that perceptions may go on existing outside the mind. This, in fact, is exactly what the imagination does suppose when it jumps the gap between similar perceptions ; and "external object" is simply the *name* we give to these imaginatively externalised perceptions. Finally, we *believe* in external objects because the *strong feeling* which accompanies our perceptions is communicated to the figment which fills the gaps, as the lover who kisses his mistress's handkerchief feels the same passion as when he kisses her lips. The upshot of the argument is to destroy our belief in external objects altogether.

The second part of the *Treatise* deals more specifically with human nature and society. It begins, characteristically, with an analysis of the emotions of *pride* and *humility*. Hume, like Hobbes, considers that the motives which activate human behaviour are essentially selfish ; but unlike Hobbes, he finds room for an emotion of *benevolence* or *sympathy*. This part of the *Treatise*, somewhat neglected nowadays, is very important in philosophical history for its influence upon Jeremy Bentham and J. S. Mill. Similarly, the *Dialogues on Natural Religion* are important as the fore-

LINCOLN'S INN, OF WHICH BENTHAM BECAME A MEMBER IN 1817

Coloured engraving by J. Marsh

THE LIBRARY OF TRINITY COLLEGE, DUBLIN
Berkeley was Fellow and Scholar of Trinity
Coloured engraving published by Robert Sayer, c.1760

runners of Victorian free thought and agnosticism. In these *Dialogues*, Hume chiefly assails that celebrated "argument from design" which attempts to prove the existence of God by the evidence of divine handiwork in the world of nature. He comes to the apparently cynical conclusion that the difference of opinion between the theist and the atheist is only a *verbal* one. It is a dispute, not about facts, but about degrees, as one might dispute whether Cleopatra was a beautiful or a very beautiful woman. The theist and the atheist have no deeper quarrel about the Universe, for if the one calls it incomprehensively divine, the other must acknowledge it divinely incomprehensible.

Yet Hume's very negativeness and scepticism have an underlying fire and passion. I still remember how, as a young man, I lay one evening on the river-bank at Cambridge, reading the last pages of the metaphysical section of the *Treatise*, while the summer sun climbed down ; and how I stared over the golden fields, inundated with despair that all was illusion, that nothing could be surely known. And at the same time I felt a surge of exultation that any man should have plumbed the very abyss of doubt and that I should have followed him there. No modern thinker touches like Hume that nerve of the spirit which caused Alcibiades to say of philosophy that it stings like a viper when it gets hold of a young and not insensitive mind.

> "The *intense* view of these manifold contradictions and imperfections in human reason has so wrought upon me, and heated my brain, that I am ready to reject all belief and reasoning, and can look upon no opinion even as more probable or likely than another. Where am I, or what ? From what causes do I derive my existence, and to what condition shall I return ? Whose favour shall I court, and whose anger must I dread ? What beings surround me ? and on whom have I any influence, or who have any influence on me ? I am confounded with all these questions, and begin to fancy myself in the most deplorable condition imaginable, environed with the deepest darkness, and utterly deprived of the use of every member and faculty."

Hume is a protagonist of the eighteenth-century cult of Reason. Gibbon, the arch-sceptic, had still to reach his prime—Gibbon who said that a letter of praise from Hume overpaid him for ten years of work. But this quotation from the First Book of the *Treatise* belongs rather to the succeeding age. It has more than a little in common with the poet who wrote :

> " 'Tis we, who, lost in stormy visions, keep
> With phantoms an unprofitable strife,
> And in mad trance strike with our spirit's knife
> Invulnerable nothings."

It belongs to the age when even philosophy was required to become romantic.

ADAM SMITH 1723-1790
Engraving by Kay from the *Wealth of Nations*. Edition of 1853

IV

AFTER Hume, the Muse of Philosophy transferred her main residence across the Rhine. Naked and unashamed she would go no
longer ; she developed a taste for showy dress.

Kant, Fichte, Hegel, Schopenhauer and Nietzsche—these were the
prophets of the new order. In modern times, when the pendulum has

swung back again, it is not easy to do them justice. All dabbled in the prophetic extravagance ; and some went in up to their necks. They did not proceed by simple observation ; they thought they could dredge up truth by devising new logical implements. Kant, for example, argued like this : space must be infinite ; space cannot be infinite ; therefore space does not exist in the real world. He arrived at a real world peopled only by *Noumena*, beings more unreal than any imagined by any other philo- sopher. Did these German philosophers make any permanent contribution to their science to match their immense contemporary prestige ? Kant was the greatest of them ; yet what, in essence, is the *Critique of Pure Reason* but a restatement of Berkeley's Idealism in more laboured terms, with the *Noumena* replacing God ? According to Bertrand Russell, Kant was a philosophic disaster !

In Britain we have, first, a period of applied philosophy. The meta- physical enquiries of the Great Age had cleared men's minds, even if they had not entirely satisfied them ; and Adam Smith, Jeremy Bentham, John Stuart Mill and Herbert Spencer, like generals who have got a secure base of operations, all crossed that indeterminate frontier which divides pure philosophy from the social sciences. Then came the full impact of the German philosophy. Carlyle was one of its chief missionaries in England. A generation of British philosophers wrote volumes entitled *A Text-Book to Kant, The Secret of Hegel*, and so on. T. H. Green's *Prolegomena* (1883) and F. H. Bradley's *Appearance and Reality* (1893) marked the climax and close of this period.

Adam Smith (1723-1790) was, like Hume, a Scot. He became Pro- fessor of Moral Philosophy at Glasgow, resigned this post after twelve years in order to travel, and in 1776, the year of Hume's death, published *The Wealth of Nations*. No philosophic work so simple in form, so immense in scope, had been written in English since Locke's *Essay*. It was the world's first full-length study of the foundations of an industrial society. Leeds, Halifax, Sheffield, Birmingham and Wolverhampton already shadow forth their giant mechanised future ; and France, Spain, the New World, India and China all supply the author with examples and arguments. Smith believed in free trade. He believed that every man's desire to better his condition would ensure continuous economic progress, if all artificial obstructions were removed. In this book of 1776 you will find a concrete plan for universal elementary education, based on the existing Scottish system of parish schools. What is said on the subject of philosophy is interesting. Smith thought that philosophy took a wrong turn when, under the influence of ecclesiastical vested interests, the ancient division into natural philosophy (science), moral philosophy (ethics) and logic was abandoned in favour of metaphysics. For the ancient division conformed to the nature of things, but metaphysics was a "cobweb science" of churchmen's disputations.

London bred Jeremy Bentham (1748-1832), as well as several generations of Bentham's before him. His father was a prominent member of the Scriveners' Company, well-to-do ; and Jeremy was that alarming thing, an infant prodigy. At the advanced age of three he was to be observed poring over Rapin's *History of England* ; at five he wrote Latin and had already been nicknamed "Philosopher" ; at eight he spoke French and resorted to Voltaire for light reading. As might be expected, he was a delicate, retiring child. The only out-of-the-way incident of his life was a two-year visit to Russia where one of his brothers was employed as an engineer. A friend wrote of him : "He never knew prosperity or adversity, passion or satiety. He never had even the experience which sickness gives. He lived from childhood to the age of eighty-two in boyish health. He knew no dejection, no heaviness of heart. He was a boy to the last."

Out of this temperamental serenity sprang the *greatest happiness* principle, the foundation-stone of the Utilitarian philosophy. Of course, Bentham was not the first to identify good with happiness ; there have been systems of hedonism since the world began. The opening sentence of his *Principles of Morals and Legislation* : "Nature has placed mankind under the governance of two sovereign masters, pain and pleasure" derives directly from Part Two of Hume's *Treatise*. But Bentham was a great populariser. He not only enunciated his principle ; he worked it out. He gathered disciples.

Bentham reckoned that if the *greatest happiness* principle were to be an effective guide to human action, we ought to be able to measure happiness, as we measure a table or a wall. He therefore set out seven dimensions of pleasure as follows :
1. Intensity.
2. Duration.
3. Certainty.
4. Propinquity.
5. Fecundity (or the chance it has of being followed by other pleasures).
6. Purity (or the chance it has of *not* being followed by pains).
7. Extent (that is, the number of people affected by it).

Benthan allowed for differences in human constitution ; there would be different pleasures for different people ; but all would be measured by the same standards. Let us take a simple pleasure like "smelling a wallflower." For Bentham this pleasure was very intense, because it reminded him of his grandmother's garden at Barking. It would not rank high for duration ; but certainty and propinquity would be 100% while the smelling went on. It would be fecund if it put Bentham into a good temper for the rest of the day. It would be pure enough ; but its extent would be limited, especially if it induced a mood of solitary contemplation instead of active good works. On the other hand, the pleasure of "hating your landlady," if it was a pleasure, would probably be a faint one ; its duration

JEREMY BENTHAM 1748-1832
Drawing by G. F. Watts

might be long, but it would be very impure, especially if, as a result of it, she brought you your shaving-water cold every morning. Add up all the pleasures and pains consequent upon any act, and according to whether the balance is pleasurable or painful, the act is good or bad. Two paradoxes now confronted the author of this system. Obviously, if good *meant* having pleasurable effect, there could not be such a thing as a bad motive. Motives like "lust" and "avarice" were, according to Bentham, simply neutral motives, "sexual desire" and "pecuniary interest," which were afterwards found to have had unpleasant effects. The second paradox was that if good was to be measured by *quantity* of pleasure, you could not say that any pleasure was *better* than another but only *greater*. Hence Bentham's notorious dictum : "Pushpin is as good as poetry." Pushpin was a child's game on the moral level of tiddlywinks. The later Utilitarians rejected this extreme consequence of Bentham's theory and admitted a *qualitative* difference between pleasures.

Bentham early resolved that his philosophy should itself conform to Utilitarian theory and be judged by its results. He wrote very little for publication ; his *Fragment on Government* and his *Introduction to the Principles of Morals and Legislation* are the books by which he is most often remembered ; but he never ceased compiling notes for his voluminous schemes of legislative reform. He had the ambition of legislating for the world ; not only the Russians and Americans, but also the Spaniards, Greeks, French, Portuguese, Mexicans and others received an offer of services ; the French gave him their citizenship and the British £23,000 in recognition of his zeal. At one time he aspired to a seat in Parliament. As he grew older, he became a political oracle, consulted especially by the men of radical views. His influence was felt in the Reform Bill, which passed into law only a few days after his death in 1832. He set political liberty high on his list of pleasures, and he considered that the only good Government in the world was that of the United States (of the rest he said that the British was the least bad). When Alexander Wedderburn, Attorney General and later Lord Chancellor of England, expressed the view that Bentham's political opinions were dangerous, Bentham retorted : "In a Government which had for its end the greatest happiness of the greatest number, Alexander Wedderburn might have been Attorney General and then Chancellor ; but he would not have been Attorney General with £15,000 a year, nor Chancellor with £25,000 and with 500 sinecures at his disposal."

John Stuart Mill stood to Bentham as Plato to Socrates. His father, James Mill, had been one of the earliest converts to the *greatest happiness* principle, and Bentham's best friend ; and John Stuart was brought up in the atmosphere of the Bentham household. He was educated by his father. A full account of this most extraordinary of all educations has been left us in Mill's *Autobiography*. His whole childhood consisted in reading classical books and taking improving walks with his father. For precocity, he out-Benthamed Bentham. He learned Greek at three. At seven he read the *Euthyphron* and five other dialogues of Plato. At eight he was teaching his sister Latin. During the walks, his father used to show him how to distinguish good arguments from bad and how to conceal his lack of religious conviction from other people. The marvel is that enough freshness was left in the child's mind to react to Bentham's Utili-

JOHN STUART MILL 1806-1873
Oil painting by G. F. Watts, 1874

tarian philosophy at fifteen years old with a sense of shock. The *greatest happiness* principle struck Mill as the final word in the science of ethics. The rigid exclusion of all that the run of mankind calls pleasure left a certain dust of dryness upon Mill's work. His intellectual pride, his very exactness of style always limited his humanity a little ; and it was not until he married, late in life, that his broadest sympathies were released. To this period belong all Mill's labours for the oppressed. He was elected to Parliament, after warning his constituents that he would do nothing for their special interests but only what he considered to be right. He was an advocate of women's suffrage and secured eighty votes in its favour from a hostile House of Commons ; the essay *On the Subjection of Women* followed three years afterwards. He fought a two years' battle for the rights of the negroes and mulattoes of Jamaica. Finally, Mill became a champion of the working people of Britain. He was the first who ever waived royalties on his books so that they should be published cheaply enough for the poor to buy. The picture survives of this most bookish of philosophers, preserved as a boy from contacts even with children of his own age, addressing a working-class audience and being asked by a heckler whether in one of his pamphlets he had not written that working men were liars. "Yes," said Mill "I wrote it." The whole audience cheered him. But he was not returned a second time to Parliament. "What was surprising," says Mill justly, "is that I should have been elected once."

The stuff of Mill's philosophy is contained in the *System of Logic*, published in 1843 when Mill was 37 years old. Now the small boy who trotted obediently at his father's heels, learning the frailties of human reason, is of an age to lay down the laws of thought for other people. His starting-point is the "proposition"—that is to say, the form of words in which we make any statement. He holds that all propositions are reducible to five primary types and that all, even the most abstract, like "Prudence is a virtue," refer to something particular in the real world. He next analyses the inductive process by which we pass from one proposition to another in enlarging our knowledge—how, for example, can we justify our "universal" scientific laws ? Mill is as suspicious as Locke and Hume before him of anything which claims to be "universal" : scientific laws must be considered approximations, based upon collections of particular instances—though Mill does not go so far as to deny the operation of invariable causes in the material world. What is the material world ? Mill affects to decline the ultimate metaphysical problems. He looks at his table (most British philosophers who address themselves to the mystery of matter begin by staring at the table !) and is content to define matter as the unknown cause of our sensations. Logic, he says, has no business with metaphysics ; on this excuse he often breaks off an argument at its most interesting point. The *System of Logic* ends with a discussion of fallacies and a long review of previous theories of knowledge ; it is, perhaps, the first book which puts into perspective what we now call modern European philosophy.

Herbert Spencer, the Philosopher of Evolution, is more difficult to classify. He believed in what H. G. Wells would call a World Brain. He published in March 1860 the prospectus of a gigantic Encyclopaedia in five parts : *First Principles ; Principles of Biology ; Principles of Psychology; Principles of Sociology* and *Principles of Morality*. The obvious comparison is with Francis Bacon's six-fold Ladder of Philosophy, with the

By courtesy of Merton College, Oxford

J. H. BRADLEY
Oil painting by W. H. Eves

J. M. E. M'TAGGART
Oil painting by Roger Fry, 1866-1934

important difference that what Herbert Spencer promised he performed. There is no consistent metaphysical point of view in Spencer's chain of treatises ; but there is a striking dominant idea. He had definitely conceived a theory of evolution before Darwin's *Origin of Species* appeared. He believed that there was a fundamental process at work in Nature : a sort of gathering together and blossoming of material particles. As in the Universe vast nebulae shrank into suns and planets, and planets shrank until they burst into life, so separate living things should be conceived as substances which were for ever concentrating and liberating new energies. Spencer believed that everything in the world, even human behaviour, was developing upon this principle. Year by year he carried the mighty labour forward, publishing *First Principles* in 1862, when he was forty-two years old, and concluding with the *Principles of Ethics*, the second volume of which appeared in 1892, when he was seventy-two. No-one in modern times has read Herbert Spencer all through. (Doubtless someone will write to *The Times* contradicting this statement). He raised a monument of mental industry which recalls the pyramids of Egypt. There they stand ; but no-one will be tempted to build in the same way again.

Traces of the contemporary German vogue may be found all over Spencer's books. Such phrases as "All our knowledge is of the phenomenal" are pure Kant. It is time to look briefly at those British philosophers who swam with the full current of the alien tradition. Sir William Hamilton, to whom Mill devoted his *Examination of Sir William Hamilton's Philosophy*, was the first of them ; but T. H. Green was probably the most important. Green had worked at Heidelberg University but spent most of his life at Oxford, finally becoming Professor of Moral Philosophy there. His earliest works were destructive criticisms of Locke and Hume. "Shut up your Mill and Spencer" he told his pupils, "and open your Kant and Hegel." There was a moral force in the man which gained him universal respect and enthusiastic disciples. But although his style was less involved than that of Kant (who habitually said : "synthetic unity of apperception" for what Locke had called "understanding") it was not much less involved. One day he was lecturing his class upon the origin of ideas. For an hour his listeners were transported in the highest realms of thought. But as he left his lecture room, one of the undergraduates plucked at his sleeve and asked timidly : "Please, Mr. Green, where did you say our ideas come from ?".

The *Prolegomena to Ethics* sets out the foundations of metaphysics, as well as of ethics, as Green understood them. First comes the flat rejection of what seemed so natural to Locke and Hume, that the raw materials of our knowledge are the sensations that force their way in upon our consciousness whether we like it or not. For when Green looked into his own mind he could not find any such things as raw sensations. He could only find complex objects held together by *relations*. It was the relations which

HERBERT SPENCER 1820-1903
Cartoon by C.G. from *Vanity Fair*,
1879

seemed to Green to be the *real* element in sensation. When Green looked at the sun, he saw the qualities of roundness, whiteness and heat inextricably related ; nor could he detach the sun from its relations with every other object of sense and knowledge. Since the relations were also the work of the mind, it followed that reality was (in Green's word) *spiritual*. He quotes with approval Kant's dictum : "The understanding makes Nature."

F. H. Bradley's *Appearance and Reality* went a stage further. Bradley (1846-1924) was a Fellow of Merton College, Oxford, and published several books on philosophical subjects besides the one which established his fame. The relations which had seemed to Green the very sign and substance of Reality struck Bradley quite the other way. It was from the relations which held the world together that Bradley deduced the *unreality* of the world. He argued somewhat like this. The world is strung together like the links of a chain. Each link is connected with the next link. But what is this connection ? Either it is something, in which case it must itself be connected with the links and so on in an infinite regress ; or it is nothing, in which case the links are not connected at all. Thus whatever is related contradicts itself. There may be two opinions upon this argument ; to my mind it reads like the arguments of the sophists in the *Euthyphron*, upon which Mill was exercising his critical faculties at the age of seven or so. With this weapon in his hands, Bradley assailed all the departments of conventional knowledge. Matter was unreal because it involved relations. Space and time were unreal, pain and pleasure mere appearances, soul and body the phantasmagoria of imperfect minds. What remained ? Only the Absolute. In the Absolute all human experience (for experience, although unreal, was nevertheless the only constituent of the Absolute) fell tidily into place, having shed its relations as a butterfly sloughs off its chrysalis. Bradley's style is clipped, vigorous, as if disarming the reader's

306

incredulity by a show of businesslike precision. His rare metaphors flicker brilliantly and impatiently through the pages. He disdains illustrations as inexact and unworthy of an adult audience. We have travelled a long way since Locke bent down to listen to the unformed babble of little children.

Mill once said that philosophy must always take one of two courses and philosophers walk in opposite ways accordingly. Either they will hold that our knowledge is built up slowly and imperfectly by experience ; or they will cleave to one or other form of the doctrine of innate ideas. This sums up the fundamental schism of the nineteenth century.

V

WE have reached the Modern Age, having proceeded, as Nature was once reputed never to do, by jumps. We have left gaps; we have suppressed many worthy names; and we have somewhat obscured that ancient truth that men who have seen the light have generally done so by climbing on another's shoulders.

How many near-great philosophers the universities have produced—great, if you take into account their influence upon their pupils and successors. Such a one was Robert Grosseteste, the first Chancellor of Oxford University, who lectured to Roger Bacon. He was an Englishman in the grand style, fearlessly outspoken, a hater of Popery, who built upon philosophy like a rock. Even Bacon writes of him with reverence. Or consider, five hundred years later, that galaxy of philosophers who won a brilliant reputation for the Scottish universities : Francis Hutcheson, professor at Glasgow, forerunner of the Utilitarians ; Thomas Reid of Aberdeen, Hume's critic and rival ; and Dugald Stewart in Edinburgh, the most quoted of J. S. Mill's authorities on logic. Hobbes made a furious attack on the universities as being stickers in the mud of reaction ; and Adam Smith, in his time, added a more gentle rebuke. Nevertheless, without the universities, British philosophy would have been poorer ; and Hobbes' assault upon the professors was the least successful of his many feuds.

When we run into the nineteenth century, the universities become even more prominent. The reason for this may be found in the increasing endowment of philosophic studies. Hutcheson has been called "the first notable British philosopher to occupy a professor's Chair"; and that was in 1729. In June 1842, that is to say, almost exactly 100 years ago, the universities of Oxford, Cambridge, Dublin, Edinburgh, Glasgow, Aberdeen, St. Andrews, London and Durham, supported between them some eighteen professorships and lectureships in pure Philosophy (excluding Divinity and Natural Philosophy). To-day the same universities can count, at a conservative estimate, more than fifty such posts. This takes no account of Professorships in Psychology and other border-line subjects. In addition, the great industrial cities have now acquired universities, each with its own Faculty of Philosophy. Birmingham has one Professorship and two Lectureships in Mental and Moral Philosophy ; the Universities of Manchester, Liverpool and Leeds make very similar provision. Where knowledge was once husbanded in channels, it now flows like a river.

At the same time, more and more young people are enabled to indulge that not ignoble curiosity which prompts us to ask philosophic questions and ponder the last uncertainties. Only in a university can such unworldly pursuits be carried on communally and single-mindedly. I still recall, with mixed astonishment and delight, the smoke-filled evenings in a friend's college rooms where, with Professor G. E. Moore for company, we used to implant our eyes upon the ceiling, trying to discover whether or not we were directly acquainted with universals, whether, in other words, we could see whiteness itself or only a white expanse of plaster ! I can still see Professor C. D. Broad lecturing in Trinity College, rosy, cherubic, repeating each sentence, like the wise thrush, twice (or was it three times ?) over, while the more industrious of his class scribbled their notes. A con-tinual half-smile lingered about his lips, as if he found the whole business irrepressibly comic ; and once or twice during the hour he would bring the house down with a sally against M'Taggart, who had lectured at Trinity before him and taught that Time was unreal, or against Leibniz' fantastic conception of a table as a colony of unintelligent souls. I now greatly regret never having heard J. M. Keynes lecture. Keynes' subject was the same which had occupied J. S. Mill : the problem of induction and the justification of general laws. His *Treatise on Probability* is held to have superseded all former studies in this highly technical province of logic. Keynes must be claimed as the only first-rank philosopher who has become a Director of the Bank of England ; he has handsomely continued the tradition of carrying philosophy into the world of affairs.

Two strong winds have blown across modern philosophy. One is the new science of psychology. This was originally a department of philosophy, springing directly from the introspective exercises of Descartes, Locke and Hume; but it developed such a practical bent in its applications to medicine and industry that its divorce from philosophy is now almost complete. The advance in psychological knowledge has modified some of the older philosophic ideas out of all recognition. It would be considered very naïve nowadays to accept Locke's "simple ideas of sensation." When we "see the sun" we have to consider a *total sense-field* out of which our faculty of *attention* selects a central object ("the sun") which we may call a *sense-datum*. Nor can our sense-datum be any longer impaled upon a point of time ; it lasts through a *specious present* containing within itself a past, a present and a future. To this experience are added certain *feelings* (*e.g.*, eye-strain) as well as *conations* (*e.g.*, a desire to shut the eyes). Another new conception with which psychology has confronted the philosophers is that of the "unconscious mental processes" of which so much has been made by Freud and his school. Most philosophers have rejected the "unconscious mind" as a misinterpretation of something which requires further analysis, but the "quasi-mnemic traces" which unconsciously influence human behaviour are a fact of which our philosophy of mind must henceforward take notice.

The other major stir has been the New Physics, the Relativity Theory and the Space-Time Hypothesis, usually associated with the name of Einstein. The intense popular interest in this subject has been demonstrated by the success of such books as Sir Arthur Eddington's *Nature of the Physical World* and Mr. Dunne's *Experiment with Time*. No doubt these books fell outside the stricter confines of philosophy. Miss Susan Stebbing's strictures upon Eddington illustrates an extreme professional view. (Miss Stebbing also illustrates the important thesis that Englishwomen may qualify, not only as Members of Parliament and aircraft designers, but also as Professors of Philosophy). Some philosophers, *e.g.* Professor A. N. Whitehead, have used Space-Time as a solvent of old philosophic dilemmas like Locke's distinction between the primary and secondary qualities of objects. According to Locke (and to most of his successors) nothing can be really coloured because the colours of things vary with the standpoint of the observer and the hour of day. Whitehead attempts to show, with the help of the Einsteinian physics, that a thing can actually *be* two different colours at once by being pervaded from two different regions of Space-Time. The argument is highly technical and may not be sound, but the fact that it is attempted shows how a revolution in physics may revolutionise philosophy, as Bacon and his friends once blazed a trail for the scientists.

A happy convention exists which holds the historian excused from extending the well-established judgments of the past to living people. But it is a fair guess that of this young century's philosophers Bertrand Russell will be longest remembered. His influence has gone far beyond his native island ; his work is well known, not only in the United States of America where he has held many university appointments, but also in the schools of philosophy of India and the Far East. He has been a controversial figure as wildly admired and reprobated as Spinoza in his time. He has suffered imprisonment and exile for his ideas.

Russell has inherited an earldom from his grandfather who was a Liberal Prime Minister of England. He was also a follower of J. S. Mill. The many links with the older philosophers form perhaps the most remarkable part of Russell's story. In his *Outline of Philosophy* he acknowledges his philosophic ancestry in these words :

"I come now to the triad of British philosophers, Locke, Berkeley and Hume —English, Irish and Scotch respectively. Perhaps from patriotic bias or from community of national temperament, I find more that I can accept and regard as still important in the writings of these three than in the philosophy of their continental predecessors."

Like Locke especially, Russell has followed his chief metaphysical works with the broadest ethical and social enquiries. *On Education, Marriage and Morals, The Conquest of Happiness* show Locke's Libertarianism and Bentham's Utilitarianism carried to the extreme conclusion. Russell's ethic is a *greatest happiness principle* from which all stoical reservations have been purged away : a sort of quintessential Utilitarianism.

"We need a morality based upon love of life, upon pleasure in growth and positive achievement . . . . A man should be regarded as "good" if he is happy, expansive, generous and glad when others are happy . . . . A man who acquires a fortune by cruelty or exploitation should be regarded as at present we regard what is called an "immoral" man and he should be so regarded even if he goes to church regularly."

Russell himself recalls how he first heard the name of Bentham as that of a very wicked man ! Russell's latest published book : *An Enquiry into Meaning and Truth*, returns to the problem of language almost exactly as it was first formulated by Francis Bacon and afterwards by Locke and Mill. To Bacon's objection that Reality is too subtle for words and to Locke's objection that all language entails abstraction, Russell envisages a primary logical language which shall copy the fundamental operations of nature. Russell matches the best of his predecessors with a beautifully direct style, capable of savage irony and elegant wit. I have always liked the riposte to the Behaviourist philosopher who found something incongruous in Keynes' marrying a famous dancer. This, said Russell, was from the Behaviourist standpoint most unreasonable (for the Behaviourists contend that all thinking is nothing more than a muscular agitation in the throat). She had cultivated the muscles of legs and arms, he the muscles of the larynx, so that both were acrobats, though belonging to different branches of the profession !

No absolutely consistent account of the universe emerges from Russell's many writings. He has undoubtedly changed his point of view more than once. There was an early period when he was much attracted to Idealism. He tells us himself that he was once very much under the spell of Bradley's *Appearance and Reality*. In one early book he even suggests a revival of the Platonic Overworld of Ideas, in which universals exist timelessly, diffusing reality upon particular things. But Russell, too, felt the impact of the new physical theories. It was necessary to re-examine the question, "What is a physical object?" and re-define the evasive relation of Matter and Mind. He returned once more to the

BERTRAND RUSSELL b. 1872
Drawing by Sir William Rothenstein

analysis of the sense-field or sense-datum, the original Lockian "idea of sensation." He found there a hard neutral core, divested of all accompanying feelings—a core which partook of the nature of neither matter nor mind. This neutral stuff, according to Russell, was the elemental stuff of which the universe was made; in certain combinations it was called mind, in other combinations it became a physical object. The sense-datum which was *perceived* formed part of a mind and a physical object simultaneously, just as some Thames-side towns belong to Berkshire in the postal sense and to Buckinghamshire topographically. It is easier to reconstruct the physical world on this basis than to explain the extraordinary variety of "events" (as Russell sometimes calls them) which

311

constitute a self or mind. As far as I know, Russell has nowhere indicated how such a task would be accomplished. But if it were, both minds and physical objects would become, for philosophers, logical constructions built upon elements which were immediately known. It is an arresting theory and one which may be worked out in detail by a later generation.

We are also confirmed in the belief, as we read Russell and other modern philosophers, that the perennial task of philosophy is to re-state and re-define truths which have been stated and defined, but imperfectly, in the past. Sometimes an old term is discarded for no better reason than that it does not sound fresh and will not serve what is essentially a fresh effort of thought. It is ironical, for instance, that Russell should abandon the word "knowledge" for the word "acquaintance"; we no longer know what we see, we are only acquainted with it! The "innate idea" of Locke's predecessors has become "the a priori concept"; the "Platonic idea" is renamed "universal." Philosophy, like political liberty, is not to be entrapped in any written constitution; it has to be struggled for, by each succeeding age, with new angles of view and new forms of expression. That is why we should read the history of philosophy imaginatively and why we should deal gently with the outworn terminologies of the past. For our own most cherished exactitudes, our "basic propositions" and "perceptual situations" and "emergent characteristics" will be ruthlessly spring-cleaned by our children and grandchildren, who will often wonder why on earth we expressed ourselves as we did.

Is there any connection between a nation's philosophy and its other activities, its foreign policies, its social and economic organisation? That depends on whether its men of action are willing to become philosophers and if its philosophers are willing to be political handicraftsmen. More than two thousand years ago Plato prophesied that there would be no good government in the world until philosophers became kings. And if this is interpreted as an allegory, we may suppose that Plato had it in mind to define human perfection as a sort of marriage between high thought and virtuous action : which must be for ever the aim of man. If we measure our British philosophers against this standard, they may fall short, but not so far as we might have expected.

INDEX

315

319

321